perfectly feminine knits

25 distinctive designs

LENE HOLME SAMSØE

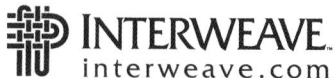
INTERWEAVE™
interweave.com

editor Nathalie Mornu

technical editor Therese Chynoweth

photographer Anders Schønnemann

stylist Birgit Axelsen

associate art director Charlene Tiedemann

cover and interior design Kerry Jackson

First published in 2012 by Lindhardt and Ringhof.
First North American edition published in 2015 by
Interweave, a division of F+W Media, Inc.

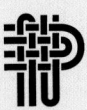

Interweave
A division of F+W Media, Inc.
4868 Innovation Dr.
Fort Collins, CO 80525
interweave.com

Manufactured in China by RR Donnelley Shenzhen

Library of Congress Cataloging-in-Publication Data
Samsøe, Lene Holme.
  Perfectly feminine knits : 25 distinctive designs /
Lene Holme Samsøe.
    pages cm
  ISBN 978-1-63250-083-0 (pbk.)
  ISBN 978-1-63250-084-7 (PDF)
  1. Knitting--Patterns. 2. Sweaters. I. Title.
  TT825.S253 2015
  746.43'2--dc23
                              2014038446

10 9 8 7 6 5 4 3 2 1

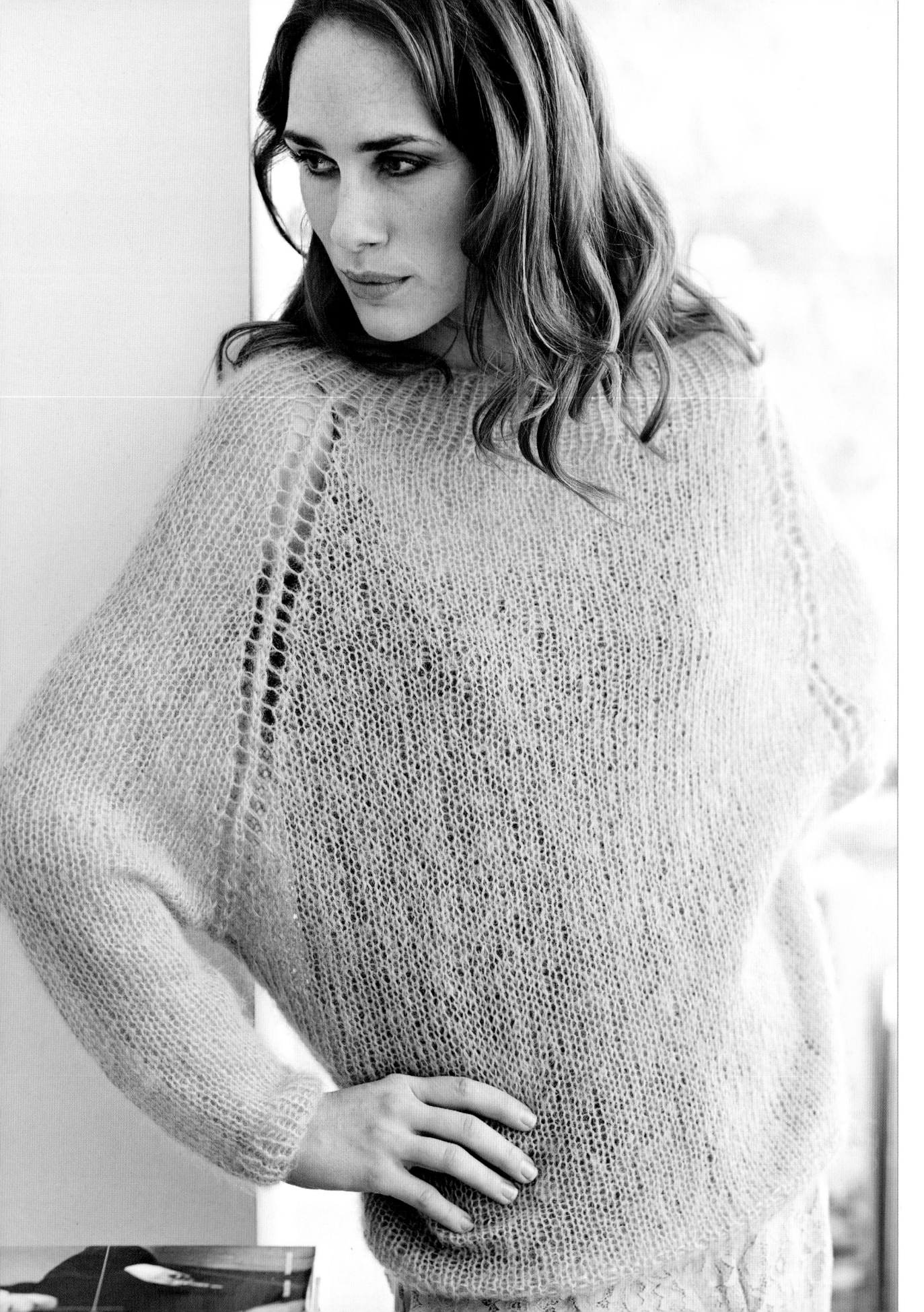

contents

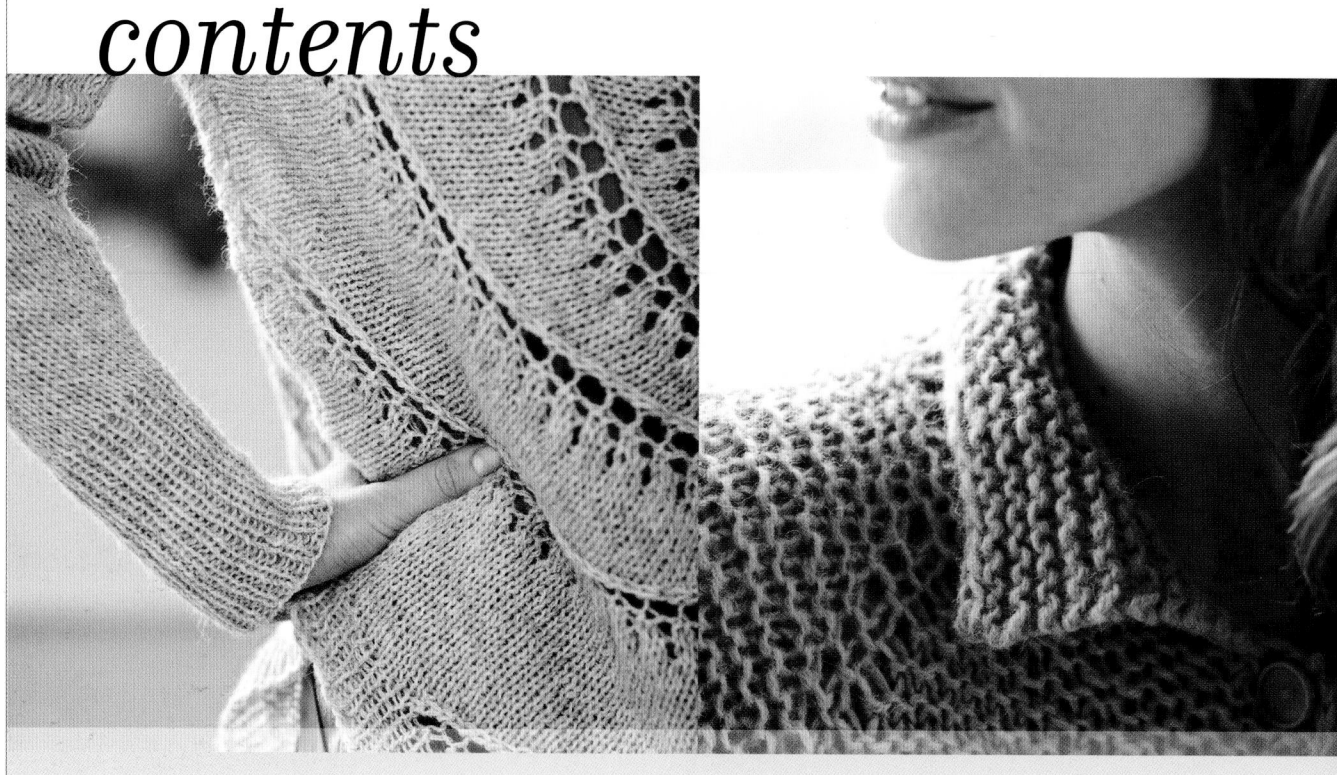

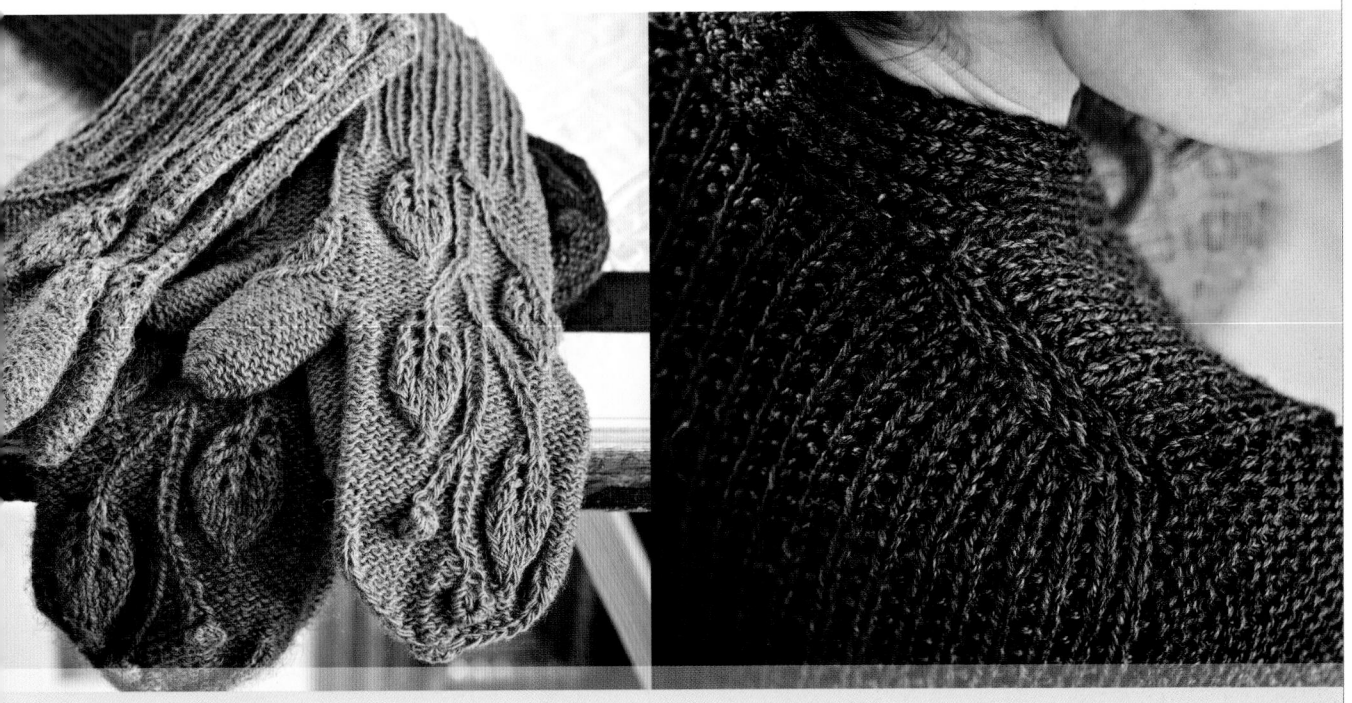

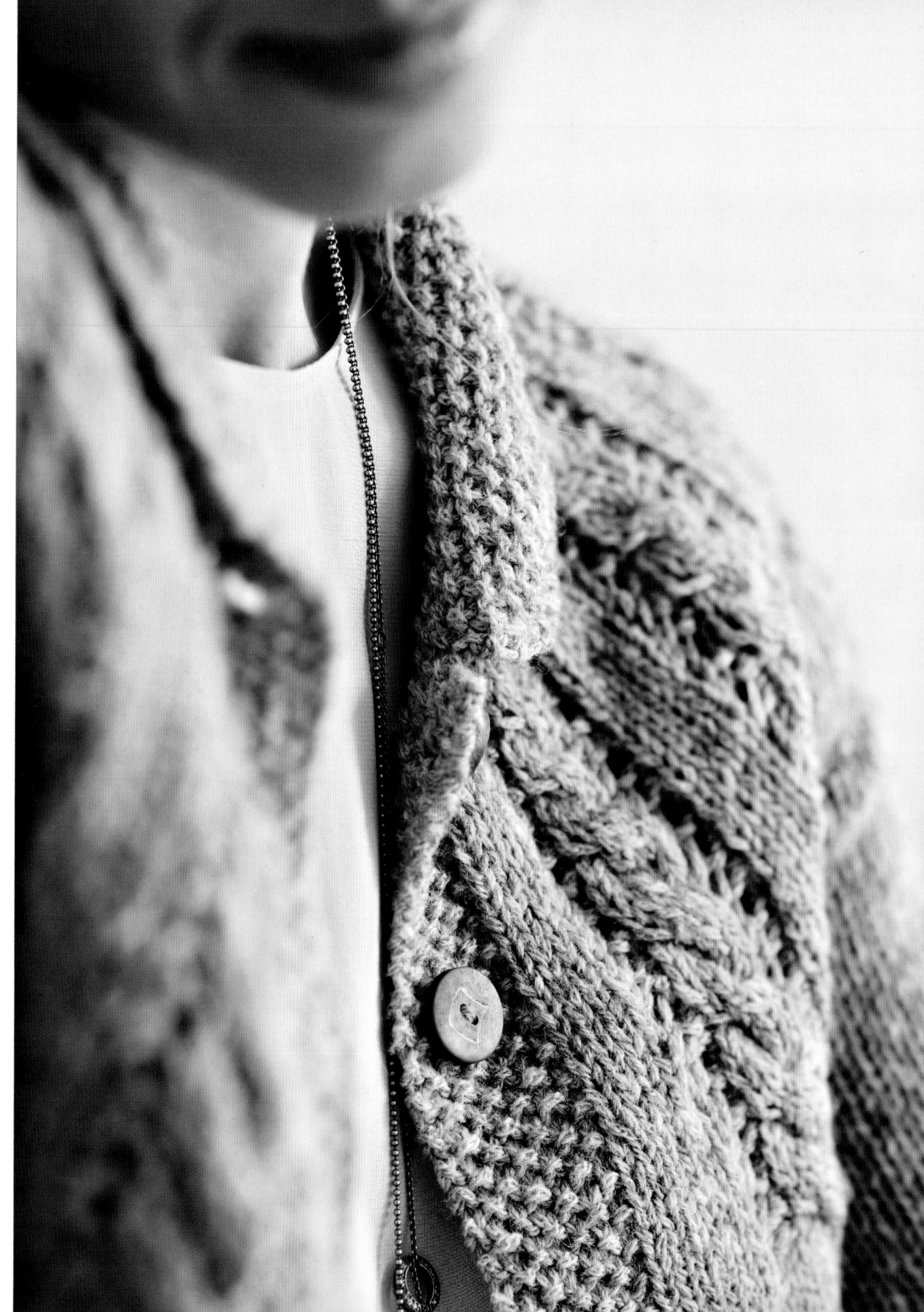

introduction

Survival of the Knittest

The great interest in handknitting, which was considered just a curious retro fad and a passing fashion a few years ago, continues at a steady pace. Knitting is meditative, but it can also be done as a social activity, and now entire online communities have built up around it—so not only is it fun to knit, it's good for the soul. In turn, knitters represent today's spirit because their craft fits perfectly with the current trend of experimenting and exploring to create something original for yourself and others. Knitting is very adaptable to the times. No wonder it has endured as a popular hobby.

You can become addicted to knitting. It isn't surprising that many knitting enthusiasts affectionately describe their local yarn stores as "yarn pushers." With yarn and needles in your hands, breathing deepens, and you can achieve a sense of quiet that purifies your thoughts—almost like yoga, but more restful!

When you knit it yourself, you can produce something that's just as attractive as a ready-made knit garment from the shops. However, for handknits, you can choose pure new wool or another natural fiber instead of the synthetics that factory-produced knitwear is unfortunately frequently made from, and which is often more expensive.

This collection includes cardigans, sweaters, ponchos, mittens, a cap, a cowl, scarves, and a shawl. Designs range from easy to more complicated models, so there's something for everyone.

I hope this book will inspire you to create new projects with knitting needles and lovely yarn in your hands.

Lene Holme Samsøe

How to Use This Book

sizes

Most of the garments in this book are worked in sizes small, medium, large, or extra-large. The measurements given below show the body measurements that each size covers.

SIZES		S 34–36	M 38–40	L 42	XL 44–46
Bust	in	32¼	35	37¾	40¼
	cm	82	89	96	102
	in	25½	27½	30	32¼
	cm	65	70	76	82
Hip	in	36¼	38½	40¼	42½
	cm	92	98	102	108

When deciding on what size to knit, it's a good idea to compare the measurements of the item you want to knit with your own measurements. The measurement schematics give you a good overview of the garment's shape. You can compare the measurements on the schematic with one of your items of clothing to decide if the fit is something you want. If a top, for example, is quite fitted with the given measurements but you prefer something looser, you can choose a larger size for a wider and roomier garment.

All the garments shown in the book were knitted in size small and are shown on models who wear size small (36).

adjustments

If your measurements differ quite a bit from those on the schematic, you can still change the pattern, in much the same way you would adjust the cutting lines on a sewing pattern.

The clothing here was designed for a person about 5 feet 4½ inches to 5 feet 7½ inches (164-172 cm) tall.

If you're taller or shorter, it might, for example, be necessary to make the sleeves longer or shorter than specified. The same applies if you have arms that are longer or shorter than average for your height. If you're much taller or shorter than average, it might also be necessary to knit the body longer or shorter as measured at the side seams. If the garment has a defined waistline, make sure that the waist hits at the right spot on your body.

materials

I always use natural fiber yarns, primarily wool, but also kid mohair, cashmere, alpaca, and silk. At the end of the book you'll find a description of each of the yarns I used. If you want to substitute yarns, try to match the original yarn's yards/ounces (or meters/grams), fiber content, and the recommended gauge. It's a good idea to buy extra yarn if you're not using the one suggested in the pattern.

instructions

Do yourself a favor: Read all the way through the instructions before you begin knitting.

Some techniques and information apply to every pattern and are not repeated in each set of instructions. These are explained below.

GAUGE

The gauge indicates how many stitches there should be in a 4-inch (10 cm) width and the number of rows (if applicable) for every 4 inches (10 cm) of length.

Before you start knitting a pattern, you must be certain that your gauge matches that specified in the instructions. Always knit a gauge swatch! Knit it with the same size needles and in the same pattern as specified in the gauge information (for example, stockinette). Make it a little larger than 4 × 4 inches

(10 × 10 cm). For example, CO 30 sts and work until the swatch is about 5½ inches (14 cm) long. BO loosely. Block the swatch as you plan to block the pieces.

Lay the swatch flat on a table and mark off 4 inches (10 cm) across with a pin on each side. If you also need to check the row gauge, mark it off in the same way. Now count the number of stitches across the width between the pins and the number of rows between the pins for the length. If you have precisely the same number of stitches and rows as indicated in the instructions, then you're good to go! If you have more stitches across than indicated in the pattern, you have knitted too tightly and should try again with needles one U.S. (one-half metric) size bigger—and vice versa. If you have fewer stitches across than specified in the pattern, then you should try needles one U.S. (one-half metric) size smaller. If your gauge varies too much from the pattern gauge, then you should try needles two or more U.S. (one or more metric) sizes smaller or larger. If your gauge varies only by a very small amount from the given gauge, then you might try using slightly smaller needles for working WS rows or, alternatively, slightly larger needles for RS rows. This advice applies only to stockinette because many knitters work the knit rows more tightly than the purl rows.

It pays to take some time with the gauge swatch because small differences in gauge can result in a big difference in the finished size of the garment. If you have 19 stitches in 4 inches (10 cm) instead of 20 as indicated in the pattern, your sweater could end up a size larger than you planned!

edge stitches

In most of the patterns in this book, the outermost stitch at each side is an edge stitch. When you sew garment pieces together, the stitching goes inside the edge stitches. Always knit the edge stitches on every row and do not include them in the pattern. Edge stitches are not shown on the charts. All increases and decreases are worked inside the edge stitches so you can seam or pick up and knit stitches along, say, the front edges without disturbing the decreases and increases.

charts

Many knitting patterns are more clearly explained with the help of charts rather than just words. I use the same symbols in the charts throughout the book, and each chart has a key for the symbols beside it. Many of the symbols look like the steps they describe. For example, a diagonal slash for a decrease slants to the right or left precisely as the decrease itself will slant. Cable crossings are symbolized with long diagonal lines, and the direction of the slant indicates whether the cable is crossed to the left or right.

Usually the first row of the chart is worked on the right side of the fabric, and the row is read from right to left. If a pattern repeat has been marked off, then repeat that section as indicated. Finish the row at the left side of the chart. The wrong side rows are worked similarly, but the chart rows should be read from left to right. There is an exception, however. If the first row of the chart is a wrong-side row, read the chart from left to right.

finishing

Careful finishing can sometimes make a garment that wasn't very smoothly knitted look wonderful, but, unfortunately, the opposite applies as well—sloppy finishing can ruin the nicest piece of knitting. I always seam garments with mattress stitch while working with the right side facing me. The benefit of working with the right side facing you is that it allows you to stitch exactly inside the edge stitches so the seam will be "knife-sharp" and almost invisible. When you sew with the wrong side facing you, sometimes the needle slides a bit unevenly from stitch to stitch.

garment care

After finishing, wet-block all of the patterns in the book except those made with the most delicate yarns. Afterward, machine-spin them at the lowest speed (400 rpm), lay them out to the correct measurements over bath towels on the floor (a warm floor is useful here), and leave them until completely dry. Flip the garment partway through the drying process so that the same surface isn't always facing down. There are, of course, other methods for drying garments, but remember to always dry knitted garments flat, never hanging!

ABBREVIATIONS

beg	begin; beginning
BO	bind off
cir	circular
cm	centimeter(s)
cn	cable needle
CO	cast on
cont	continue(s); continuing
dec	decrease(s); decreasing
dpn	double-pointed needle(s)
g	gram(s)
in	inch(es)
inc	increase(s); increasing
k	knit
k2tog	knit 2 stitches together
M1	make 1 increase (if not otherwise specified, work as M1L)
M1L	(make 1 left) lift the strand between 2 stitches from front to back and knit into back of strand
m1p	make 1 purlwise

M1R	(make 1 right) lift the strand between 2 stitches from back to front and knit into front of strand
m	meter(s)
mm	millimeter(s)
p	purl
p3tog	purl 3 together
patt	pattern
pm	place marker
psso	pass slip stitch over
rem	remain(s); remaining
rep	repeat; repeating
rev St st	reverse stockinette stitch = purl on RS, knit on WS
rnd(s)	round(s)
RS	right side
s2kp	slip 2, knit 1, pass the slipped stitches over
sk2p	slip 1, knit 2 together, pass the slipped stitches over
sl	slip
slm	slip marker

ssk	slip 2 stitches knitwise, one at a time, from left needle to right needle, insert left needle tip through both front loops and knit together from this position (1 stitch decreased)
ssp	slip, slip, purl
St st	stockinette stitch = knit on RS, purl on WS
tbl	through the back loop
tog	together
WS	wrong side
wyb	with yarn in back
yd	yard(s)
yo	yarnover
*	repeat starting point
( )	alternate measurements and/or instructions

glossary

KITCHENER STITCH

Step 1: Bring threaded needle through front stitch as if to purl and leave stitch on needle (**Figure 1**).

Step 2: Bring threaded needle through back stitch as if to knit and leave stitch on needle (**Figure 2**).

Step 3: Bring threaded needle through first front stitch as if to knit and slip this stitch off needle. Bring threaded needle through next front stitch as if to purl and leave stitch on needle (**Figure 3**).

Step 4: Bring threaded needle through first back stitch as if to purl (figure 1 at right) and slip this stitch off needle. Bring needle through next back stitch as if to knit and leave stitch on needle (**Figure 4**).

Repeat Steps 3 and 4 until no stitches remain on needles.

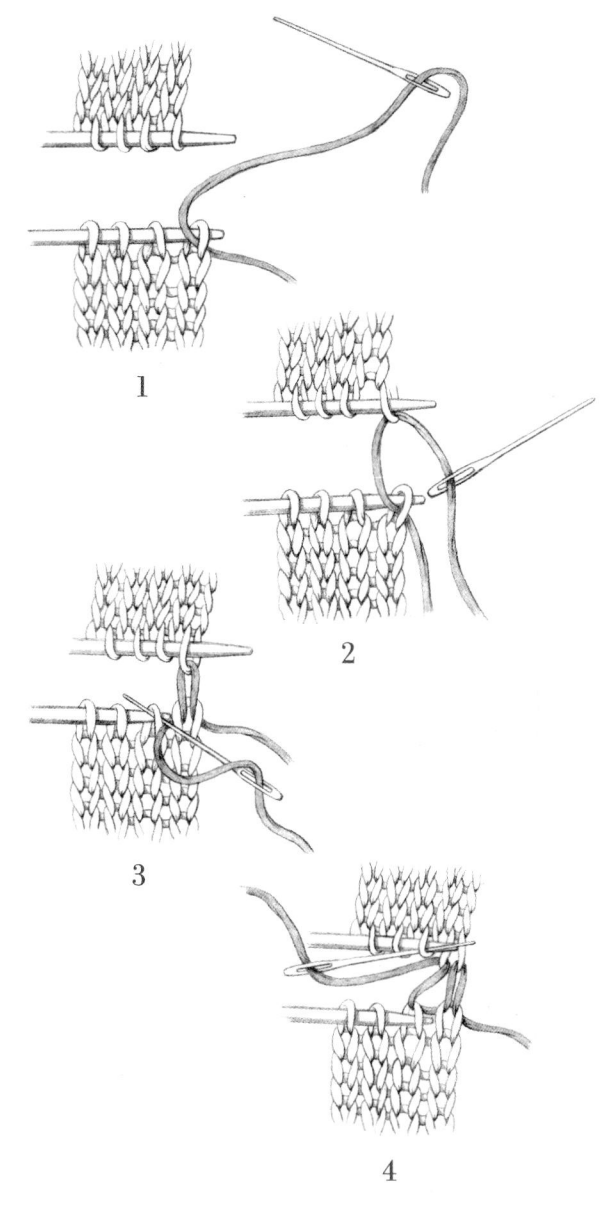

M1L (INCREASING AFTER MARKED STS)

Insert your left needle through the strand between 2 sts from front to back (**Figure 1**). Knit the lifted strand through the back (**Figure 2**).

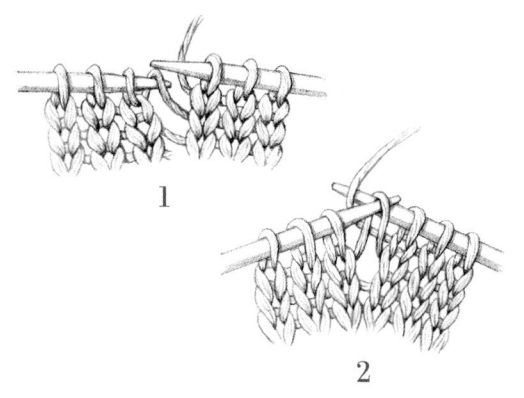

M1R (INCREASING BEFORE MARKED STS)

Insert the left needle through the strand between 2 sts from back to front **(Figure 1)**. Knit the lifted strand through the front **(Figure 2)**.

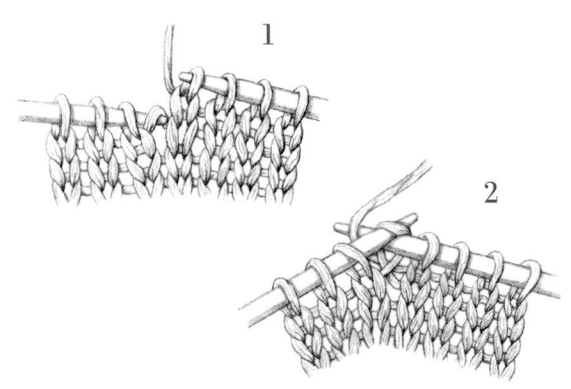

MATTRESS STITCH

Mattress stitch is worked from the right side, allowing you to match the stitches on one piece to those of the other so they line up perfectly and conceal the seaming yarn.

Start at the cast-on edge, using the tail left over from casting on (thread it on a tapestry needle), and work up. *Note: If the tail isn't long enough to work the entire seam, join a length of yarn about twice as long as the seam; don't tie a knot or the ends, but instead leave a few inches (roughly 10 cm) of the seaming yarn loose. Then, after you've sewn the seam, tighten the end and then work the tail into the seam.*

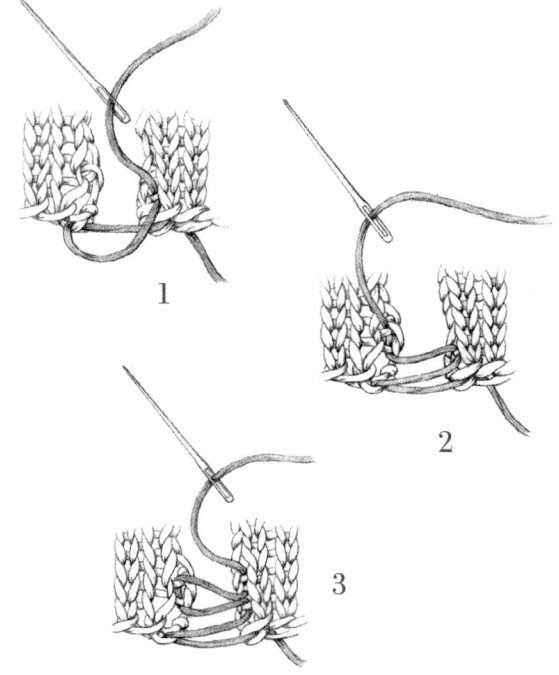

With the right sides of the knitting facing you, use the needle to pick up just one bar (this is important; it prevents a half-row displacement) between the first two stitches on one piece **(Figure 1)**. Moving to the other piece, pick up the corresponding bar plus the bar above it **(Figure 2)**. *Pick up the next two bars on the first piece, then the next two bars on the other **(Figure 3)**. Repeat from * until you reach the end of the seam. Finish by picking up the last bar (or pair of bars) at the end of the first piece. Picking up the bars in the center of the edge stitches—instead of between the last two stitches—will reduce bulk.

THREE-NEEDLE BIND-OFF

This technique binds off stitches at the same time as it joins two pieces of knitting together.

The stitches you wish to join should be placed on two needles. Holding the needles parallel so that the right sides of the pieces face each other, *insert a third needle into the first stitch on each of the two needles **(Figure 1)** and knit them together as if they were a single stitch **(Figure 2)**. Knit the next stitch on both needles in the same way, then, using the left needle tip, lift the first stitch over the second and off the needle **(Figure 3)**. Repeat from * until just one stitch remains on the third needle. Cut the yarn and pull its tail through the remaining stitch to secure the work.

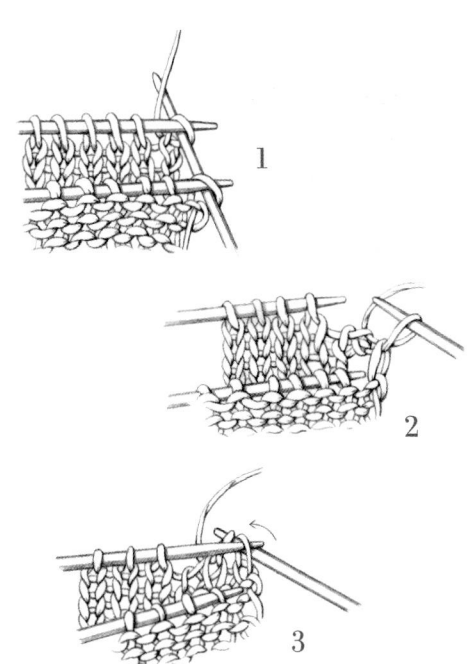

SHORT-ROWS

Work the required number of stitches to the turning point, then turn the work. Place a removable marker—such as a split-ring marker, safety pin, or waste yarn—on the turning yarn **(Figure 1)**. When it's time to close the gap on a subsequent row, slip the stitch immediately before the turning yarn, pull up on the marker and place the turning yarn on the needle, then transfer the slipped stitch back onto the left needle **(Figure 2)** and work the turning yarn together with the next stitch as follows:

* If knit stitch follows, k2tog.

* If purl stitch follows, ssp.

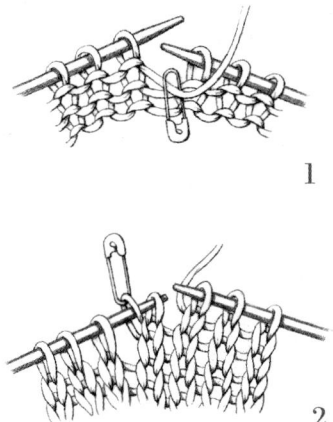

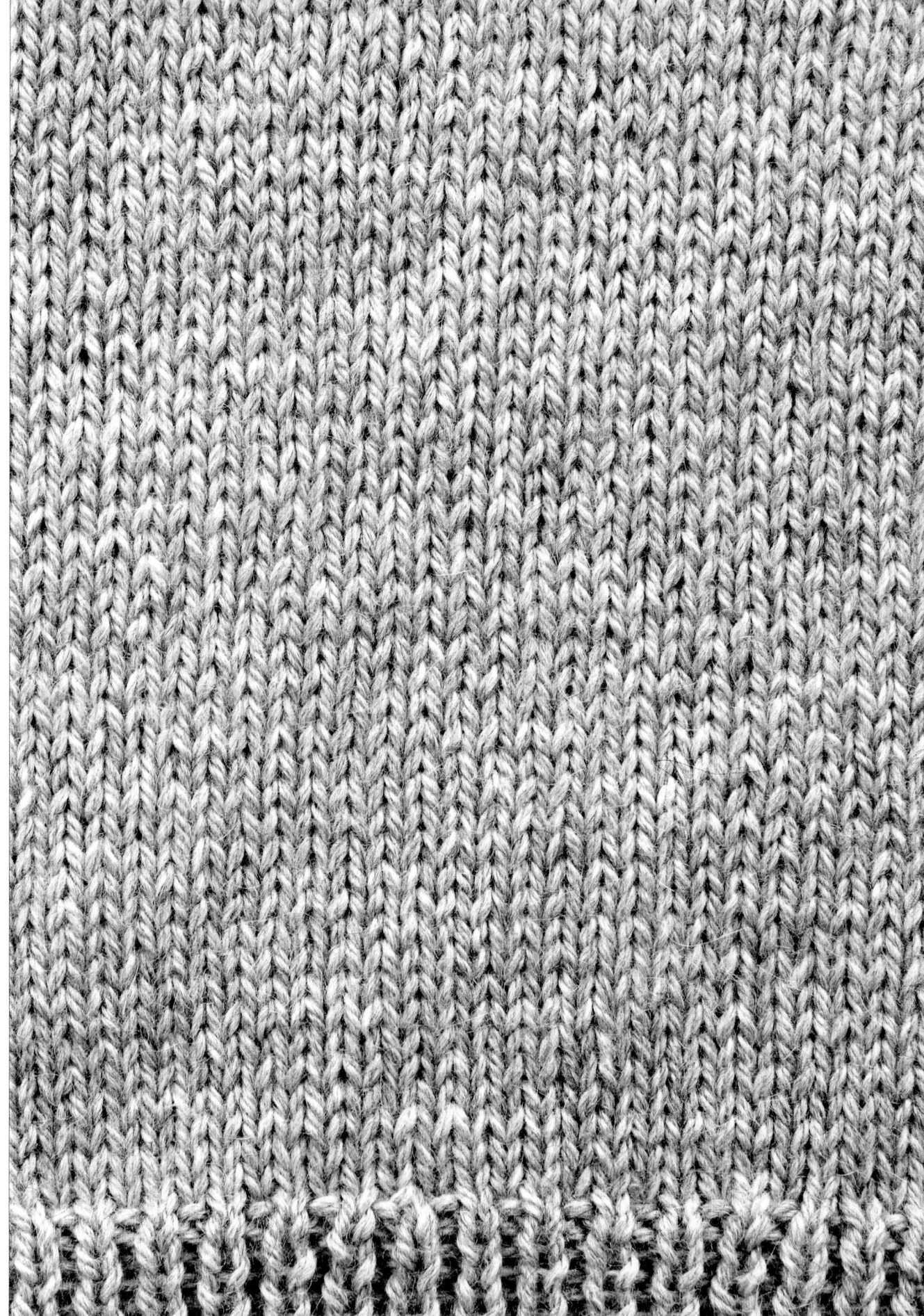

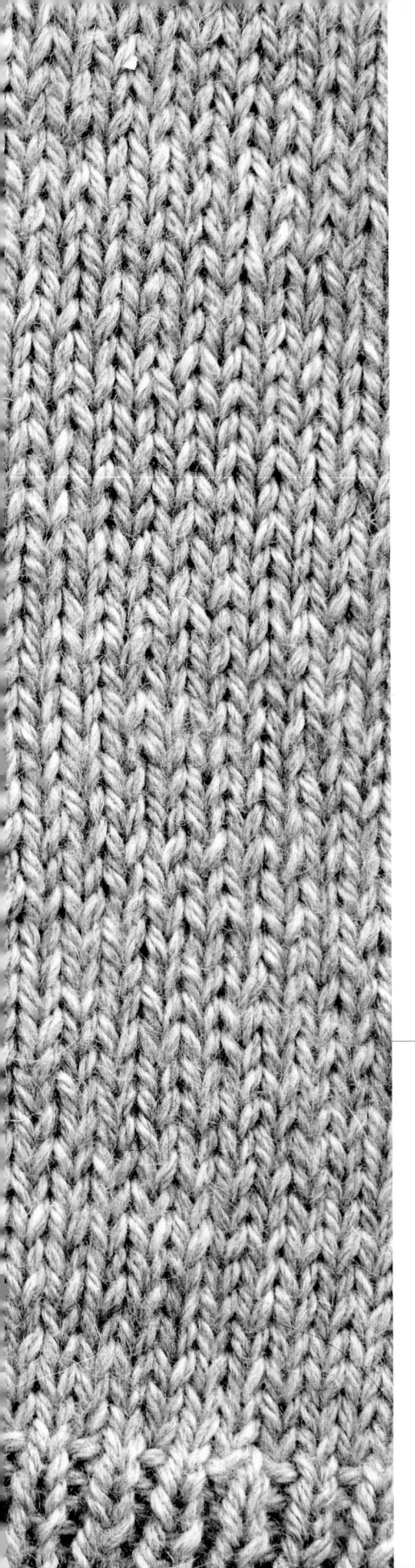

Knit and Purl

Knit and purl stitches are the basics of knitting. If
you can do these, you have enough technique mastery
to produce beautiful garments in stockinette, relief
patterns, brioche, and ribbing. The designs in this
chapter are all worked with various easy combinations
of knit and purl stitches.

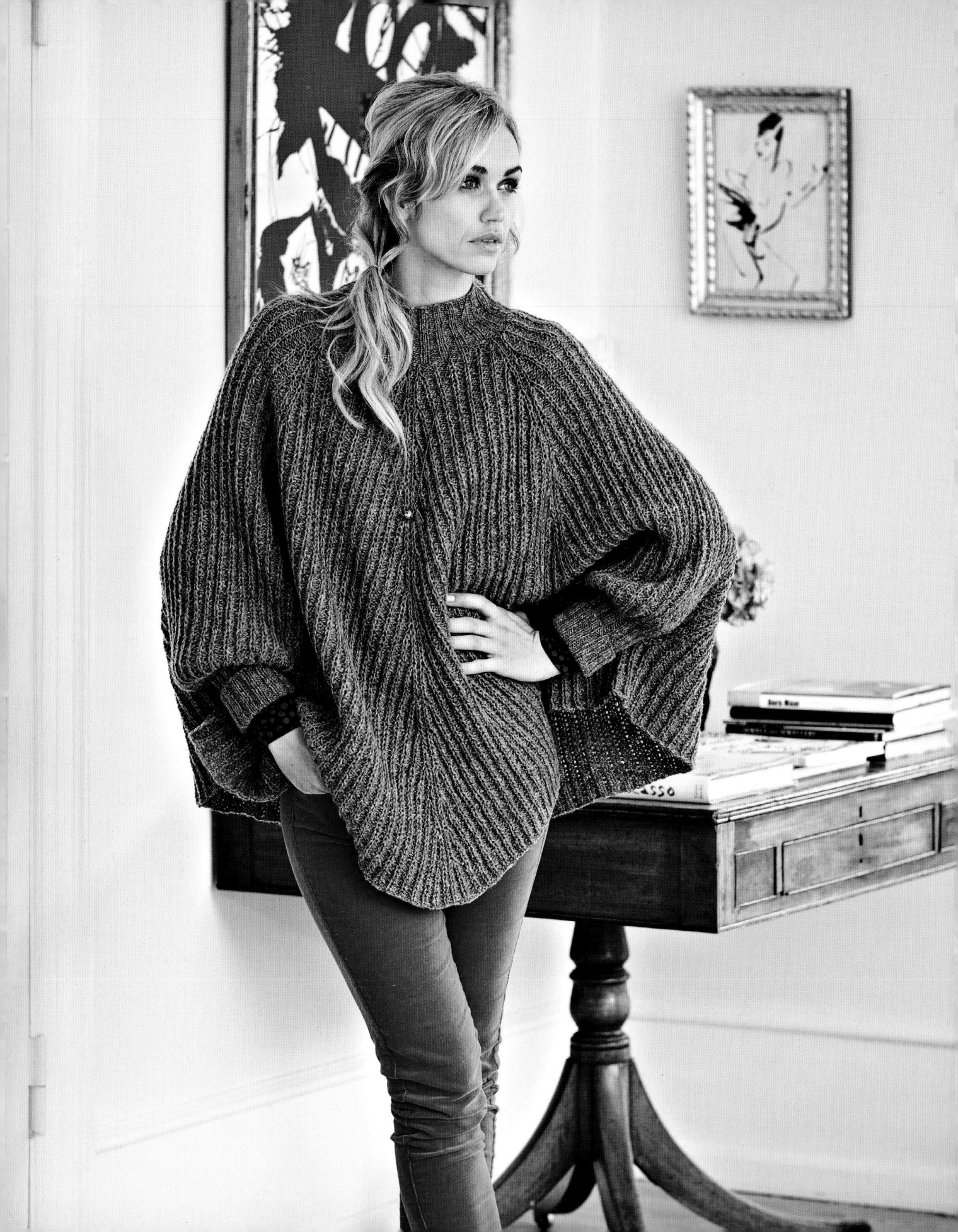

josina

poncho with sleeves

You could just about live in this poncho! Anyone, from small to large, can wear this one-size-fits-all accessory. It's knitted from the top down, so it's easy to adjust the length.

FINISHED SIZE
One size (S–XL).

About 26½" (67.5 cm) from shoulder to bottom of center front or back, excluding neckband.

YARN
Sportweight (#2 Fine).

Shown here: Sandnes Garn Tove (100% wool; 174 yd [160 m]/50 g): gray #1053, 10 balls.

NEEDLES
Sizes U.S. 6 and 8 (4 and 5 mm): 16" (40 cm) circular (cir). Size U.S. 8 (5 mm): 32" (80 cm) cir. Size U.S. 6 (4 mm): set of 5 double-pointed (dpn).

Adjust needle size if necessary to obtain the correct gauge.

NOTIONS
Markers (1 in a first color to mark beg of rnd, 4 of a second color to mark raglan seam lines, 2 of a third color to mark center sts of front and center back); stitch holders; tapestry needle.

GAUGE
19 sts and 30 rnds = 4" (10 cm) in brioche pattern on size U.S. 8 (5 mm) needles.

NOTE
Place raglan and center markers in center st of each set of sts to be marked and move them up as work progresses.

stitch guide

BRIOCHE STITCH

K1, inserting tip of right needle in st below next st on tip of left needle, then slip st off tip of left needle. That stitch will loosen but will be held in place by the brioche st and will not ravel.

BRIOCHE PATTERN (multiple of 3 sts + 2)

RND 1: P2, *k1, p2; rep from * to end.
RND 2: P2, *brioche st, p2; rep from * to end.
Repeat Rnds 1 and 2.

BRIOCHE PANEL (panel of 3 sts at raglan and center front and back)

RND 1: K1, p1, k1.
RND 2: Brioche st, p1, brioche st.
Repeat Rnds 1 and 2.

INCREASE A (inc-A)

Work (brioche st, yo, brioche st) in the same st—2 sts inc'd.

INCREASE B (inc-B)

With tip of left needle, lift the strand between the needles from front to back, then purl the lifted loop through the back—1 st inc'd.

yoke

Note: The poncho is worked from the top down.

With short smaller cir needle, CO 108 sts. Place marker (pm) and join for working in rnds, being careful not to twist sts.

Work in k2 p2 rib for 3¼" (8.5 cm).

Change to larger cir needle and set up patt as follows:

RND 1: P1, pm in this st for raglan, k1 (these are the last 2 of 3 Brioche Panel raglan sts), work 14 sts in brioche patt, k1, p1, pm in this st for center back, k1, work 14 sts in brioche patt, k1, p1, pm in this st for raglan, k1, work 17 sts in brioche patt for sleeve, k1, p1, pm in this st for raglan, k1, work 14 sts in brioche patt, k1, p1, pm in this st for center front, k1, work 14 sts in brioche patt, k1, p1, pm in this st for raglan, k1, 17 sts in brioche patt for sleeve, k1 (this is the first st of 3 Brioche Panel raglan sts).

Work 2 rnds even in established patt, keeping raglan sts and center front and back in Brioche Panel.

RND 4 (INC): *P1, inc-A, work in patt to 1 st before next marked st, inc-A; rep from * around—24 sts inc'd.

Work 3 rnds even, working new sts into patt and purl each yo on inc rnd.

RND 8 (INC): *P1, inc-B, work in patt to next marked st, inc-B; rep from * around—12 sts inc'd.

RNDS 9–15: Work even in established patt.

Repeat Rnds 4–15 nine more times—468 sts, with 77 sts for each sleeve, 74 sts on each side of center front and back, 12 raglan sts, and 6 center sts. *Note: The new patt st counts can easily be made by counting the new brioche sts out from the marked sts. Change to a longer cir needle when necessary.*

Piece should measure about 16½" (42 cm) along center back, excluding neckband.

Working inc at center front and back, and at back and front raglan edges only, rep Rnds 4–15 three more times, then rep Rnds 4–8 once more, and inc at center front and back, and at back and front raglans only (16 sts inc'd each rep of Rnd 4, and 8 sts inc'd each rep of Rnd 8)—564 sts, with 77 sts for each sleeve, 98 sts each side of center front and back, 12 raglan sts, and 6 center sts.

DIVIDE BODY AND SLEEVES

NEXT RND: Work 203 back sts, place next 79 sts on holder for sleeve, work 203 front sts, place rem 79 sts on holder for sleeve—406 sts.

Rep Rnds 10-15 once, then rep Rnds 4-8 once more—418 sts. Piece should measure about 23¾" (60.5 cm) along center back, excluding neckband.

Cont even for 1½" (3.8 cm) or until poncho is desired length.

BO loosely, adding a yo after every other brioche st as follows: yo, pass first st over yo and off needle, p1, pass yo over st and off needle.

sleeve cuffs

Return held sts for sleeve to dpn. Pm and join for working in rnds.

NEXT RND: Sl 1, *p2tog, brioche st; rep from * to last 3 sts, p2tog, pm for beg of rnd—53 sts rem.

NEXT RND: K2tog, k1, p2, (k2, p2) to end of rnd—52 sts rem.

Cont in k2, p2 rib until cuff measures 5½" (14 cm) or desired length. BO in rib.

finishing

Weave in ends. Sew underarm seams.
Block to finished measurements.

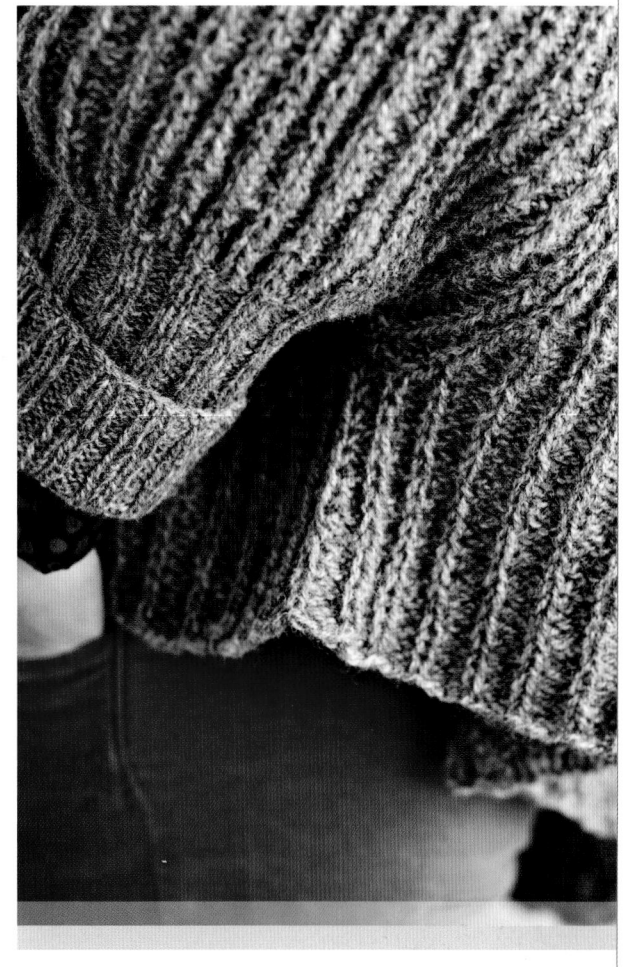

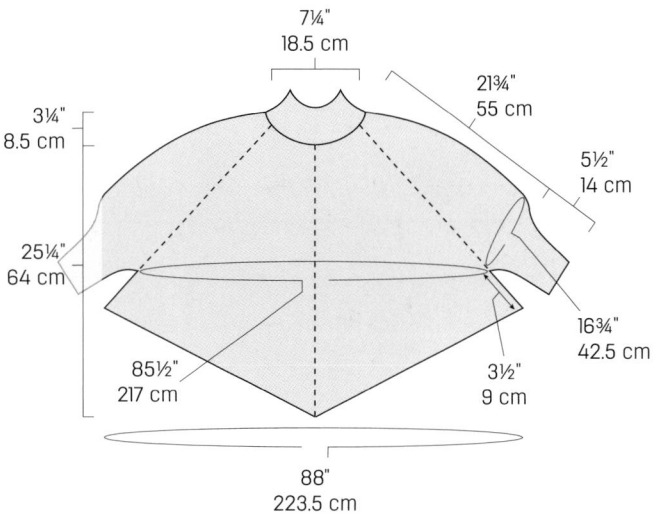

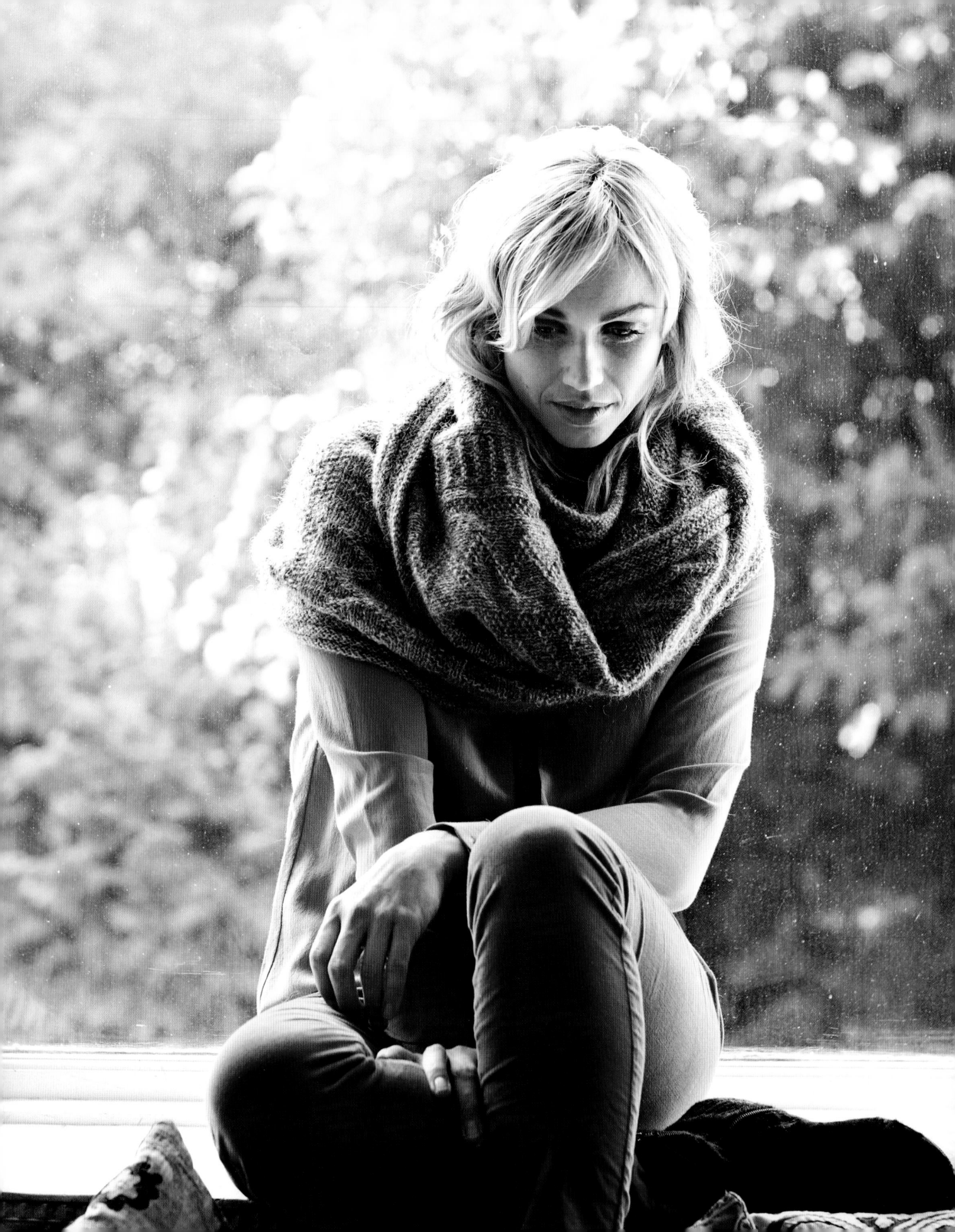

greta

guernsey cowl

This extra-large cowl in an easy knit and purl pattern is inspired by motifs used on the classic fishermen's sweaters from the island of Guernsey. This cowl will warm more than your neck because you can wrap it snugly around your shoulders on an especially cold day.

FINISHED SIZE
One size.

74¾" (190 cm) in circumference.

16¼" (41.5 cm) long.

YARN
DK weight (#3 Light).

Shown here: Hjelholt's Wool Mill Danish Pels (Gotland) wool 5.5/2 (100% wool; 300 yd [275 m]/100 g): gray #1, 4 skeins.

NEEDLES
Sizes U.S. 4 and 6 (3.5 and 4 mm): 32–47" (80–120 cm) circular (cir).

Adjust needle size if necessary to obtain the correct gauge.

GAUGE
19½ sts and 31 rnds = 4" (10 cm) in pattern on size U.S. 6 (4 mm) needles.

neck

With smaller cir needle, CO 365 sts. Place marker (pm) for beg of rnd and join for working in rnds, being careful not to twist sts.

*Purl 3 rnds, knit 3 rnds; rep from * 2 more times.

Change to larger cir needle. Rep Rnds 1-12 of chart until piece measures about 15¼" (38.5 cm) from beg, ending with Rnd 12 of rep so patt will match at beg and end.

Change to smaller cir needle.

*Knit 3 rnds, purl 3 rnds; rep from * 2 more times. BO loosely pwise.

finishing

Weave in ends. Block to finished measurements.

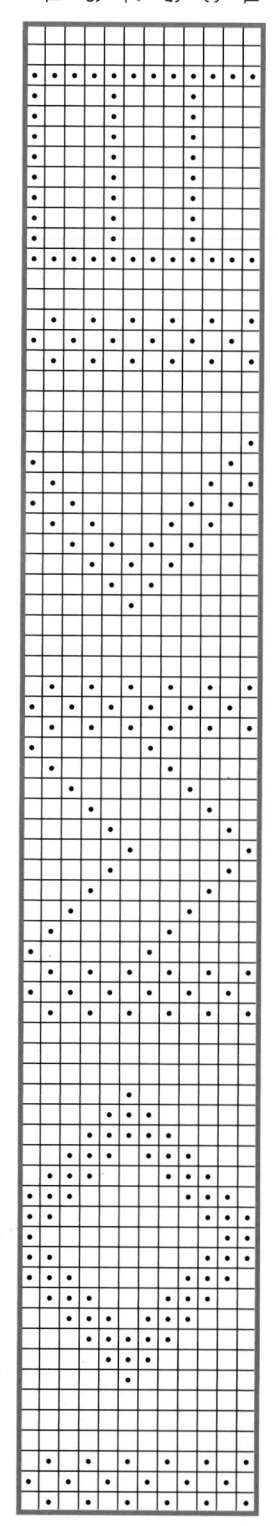

GRETA CHART

pattern repeat

k on RS; p on WS

p on RS; k on WS

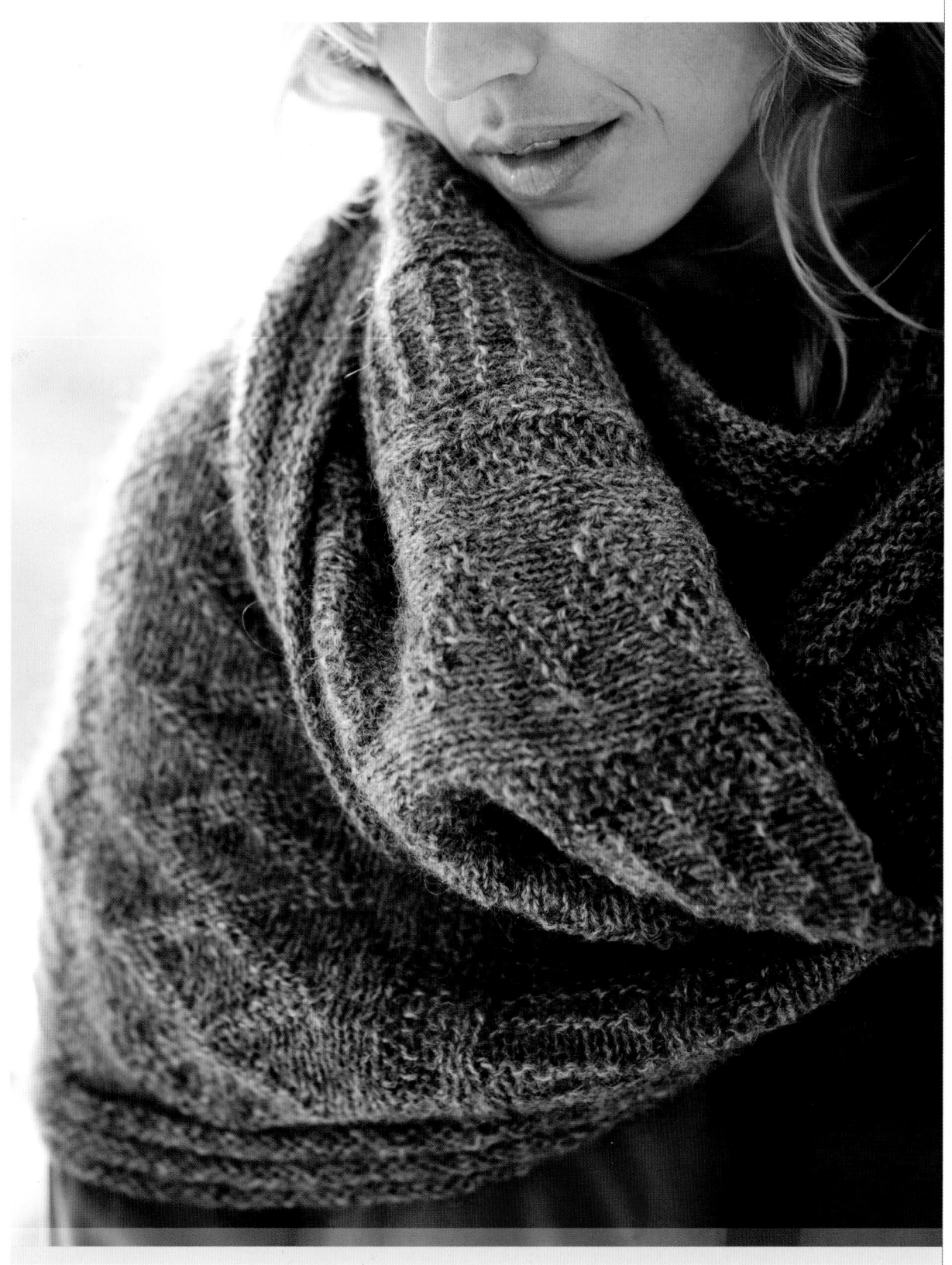

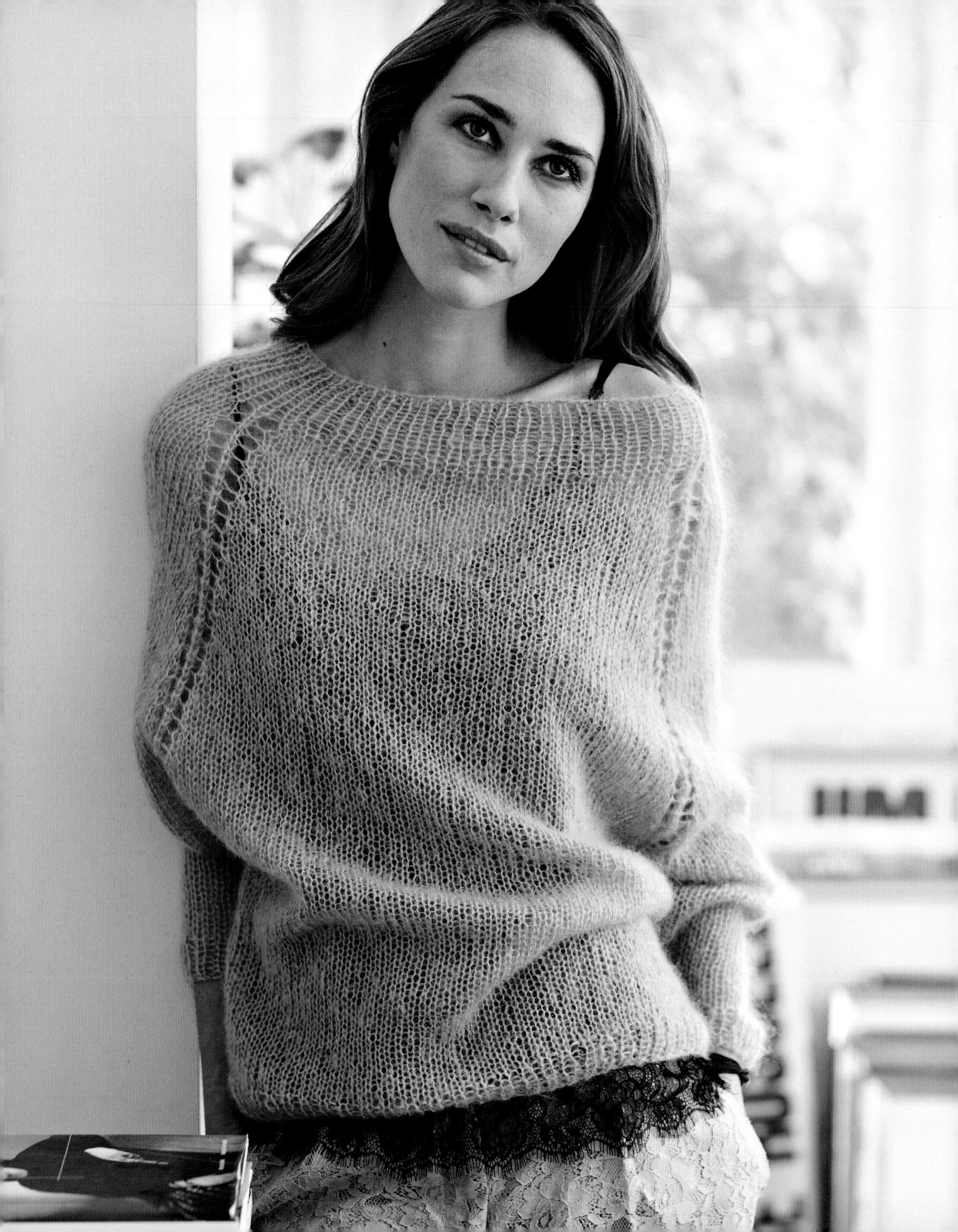

ruby

oversized raglan top

Two lines of lacy knitting punctuate the deep raglan
seams in this loose-fitting pullover made of fluffy yarn.

FINISHED SIZE		S	M	L	XL
Bust	in	44¼	48	51¾	55½
	cm	112.5	122	131.5	141
Total length	in	22½	22¾	22¾	23½
	cm	57	58	58	59.5

YARN
Laceweight (#0 Lace).

Shown here: Canard's Brushed
Lace Mohair (72% kid mohair,
28% mulberry silk; 229 yd
[210 m]/50 g): sand #3005, 6
(7, 8, 9) balls.

NEEDLES
Size U.S. 10 (6 mm): 16 and 32" (40
and 80 cm) circular (cir). Size U.S.
8 (5 mm): 16" (40 cm) cir.

*Adjust needle sizes if necessary to
obtain the correct gauge.*

NOTIONS
Markers (1 of a first color to mark
beg of rnd, 4 of a second color
to mark raglan lines); tapestry
needle.

GAUGE
13 sts and 21 rows = 4" (10 cm) in
St st with yarn held double on
size U.S. 10 (6 mm) needles.

NOTE
The top is worked from the
bottom up with yarn held double
throughout.

back

With larger long cir needle and 2 strands of yarn held tog, loosely CO 66 (72, 78, 84) sts. Do not join.

Beg with a WS row, work 7 rows in k1, p1 rib.

Cont in St st until piece measures 2¼" (5.5 cm) from CO edge, ending with a WS row.

NEXT (INC) ROW: (RS) K1, M1, knit to last st, M1, k1—2 sts inc'd.

Rep inc row every 10 rows 3 more times—74 (80, 86, 92) sts.

Cont even until piece measures 9½ (9, 8¾, 8¼)" (24 [23, 22, 21] cm). Set aside.

front

Work front same as for back.

sleeves (make 2)

With larger short cir needle and 2 strands of yarn held tog, loosely CO 30 (30, 32, 32) sts. Do not join.

Beg with a WS row, work 7 rows in k1, p1 rib.

Cont in St st until piece measures 2¼" (5.5 cm) from CO edge, ending with a WS row.

NEXT (INC) ROW: (RS) K1, M1, knit to last st, M1, k1—2 sts inc'd.

Rep inc row every RS row 0 (2, 3, 9) times, then every 4 rows 7 (7, 7, 3) times—46 (50, 54, 58) sts. Cont even until piece measures 10¼ (9¾, 9½, 9)" (26 [25, 24, 23] cm) from CO edge. Set aside.

yoke

With RS facing, place sts for all pieces on larger long cir needle as follows: 74 (80, 86, 92) back sts, 46 (50, 54, 58) sleeve sts, 74 (80, 86, 92) front sts, then 46 (50, 54, 58) sleeve sts—240 (260, 280, 300) sts.

NEXT RND: Sl last st of right sleeve to tip of left needle, k2tog, k1, place marker (pm), k70 (76, 82, 88), pm, k1, k2tog, k1, pm, k42 (46, 50, 54), pm, k1, k2tog, k1, pm, k70 (76, 82, 88), pm, k1, k2tog, k1, pm, k42 (46, 50, 54), place beg-of-rnd marker—236 (256, 276, 296) sts; 70 (76, 82, 88) sts each for front and back, 42 (46, 50, 54) sts for each sleeve, and 12 sts for raglans.

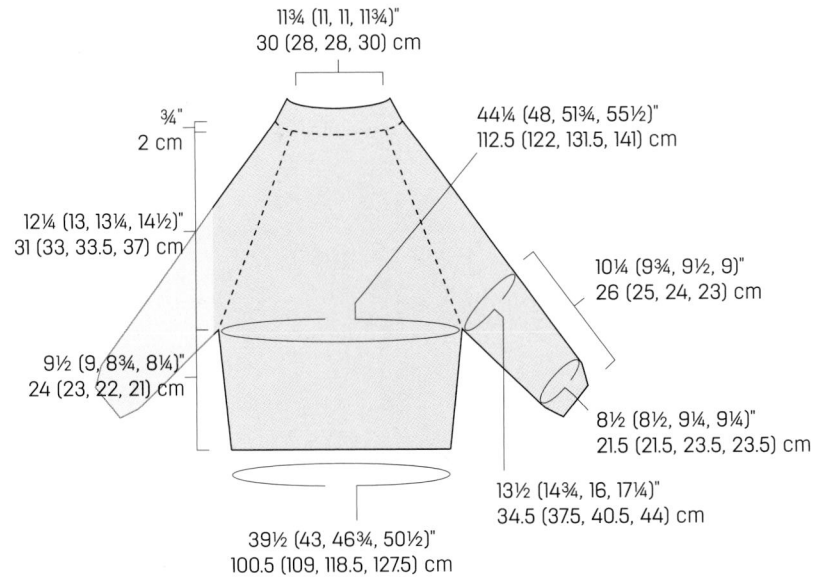

11¾ (11, 11, 11¾)"
30 (28, 28, 30) cm

¾"
2 cm

44¼ (48, 51¾, 55½)"
112.5 (122, 131.5, 141) cm

12¼ (13, 13¼, 14½)"
31 (33, 33.5, 37) cm

10¼ (9¾, 9½, 9)"
26 (25, 24, 23) cm

9½ (9, 8¾, 8¼)"
24 (23, 22, 21) cm

8½ (8½, 9¼, 9¼)"
21.5 (21.5, 23.5, 23.5) cm

13½ (14¾, 16, 17¼)"
34.5 (37.5, 40.5, 44) cm

39½ (43, 46¾, 50½)"
100.5 (109, 118.5, 127.5) cm

RND 1: *Yo, s2kp (see page 10), yo, slm, knit to next m, slm; rep from * 3 more times.

RND 2: Knit.

Rep these 2 rnds for lace patt and beg shaping raglan as foll.

NEXT (DEC) RND: *Yo, sk2p, yo, sm, k2tog, knit to 2 sts before next m, ssk, slm; rep from * to end of rnd—8 sts dec'd.

Size S only
Rep dec rnd every 4 rnds 15 more times—108 sts rem; 38 sts each for front and back, 10 sts for each sleeve, and 12 raglan sts.

Size M only
Rep raglan dec on sleeves every 4 rnds 16 more times. At the same time, rep raglan dec on back and front as follows: every 4 rnds 3 more times, (every other rnd twice, every 4 rnds 4 times) twice, every other rnd twice, then every 4 rnds twice more—108 sts rem; 36 sts each for front and back, 12 sts for each sleeve, and 12 raglan sts.

Sizes L and XL only
Rep raglan dec on sleeves every 4 rnds 16 (18) more times. At the same time, rep raglan on back and front as foll: (every 2 rnds once, then every 4 rnds once) 11 (12) times—116 (120) sts rem; 36 (38) sts each for front and back, 16 sts for each sleeve, and 12 raglan sts.

All sizes
NEXT (DEC) RND: *K25 (25, 12, 13), k2tog; rep from * 3 (3, 7, 7) more times, k0 (0, 4, 0)—104 (104, 108, 112) sts.

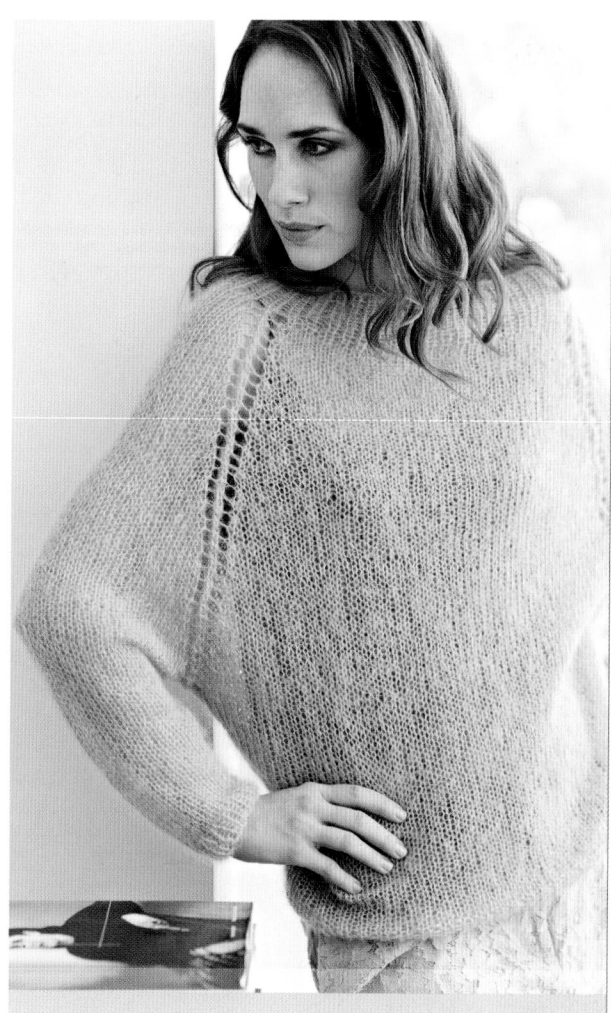

Work 5 rnds in k1, p1 rib. Change to smaller cir needle and cont in established patt until ribbing measures 2¾-3¼" (7-8.5 cm). BO all sts loosely in rib.

finishing
Weave in ends. Sew the sleeve and side seams. Block to finished measurements.

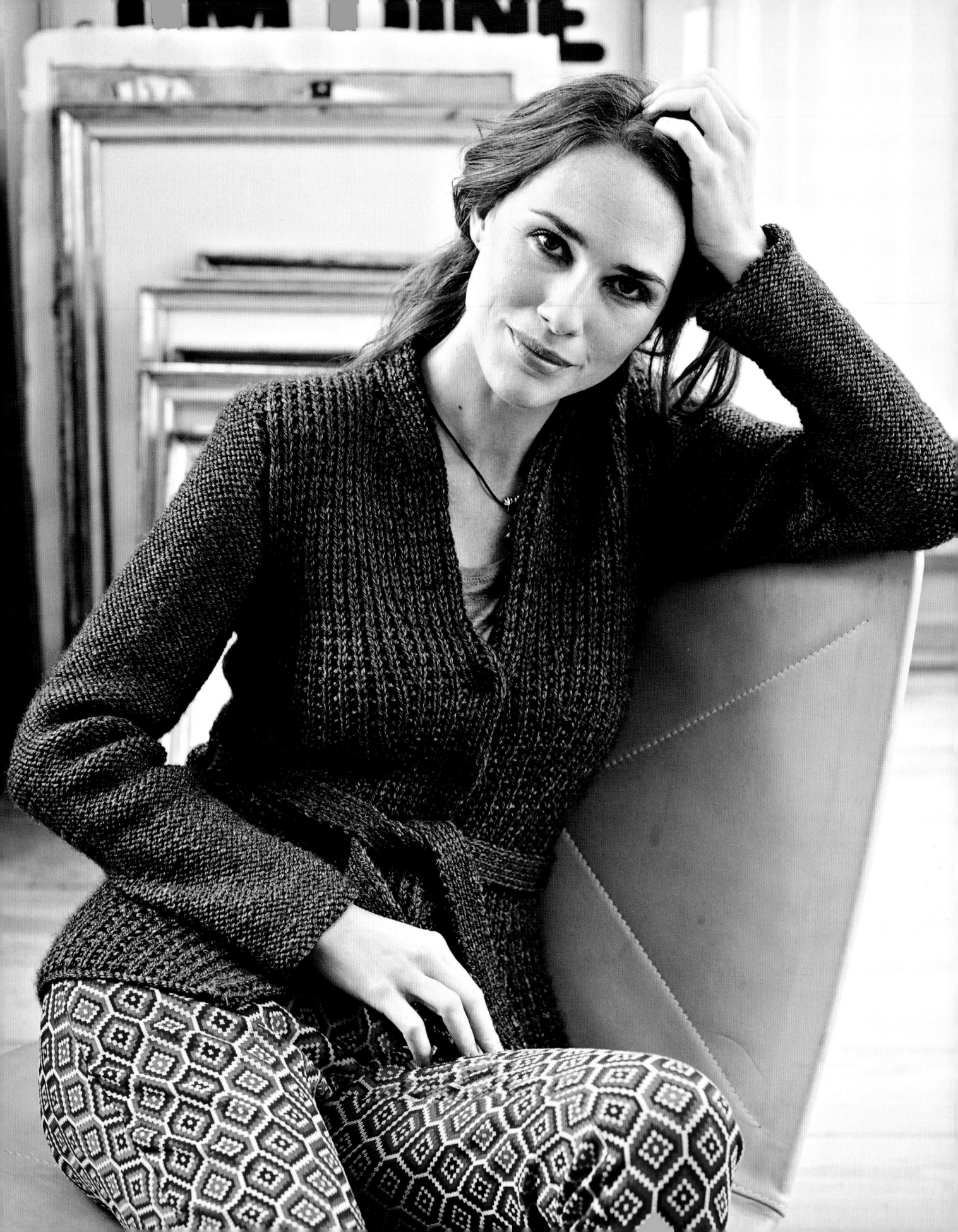

vera

belted sweater

The lovely neck shaping of this belted sweater is surprisingly easy to do, while the rest of the garment is slightly more complex. Its silhouette is cleanly shaped with increases and decreases.

FINISHED SIZE		S	M	L	XL
Bust including 1" (2.5 cm) overlap	in	37¾	41¼	43¾	47¼
	cm	96	105	111	120
Total length	in	24	24½	24½	25¼
	cm	61	62	62	64

YARN
Aran weight (#4 Medium).

Shown here: Onion Organic Wool+Nettles (70% wool, 30% nettles; 87 yd [80 m]/50 g): charcoal #601, 11 (12, 13, 14) balls.

NEEDLES
Size U.S. 10 (6 mm): straight.

Adjust needle size if necessary to obtain the correct gauge.

NOTIONS
Markers; stitch holder; spare size U.S. 10 (6 mm) needle; 4 large snaps ¾" (18 mm) diameter; tapestry needle.

GAUGE
16 sts and 22 rows = 4" (10 cm) in broken rib.

16 sts and 21 rows = 4" (10 cm) in St st.

NOTE
The armhole on the front is slightly longer than the back, and the shoulder seam will fall slightly to the back of the shoulder.

back

CO 77 (83, 89, 95) sts.

Work in Broken Rib patt until piece measures 4" (10 cm) from CO edge, ending with a WS row.

SHAPE WAIST

NEXT (DEC) ROW: (RS) K17 (19, 19, 21) sts, sk2p, place marker (pm) on dec st, k37 (39, 45, 47) sts, sk2p, pm on dec st, k17 (19, 19, 21) sts—4 sts dec'd.

Work 7 rows even.

NEXT (DEC) ROW: Knit to marked st, sk2p, knit to 2 sts before marked st, sk2p, k17 (19, 19, 21) sts—4 sts dec'd.

Rep last 8 rows 2 more times—61 (67, 73, 79) sts rem.

Cont even until piece measures 11¾ (12¼, 12¼, 12¼)" (30 [31, 31, 31] cm) from CO edge, ending with a WS row.

NEXT (INC) ROW: (RS) K1, M1, knit to last st, M1, k1—2 sts inc'd.

Working new sts into established patt, rep inc row every 6 rows 3 more times—69 (75, 81, 87) sts. Remove markers.

Cont even until piece measures 16½ (16½, 16¼, 16¼)" (42 [42, 41.5, 41.5] cm) from CO edge, ending with a WS row.

SHAPE ARMHOLES

BO 4 sts at beg of next 2 rows—61 (67, 73, 79) sts.

NEXT (DEC) ROW: (RS) K3, sk2p, knit to last 6 sts, k3tog, knit to end of row—4 sts dec'd.

Rep dec row every RS row 1 (1, 2, 2) more time(s)—53 (59, 61, 67) sts rem.

Cont even until armhole measures 6¼ (6¾, 7, 7½)" (16 [17, 18, 19] cm), ending with a WS row.

SHAPE SHOULDERS

NEXT (DEC) ROW: (RS) K3, sk2p, knit to last 6 sts, k3tog, knit to end of row—4 sts dec'd.

NEXT (DEC) ROW: (WS) Work 3 sts in established patt, p3tog, work to last 6 sts, p3tog tbl, work to end of row—4 sts dec'd.

Rep last 2 rows 3 (4, 4, 5) more times—21 (19, 21, 19) sts rem.

BO rem sts.

left front

CO 43 (47, 49, 53) sts.

Work in Broken Rib patt until piece measures 4" (10 cm) from CO edge, ending with a WS row.

SHAPE WAIST

NEXT (DEC) ROW: (RS) K17 (19, 19, 21) sts, sk2p, pm on dec st, k23 (25, 27, 29) sts—2 sts dec'd.

Work 7 rows even.

NEXT (DEC) ROW: K17 (19, 19, 21) sts, sk2p, knit to end of row—2 sts dec'd.

Rep last 8 rows 2 more times—35 (39, 41, 45) sts rem. Remove marker.

Cont even until piece measures 11¾ (12¼, 12¼, 12¼)" (30 [31, 31, 31] cm) from CO edge, ending with a WS row.

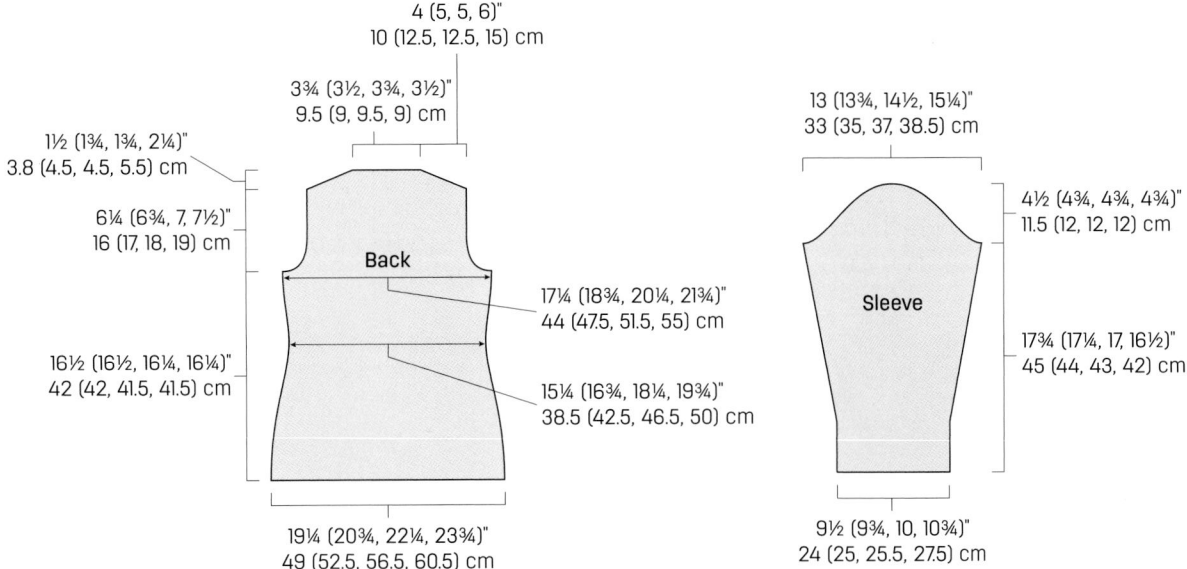

4 (5, 5, 6)"
10 (12.5, 12.5, 15) cm

3¾ (3½, 3¾, 3½)"
9.5 (9, 9.5, 9) cm

1½ (1¾, 1¾, 2¼)"
3.8 (4.5, 4.5, 5.5) cm

6¼ (6¾, 7, 7½)"
16 (17, 18, 19) cm

Back

17¼ (18¾, 20¼, 21¾)"
44 (47.5, 51.5, 55) cm

16½ (16½, 16¼, 16¼)"
42 (42, 41.5, 41.5) cm

15¼ (16¾, 18¼, 19¾)"
38.5 (42.5, 46.5, 50) cm

19¼ (20¾, 22¼, 23¾)"
49 (52.5, 56.5, 60.5) cm

13 (13¾, 14½, 15¼)"
33 (35, 37, 38.5) cm

Sleeve

4½ (4¾, 4¾, 4¾)"
11.5 (12, 12, 12) cm

17¾ (17¼, 17, 16½)"
45 (44, 43, 42) cm

9½ (9¾, 10, 10¾)"
24 (25, 25.5, 27.5) cm

NEXT (INC) ROW: (RS) Knit to last 12 sts, M1, knit to end of row—1 st inc'd.

NEXT ROW: Work 12 sts in established patt, p1, work to end of row.

Rep inc row—1 st inc'd.

NEXT ROW: Work 12 sts in established patt, k1, work to end of row.

Work 6 rows even.

Rep last 10 rows 3 more times and, at the same time, when piece measures 16½ (16½, 16¼, 16¼)" (42 [42, 41.5, 41.5] cm) from CO edge, shape armhole at beg of RS rows as follows.

SHAPE ARMHOLE

NEXT ROW: (RS) BO 4 sts, knit to end of row.

Work 1 WS row in established patt.

NEXT (DEC) ROW: (RS) K3, sk2p, work in established patt to end of row—2 sts dec'd at armhole.

Rep armhole dec row every RS row 1 (1, 2, 2) more time(s)—35 (39, 39, 43) sts rem when all shaping is complete.

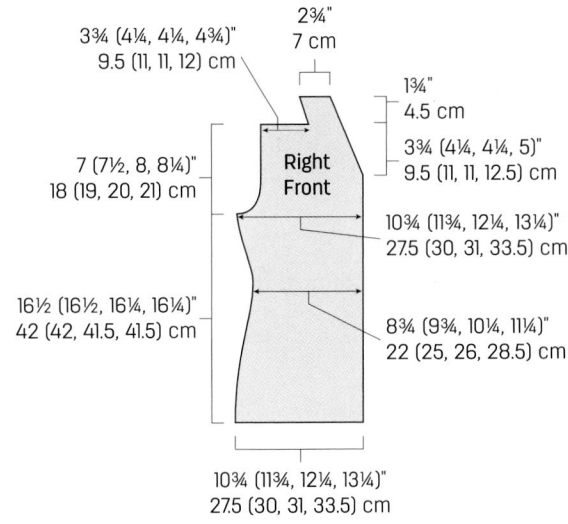

3¾ (4¼, 4¼, 4¾)"
9.5 (11, 11, 12) cm

2¾"
7 cm

1¾"
4.5 cm

3¾ (4¼, 4¼, 5)"
9.5 (11, 11, 12.5) cm

7 (7½, 8, 8¼)"
18 (19, 20, 21) cm

Right
Front

10¾ (11¾, 12¼, 13¼)"
27.5 (30, 31, 33.5) cm

16½ (16½, 16¼, 16¼)"
42 (42, 41.5, 41.5) cm

8¾ (9¾, 10¼, 11¼)"
22 (25, 26, 28.5) cm

10¾ (11¾, 12¼, 13¼)"
27.5 (30, 31, 33.5) cm

Cont even until armhole measures 3¼ (3¼, 3½, 3¼)" (8.5 [8.5, 9, 8.5] cm), ending with a WS row.

SHAPE NECK

NEXT (DEC) ROW: (RS) Knit to last 11 sts, ssk, knit to end of row—1 st dec'd.

NEXT ROW: (WS) (K1, p1) 5 times, (p1, k1) to end of row.

Rep dec row—1 st dec'd.

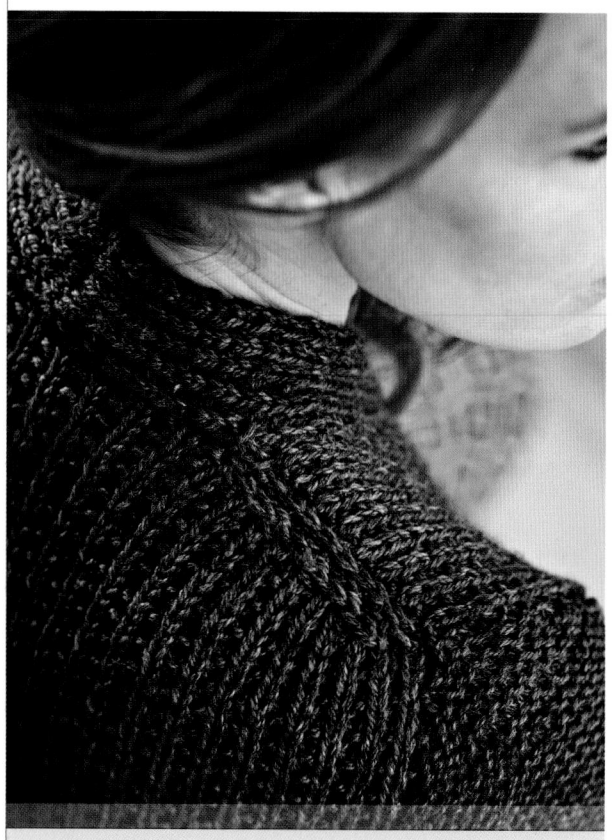

NEXT ROW: (WS) (K1, p1) to last st, k1.

Rep last 4 rows 4 (5, 5, 6) more times—25 (27, 27, 29) sts rem.

Armhole should measure about 7 (7½, 8, 8¼)" (18 [19, 20.5, 21] cm).

COLLAR/NECKBAND

NEXT ROW: (RS) BO 15 (17, 17, 19) sts, knit to end of row—10 sts rem.

NEXT (INC) ROW: Work in established patt to end of row, CO 1 st—11 sts.

Cont even in established patt until collar/neck-band reaches center of back neck BO sts, when slightly stretched, ending with a WS row. Place sts on holder.

right front

CO 43 (47, 49, 53) sts.

Work in Broken Rib patt until piece measures 4" (10 cm) from CO edge, ending with a WS row.

SHAPE WAIST

NEXT (DEC) ROW: (RS) K23 (25, 27, 29) sts, sk2p, pm on dec st, k17 (19, 19, 21) sts—2 sts dec'd.

Work 7 rows even.

NEXT (DEC) ROW: Knit to 2 sts before marked st, sk2p, k17 (19, 19, 21) sts—2 sts dec'd.

Rep last 8 rows 2 more times—35 (39, 41, 45) sts rem. Remove marker.

Cont even until piece measures 11¾ (12¼, 12¼, 12¼)" (30 [31, 31, 31] cm) from CO edge, ending with a WS row.

NEXT (INC) ROW: (RS) K12, M1, knit to end of row—1 st inc'd.

NEXT ROW: Work to last 13 sts in established patt, p1, work to end of row.

Rep inc row—1 st inc'd.

NEXT ROW: Work to last 13 sts in established patt, k1, work to end of row.

Work 6 rows even.

Rep last 10 rows 3 more times and, at the same time, when piece measures 16½ (16½, 16¼, 16¼)" (42 [42, 41.5, 41.5] cm) from CO edge, shape armhole at beg of WS rows as follows.

SHAPE ARMHOLE

NEXT ROW: (WS) BO 4 sts, work to end of row.

NEXT (DEC) ROW: (RS) Work to last 6 sts, sk2p, k3—2 sts dec'd at armhole.

Rep armhole dec row every RS row 1 (1, 2, 2) more time(s)—35 (39, 39, 43) sts rem when all shaping is complete.

Cont even until armhole measures 3¼ (3¼, 3½, 3¼)" (8.5 [8.5, 9, 8.5] cm), ending with a WS row.

SHAPE NECK

NEXT (DEC) ROW: (RS) K9, k2tog, knit to end of row—1 st dec'd.

NEXT ROW: (WS) Work in established patt to last 10 sts, p2, work in patt to end of row.

Rep dec row—1 st dec'd.

NEXT ROW: (WS) (K1, p1) to last st, k1.

Rep last 4 rows 4 (5, 5, 6) more times—25 (27, 27, 29) sts rem.

Knit 1 row even.

Armhole should measure about 7 (7½, 8, 8¼)" (18 [19, 20.5, 21] cm).

COLLAR/NECKBAND

NEXT ROW: (WS) BO 15 (17, 17, 19) sts, work to end of row—10 sts rem.

NEXT (INC) ROW: K10, CO 1 st—11 sts.

Cont even in established patt until collar/neckband reaches center of back neck BO sts, when slightly stretched, ending with a WS row.

Return held 11 sts for left collar/neckband to separate needle, with needle tips facing in the same direction when RS are held tog. Using spare needle, join collars using three-needle BO (see Glossary, page 13).

sleeves (make 2)

CO 38 (39, 40, 43) sts.

Work in rev St st (purl RS rows, knit WS rows) until piece measures 6¼ (4¾, 3¼, 3¼)" (16 [12, 8.5, 8.5] cm) from CO edge, ending with a RS row.

NEXT (INC) ROW: (WS) K1, M1, knit to last st, M1, k1—2 sts inc'd.

Rep inc row every 8 rows 6 (7, 8, 8) more times—52 (55, 58, 61) sts.

Cont even until piece measures 17¾ (17¼, 17, 16½)" (45 [44, 43, 42] cm) from CO edge, ending with a WS row.

SHAPE CAP

BO 3 (3, 4, 5) sts at beg of next 2 rows, then 2 sts at beg of next 4 rows—38 (41, 42, 43) sts rem.

NEXT (DEC) ROW: (RS) P1, p2tog tbl, purl to last 3 sts, p2tog, p1—2 sts dec'd.

Rep dec row every RS row 4 (5, 5, 5) more times. BO 2 sts at beg of next 4 rows, 3 sts at beg of next 2 rows, then 4 (4, 5, 5) sts at beg of next 2 rows—6 (7, 6, 7) sts rem.

BO rem sts.

belt

CO 10 sts.

Work in k1, p1 rib until piece measures about 51¼ (53¼, 55½, 57¾)" (130 [135.5, 141, 146.5] cm), or desired length. BO all sts in rib.

finishing

Weave in ends.

Sew shoulder seams. Sew collar to back neck edge. Sew sleeve and side seams, leaving 1¼-1½" (3.2-3.8 cm) open at each side of waist for belt. Sew in sleeves. Sew on 4 snaps evenly spaced along front edge.

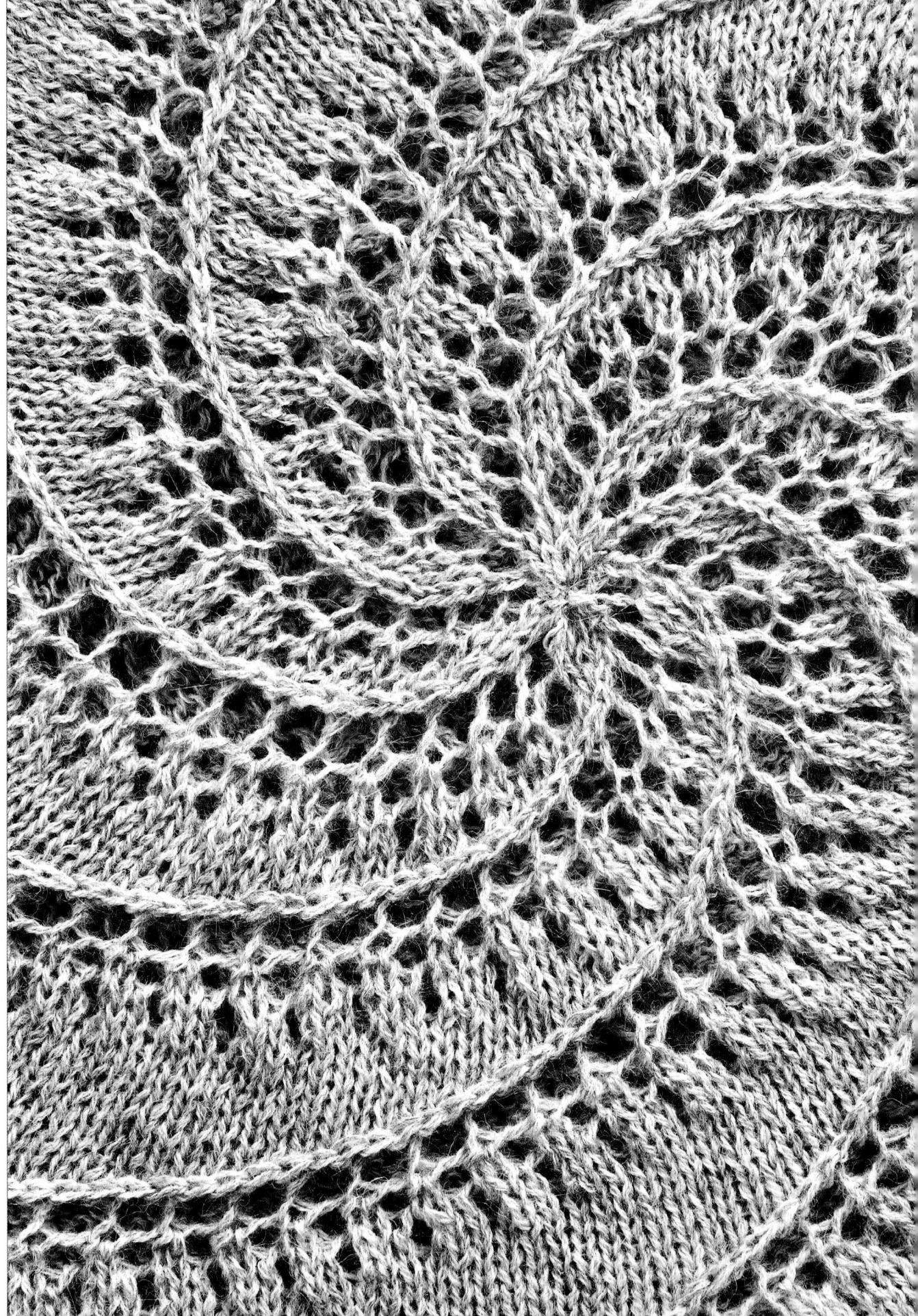

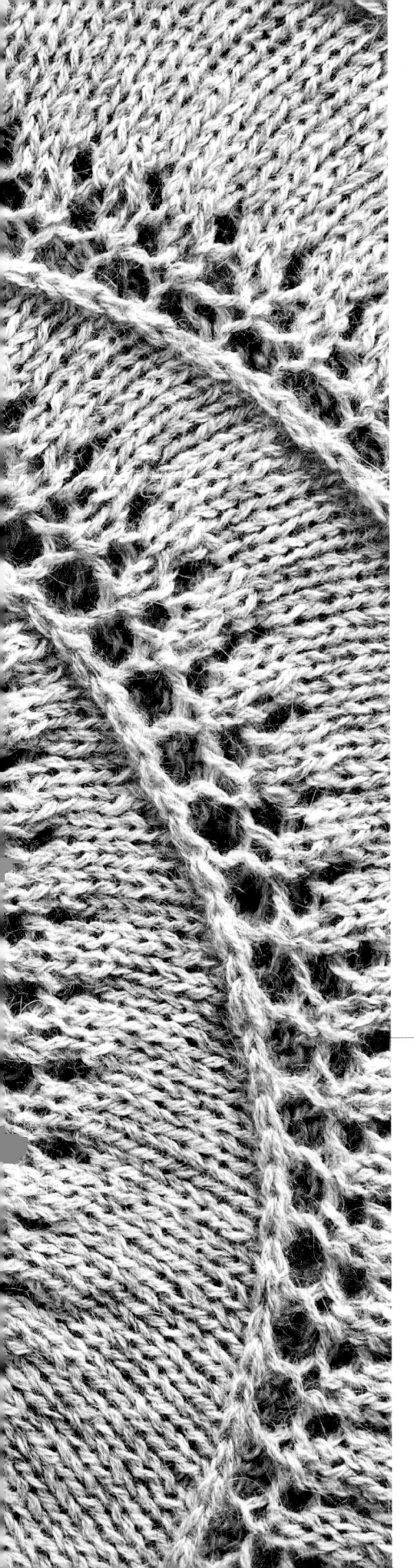

Lace

Yarnovers and decreases form the foundation of all lace motifs, and you can create the finest patterns from these stitches. The patterning looks complex, but once you've learned the system, lace motifs aren't really all that complicated to knit. All the patterns in this chapter are knitted with light, airy yarns to take full advantage of the transparency of the feminine lace motifs.

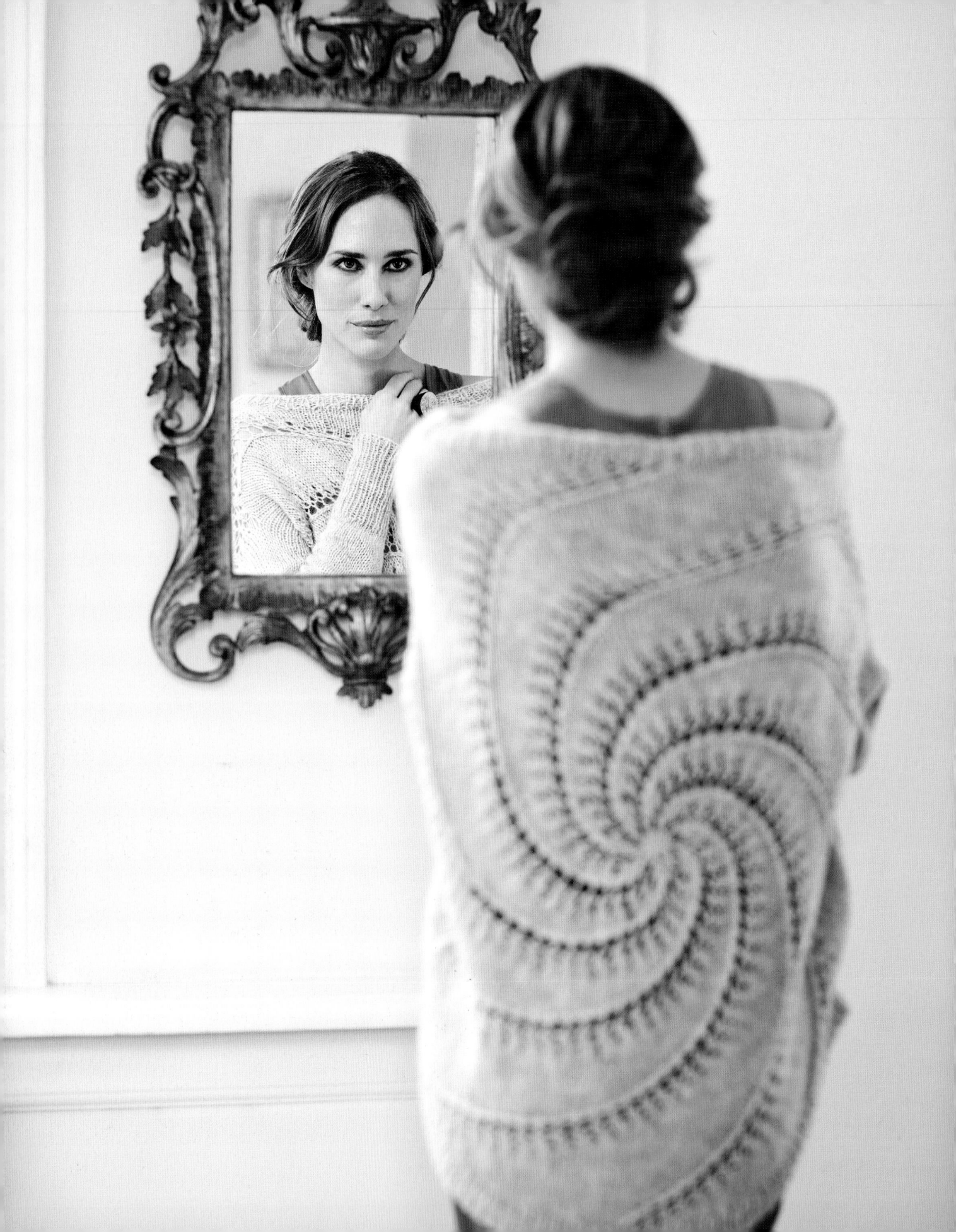

cille
spiral-lace top

Two circles form the front and back of this oh-so-cool top with very narrow sleeves. The garment can be worked with either a wide, open neckline or a high, narrow neckband.

FINISHED SIZE		S–M	L–XL
Bust	in	48	51
	cm	122	129.5
Total length	in	25¼	26¾
	cm	64	68

YARN
For Sand Top with Wide Neck
Fingering weight (#1 Super Fine).

Shown here: Isager Tvinni or Tvinni Tweed (100% merino wool; 279 yd [255 m]/50 g): 4 (4) skeins, #6s.

Laceweight (#0 Lace).

Isager Alpaca 1 (100% alpaca; 437 yd [400 m]/50 g): 3 (3) skeins, #2s.

For Blue-Gray Top with Narrow Neck (shown on page 43)
Fingering weight (#1 Super Fine).

Shown here: Isager Tvinni or Tvinni Tweed (100% merino wool; 278 yd [255 m]/50 g): 4 (4) skeins, #42.

Laceweight (#0 Lace).

Isager Alpaca 1 (100% alpaca; 437.5 yd [400 m]/50 g): 3 (3) skeins, #4.

NEEDLES
Size S–M: Size U.S. 10 (6 mm): set of 5 dpn and 16 and 24" (40 and 60 cm) circular (cir); two 32" (80 cm) cir; size U.S. 8 (5 mm): straight and 32" (80 cm) cir.

Size L–XL: Size U.S. 10¾–11 (7–8 mm): set of 5 dpn and 16 and 24" (40 and 60 cm) cir; two 32" (80 cm) cir; size U.S. 10 (6 mm): straight and 32" (80 cm) cir.

Adjust needle size if necessary to obtain the correct gauge.

NOTIONS
Markers; stitch holder.

GAUGE
Size S–M: 18 sts = 4" (10 cm) in St st on larger needles with 1 strand of each yarn held tog.

17 sts = 4" (10 cm) in lace patt on larger needles with 1 strand of each yarn held tog.

Size L–XL: 17 sts = 4" (10 cm) in St st on larger needles with 1 strand of each yarn held tog.

16 sts = 4" (10 cm) in lace patt on larger needles with 1 strand of each yarn held tog.

back

With larger size dpn, and 1 strand of each yarn held tog, CO 8 sts. Distribute sts evenly over 4 dpn with 2 sts on each needle. Place marker (pm), and join for working in rnds, being careful not to twist sts. Work in patt below, changing to cir needle when there are too many sts to work comfortably on dpn. Each repeat is worked twice over each dpn/section.

RND 1: Knit.

RND 2 (AND ALL FOLLOWING RNDS NOT LISTED THROUGH RND 14): Knit.

RND 3: *Yo, k1; rep from * around—16 sts; 4 sts on each dpn.

RND 5: *Yo, k2; rep from * around—24 sts; 6 sts on each dpn.

RND 7: *Yo, k3; rep from * around—32 sts; 8 sts on each dpn.

RND 9: *(Yo, k1) twice, k2tog; rep from * around—40 sts; 10 sts on each dpn.

RND 11: *Yo, k1, yo, k2, k2tog; rep from * around—48 sts; 12 sts on each dpn.

RND 13: *Yo, k1, yo, k3, k2tog; rep from * around—54 sts; 14 sts on each dpn.

RND 15: *Yo, k1, (yo, k2) twice, k2tog; rep from * around—72 sts; 18 sts on each dpn.

RND 16: *K7, k2tog; rep from * around—64 sts; 16 sts on each dpn.

RND 17: *Yo, k1, yo, k2, yo, k3, k2tog; rep from * around—80 sts; 20 sts on each dpn.

RND 18: *K8, k2tog; rep from * around—72 sts; 18 sts on each dpn.

RND 19: *Yo, k1, yo, k2, yo, k4, k2tog; rep from * around—88 sts; 22 sts on each dpn.

RND 20: *K9, k2tog; rep from * around—80 sts; 20 sts on each dpn.

RND 21: *Yo, k1, yo, k2, yo, k5, k2tog; rep from * around—96 sts; 24 sts in each section.

RND 22: *K10, k2tog; rep from * around—88 sts; 22 sts in each section.

RND 23: *Yo, k1, yo, k2, yo, k6, k2tog; rep from * around—104 sts; 26 sts in each section.

RND 24: *K11, k2tog; rep from * around—96 sts; 24 sts in each section.

RND 25: *Yo, k1, yo, k2, yo, k7, k2tog; rep from * around—112 sts; 28 sts in each section.

RND 26: *K12, k2tog; rep from * around—104 sts; 26 sts in each section.

RND 27: *Yo, k1, yo, k2, yo, k8, k2tog; rep from * around—120 sts; 30 sts in each section.

RND 28: *K13, k2tog; rep from * around—112 sts; 28 sts in each section.

RND 29: *Yo, k1, yo, k2, yo, k9, k2tog; rep from * around—128 sts; 32 sts in each section.

RND 30: *K14, k2tog; rep from * around—120 sts; 30 sts in each section.

RND 31: *Yo, k1, yo, k2, yo, k10, k2tog; rep from * around—136 sts; 34 sts in each section.

RND 32: *K15, k2tog; rep from * around—128 sts; 32 sts in each section.

RND 33: *Yo, k1, yo, k2, yo, k11, k2tog; rep from * around—144 sts, with 36 sts in each section.

RND 34: *K16, k2tog; rep from * around—136 sts, with 34 sts in each section.

RND 35: *Yo, k1, yo, k2, yo, k12, k2tog; rep from * around—152 sts; 38 sts in each section.

RND 36: *K17, k2tog; rep from * around—144 sts, with 36 sts in each section.

RND 37: *Yo, k1, yo, k2, yo, k13, k2tog; rep from * around—160 sts; 40 sts in each section.

RND 38: *K18, k2tog; rep from * around—152 sts; 38 sts in each section.

RND 39: *Yo, k1, yo, k2, yo, k14, k2tog; rep from * around—168 sts; 42 sts in each section.

RND 40: *K19, k2tog; rep from * around—160 sts; 40 sts in each section.

RND 41: *Yo, k1, yo, k2, yo, k15, k2tog; rep from * around—176 sts; 44 sts in each section.

RND 42: *K20, k2tog; rep from * around—168 sts; 42 sts in each section.

RND 43: *Yo, k1, yo, k2, yo, k16, k2tog; rep from * around—184 sts; 46 sts in each section.

RND 44: *K21, k2tog; rep from * around—176 sts; 44 sts in each section.

RND 45: *Yo, k1, yo, k2, yo, k17, k2tog; rep from * around—192 sts; 48 sts in each section.

RND 46: *K22, k2tog; rep from * around—184 sts; 46 sts in each section.

RND 47: *Yo, k1, yo, k2, yo, k18, k2tog; rep from * around—200 sts, with 50 sts in each section.

RND 48: *K23, k2tog; rep from * around—192 sts, with 48 sts in each section.

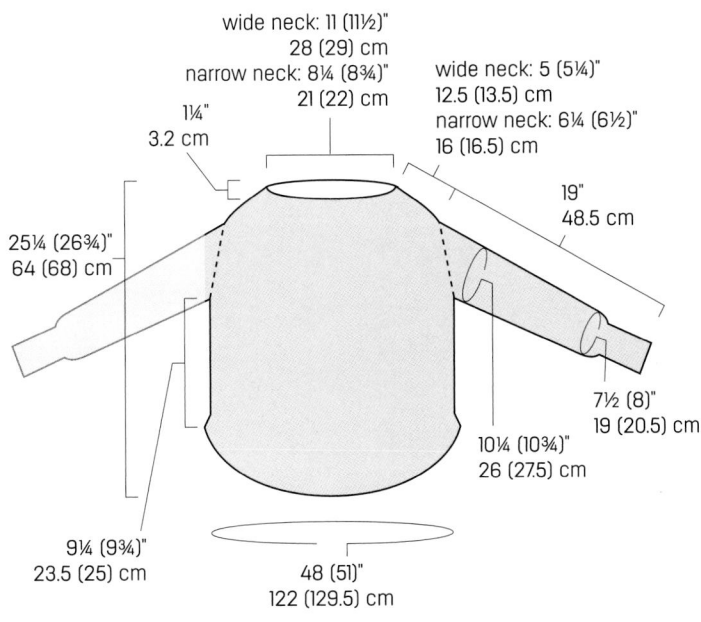

wide neck: 11 (11½)"
28 (29) cm
narrow neck: 8¼ (8¾)"
21 (22) cm

wide neck: 5 (5¼)"
12.5 (13.5) cm
narrow neck: 6¼ (6½)"
16 (16.5) cm

1¼"
3.2 cm

19"
48.5 cm

25¼ (26¾)"
64 (68) cm

7½ (8)"
19 (20.5) cm

10¼ (10¾)"
26 (27.5) cm

9¼ (9¾)"
23.5 (25) cm

48 (51)"
122 (129.5) cm

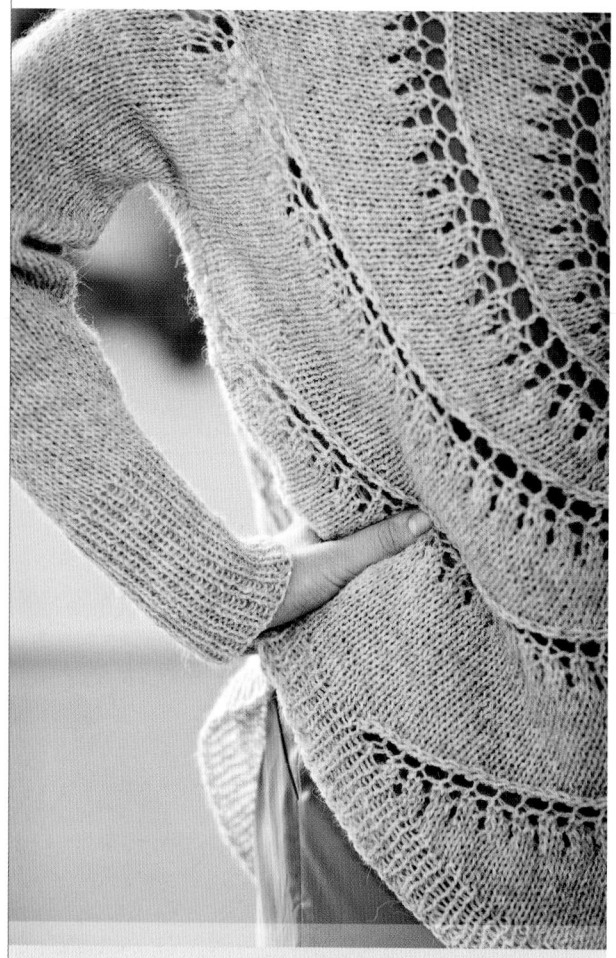

RND 49: *Yo, k1, yo, k2, yo, k19, k2tog; rep from * around—208 sts; 52 sts in each section.

RND 50: *K24, k2tog; rep from * around—200 sts; 50 sts in each section.

RND 51: *Yo, k1, yo, k2, yo, k20, k2tog; rep from * around—216 sts; 54 sts in each section.

RND 52: *K25, k2tog; rep from * around—208 sts; 52 sts in each section.

RND 53: *Yo, k1, yo, k2, yo, k21, k2tog; rep from * around—224 sts; 56 sts in each section.

RND 54: *K26, k2tog; rep from * around—216 sts; 54 sts in each section.

RND 55: *Yo, k1, yo, k2, yo, k22, k2tog; rep from * around—232 sts; 58 sts in each section.

RND 56: *K27, k2tog; rep from * around—224 sts; 56 sts in each section.

RND 57: *Yo, k1, yo, k2, yo, k23, k2tog; rep from * around—240 sts; 60 sts in each section.

RND 58: *K28, k2tog; rep from * around—232 sts; 58 sts in each section.

RND 59: *Yo, k1, yo, k2, yo, k24, k2tog; rep from * around—248 sts; 62 sts in each section.

RND 60: *K29, k2tog; rep from * around—240 sts; 60 sts in each section.

RND 61: *Yo, k1, yo, k2, yo, k25, k2tog; rep from * around—256 sts; 64 sts in each section.

RND 62: *K30, k2tog; rep from * around—248 sts; 62 sts in each section.

RND 63: *Yo, k1, yo, k2, yo, k26, k2tog; rep from * around—264 sts; 66 sts in each section.

RND 64: *K31, k2tog; rep from * around—256 sts; 64 sts in each section.

RND 65: *Yo, k1, yo, k2, yo, k27, k2tog; rep from * around—272 sts; 68 sts in each section.

RND 66: *K32, k2tog; rep from * around—264 sts; 66 sts in each section.

RND 67: *Yo, k1, yo, k2, yo, k28, k2tog; rep from * around—280 sts; 70 sts in each section.

RND 68: *K33, k2tog; rep from * around—272 sts; 68 sts in each section.

RND 69: *Yo, k1, yo, k2, yo, k29, k2tog; rep from * around—288 sts; 72 sts in each section.

RND 70: *K34, k2tog; rep from * around—280 sts; 70 sts in each section.

RND 71: *Yo, k1, yo, k2, yo, k30, k2tog; rep from * around—296 sts; 74 sts in each section.

RND 72: *K35, k2tog; rep from * around—288 sts; 72 sts in each section.

RND 73: *Yo, k1, yo, k2, yo, k31, k2tog; rep from * around—304 sts; 76 sts in each section.

RND 74: *K36, k2tog; rep from * around—296 sts; 74 sts in each section.

RND 75: *Yo, k1, yo, k2, yo, k32, k2tog; rep from * around—312 sts; 78 sts in each section.

RND 76: *K37, k2tog; rep from * around—304 sts; 76 sts in each section.

ROW 77: *Yo, k1, yo, k2, yo, k33, k2tog; rep from * around—320 sts; 80 sts in each section.

RND 78: *K38, k2tog; rep from * around—312 sts; 78 sts in each section.

RND 79: *Yo, k1, yo, k2, yo, k34, k2tog; rep from * around—328 sts; 82 sts in each section.

RND 80: *K39, k2tog; rep from * around—320 sts; 80 sts in each section.

Piece should measure about 24 (25½)" (61 [65] cm) in diameter. Set aside.

front

Work as for back through Rnd 72.

SHAPE NECK

Note: The number of sts for the narrow neck are listed first, with the number of sts for the wide neck given in parentheses.

SET-UP ROW: K0 (6), place last 17 (29) sts from RH needle onto a holder—271 (259) sts rem in work. Cont working back and forth.

ROW 73 (RS): BO 2 sts, knit until there are 32 (26) sts on RH needle after BO gap, k2tog, (yo, k1, yo, k2, yo, k31, k2tog) 6 times, yo, k1, yo, k2, yo, k16 (10)—283 (271) sts.

ROW 74 (WS): BO 2 sts, purl until there are 20 (14) sts on RH needle after BO gap, p2tog, (p36, p2tog) 6 times, p31 (25)—274 (262) sts.

ROW 75: BO 2 sts, knit until there are 28 (22) sts on RH needle after BO gap, k2tog, (yo, k1, yo, k2, yo, k32, k2tog) 6 times, yo, k1, yo, k2, yo, k17 (11)—286 (274) sts.

ROW 76: BO 2 sts, purl until there are 21 (15) sts on RH needle after BO gap, p2tog, (p37, p2tog) 6 times, p27 (21)—277 (265) sts.

ROW 77: BO 2 sts, knit until there are 24 (18) sts on RH needle after BO gap, k2tog, (yo, k1, yo, k2, yo, k33, k2tog) 6 times, yo, k1, yo, k2, yo, k18 (12)—289 (277) sts.

ROW 78: BO 2 sts, purl until there are 22 (16) sts on RH needle after BO gap, p2tog, (p38, p2tog) 6 times, p23 (17)—280 (268) sts.

ROW 79: BO 2 sts, knit until there are 20 (14) sts on RH needle after BO gap, k2tog, (yo, k1, yo, k2, yo, k34, k2tog) 6 times, yo, k1, yo, k2, yo, k19 (13)—292 (280) sts.

ROW 80: BO 2 sts, purl until there are 23 (17) sts on RH needle after BO gap, p2tog, (p39, p2tog) 6 times, p19 (13)—283 (271) sts.

Front should measure the same as the back, and there should be the same number of sts in St st on each side of neck shaping. Pm on back with 37 (49) sts for neck to match front neck. *Note: Due to the nature of the pattern, the k2tog from front and back will not match, but the pattern does line up with those on the opposite side.*

shoulder seams

Hold needles for back and front tog with RS tog and WS facing out and lace spiral meeting at shoulders. Join 28 (22) sts on each side of neck for shoulders using three-needle BO (see Glossary, page 13)—227 sts rem each for front and back.

sleeves (make 2)

Note: The sleeves are narrow and fit closely. If you want them wider, use a few more sts for each sleeve and make the side seam correspondingly shorter. You can also choose to omit the dec at each side of the sleeve and work the sleeve without shaping.

With RS facing, place next 24 sts from front and 24 sts from back on shortest large cir needle for your size—48 sts. Do not join.

Holding 1 strand of each yarn tog, work back and forth in St st (knit RS rows, purl WS rows) until sleeve measures 4" (10 cm), ending with a WS row.

NEXT (DEC) ROW: (RS) K1, ssk, knit to last 3 sts, k2tog, k1—2 sts dec'd.

Rep dec row on a RS row every 1½" (3.8 cm) 6 more times—34 sts rem.

Cont even until sleeve measures about 14¼" (36 cm), ending with a WS row.

Change to smaller cir needle. Work in k1, p1 rib for 4¾" (12 cm). BO loosely in rib.

After 2nd sleeve, 179 sts rem on hold each for front and back.

side seams

Place next 34 sts below sleeve sts on separate needles or long large cir needle. Holding pieces with RS tog and WS facing out, use a spare needle to join side seams using three-needle BO.

After 2nd side seam, 111 sts rem on hold each for front and back.

lower edge

Place rem back and front sts on longer large cir needle—222 sts. Pm and join for working in rnds. Work in k1, p1 rib for 1¼" (3.2 cm). BO loosely in rib. *Note: It's important to bind off loosely so the edge doesn't pull in and under. If the edge is too tight, the rest of the sweater will balloon out.*

neckband

Make the narrow neck for a warmer design that covers more skin; or go with the wide neck and a more casual look.

NARROW NECK

With smaller cir needle and RS facing, hold 1 strand of each yarn tog and pick up and k13 sts along left neck edge, knit held 17 front sts, pick up and k13 sts along right neck edge, then 37 sts along back neck edge—80 sts. Pm for beg of rnd, and join for working in rnds. Work in k1, p1 rib for 3¼" (8.5 cm). BO loosely in rib.

WIDE NECK

With smaller cir needle and RS facing, hold 1 strand of each yarn tog and pick up and k13 sts along left neck edge, knit held 29 front sts, pick up and k13 sts along right neck edge, then 49 sts along back neck edge—104 sts. Pm for beg of rnd, and join for working in rnds. Work in k1, p1 rib for 5 rnds. BO loosely in rib.

finishing

Weave in ends. Block to finished measurements.

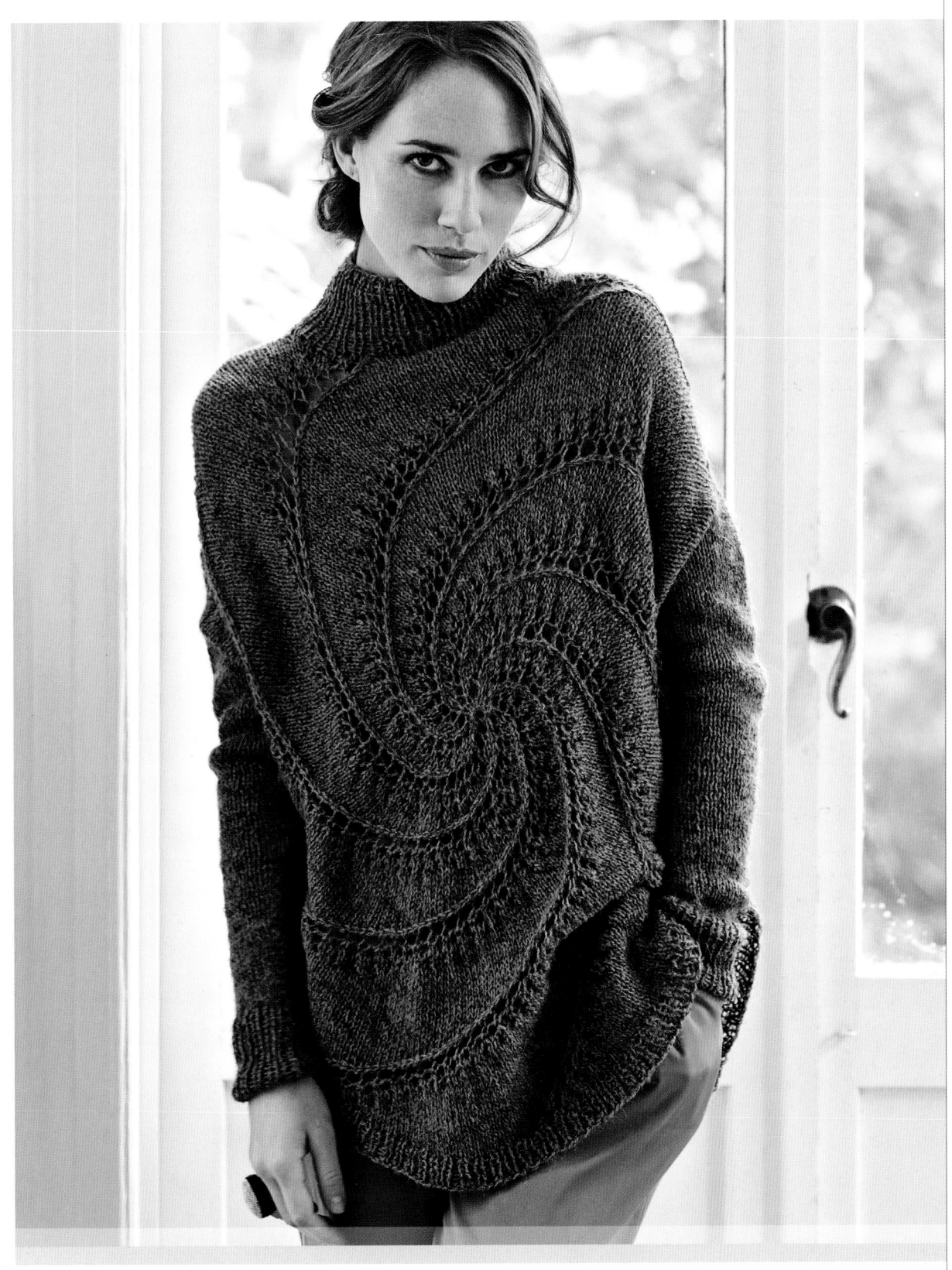

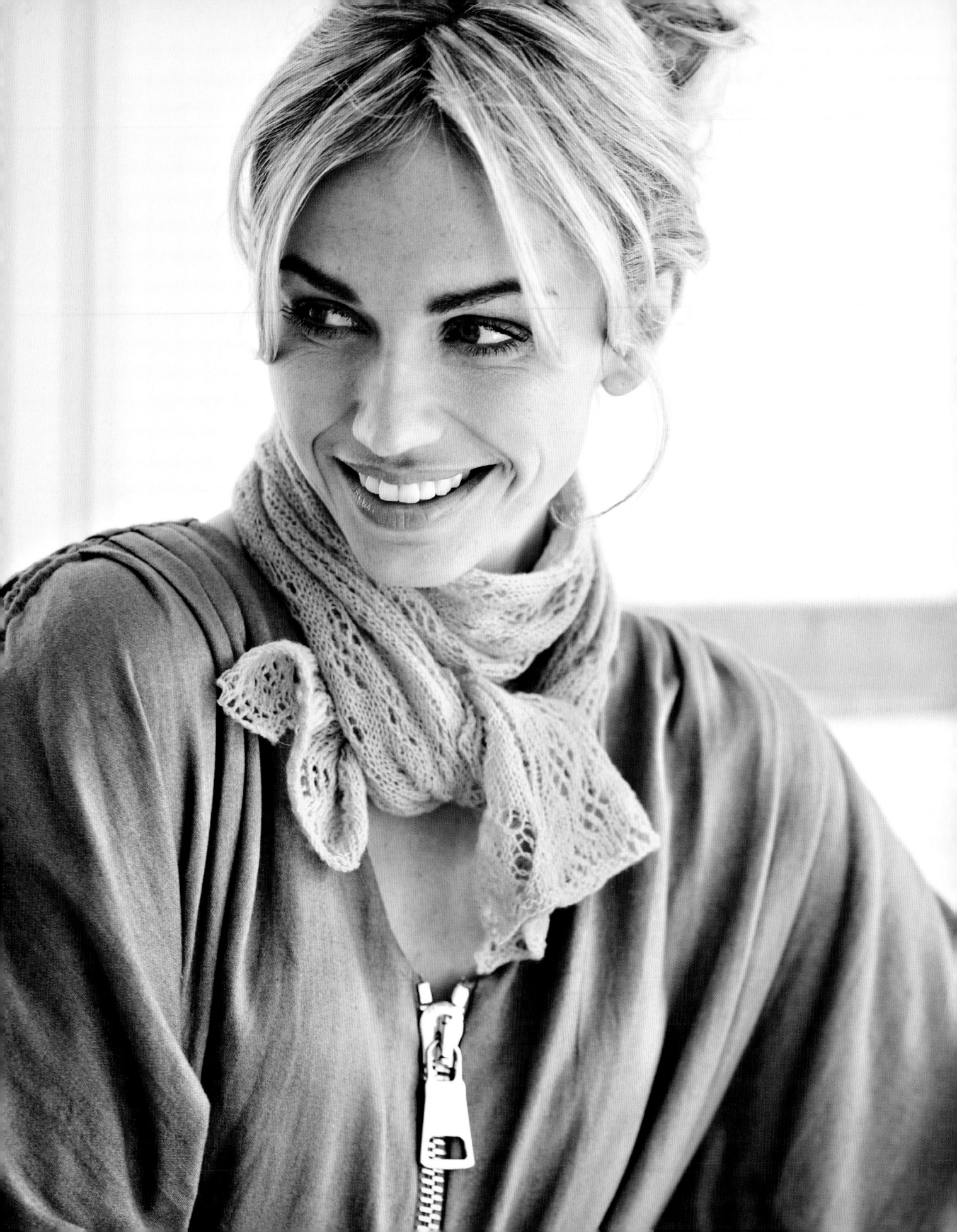

dora

sawtooth-edged scarf

The classic pattern in this ultra-feminine lace scarf is as pretty as a flower in bloom. The sawtooth edges at the sides are worked at the same time as the body of the scarf.

FINISHED SIZE
The yellow scarf measures about 51" (129.5 cm). The gray scarf on the next page is about 83½" (212 cm) long. Both are 11" (28 cm) wide after blocking.

YARN
Laceweight (#0 Lace).

Shown here: Gepard Cashmere Lace 1 (100% cashmere; 382 yd [350 m]/25 g): gray #8165, 3 balls, or yellow #2, 2 balls.

NEEDLES
Size U.S. 4 (3.5 mm): straight.

Adjust needle size if necessary to obtain the correct gauge.

GAUGE
26 sts and 32 rows = 4" (10 cm) in lace pattern.

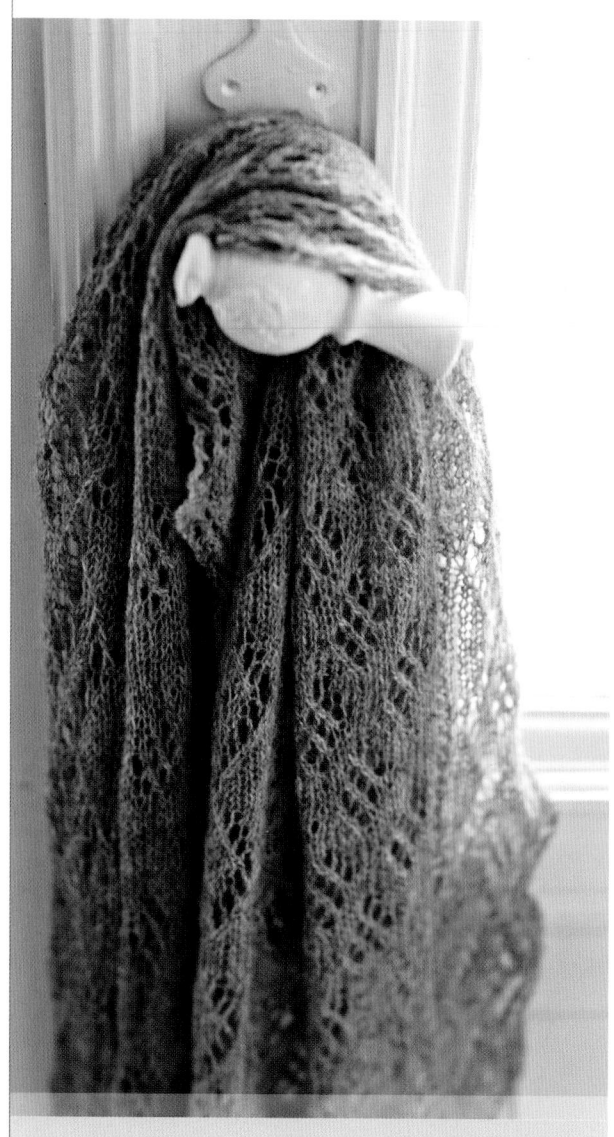

scarf

Note: Numbers for the shorter scarf are listed first, and numbers for the longer scarf are in parentheses.

CO 65 sts.

Knit 2 rows.

Cont in pattern following chart; work Rows 1–42 once, then rep Rows 23–42 eighteen (thirty-one) more times. Knit 2 rows. Piece should measure about 51 (83½)" (129.5 [212] cm) from CO.

BO knitwise.

finishing

Weave in ends. Block to finished measurements.

DORA CHART

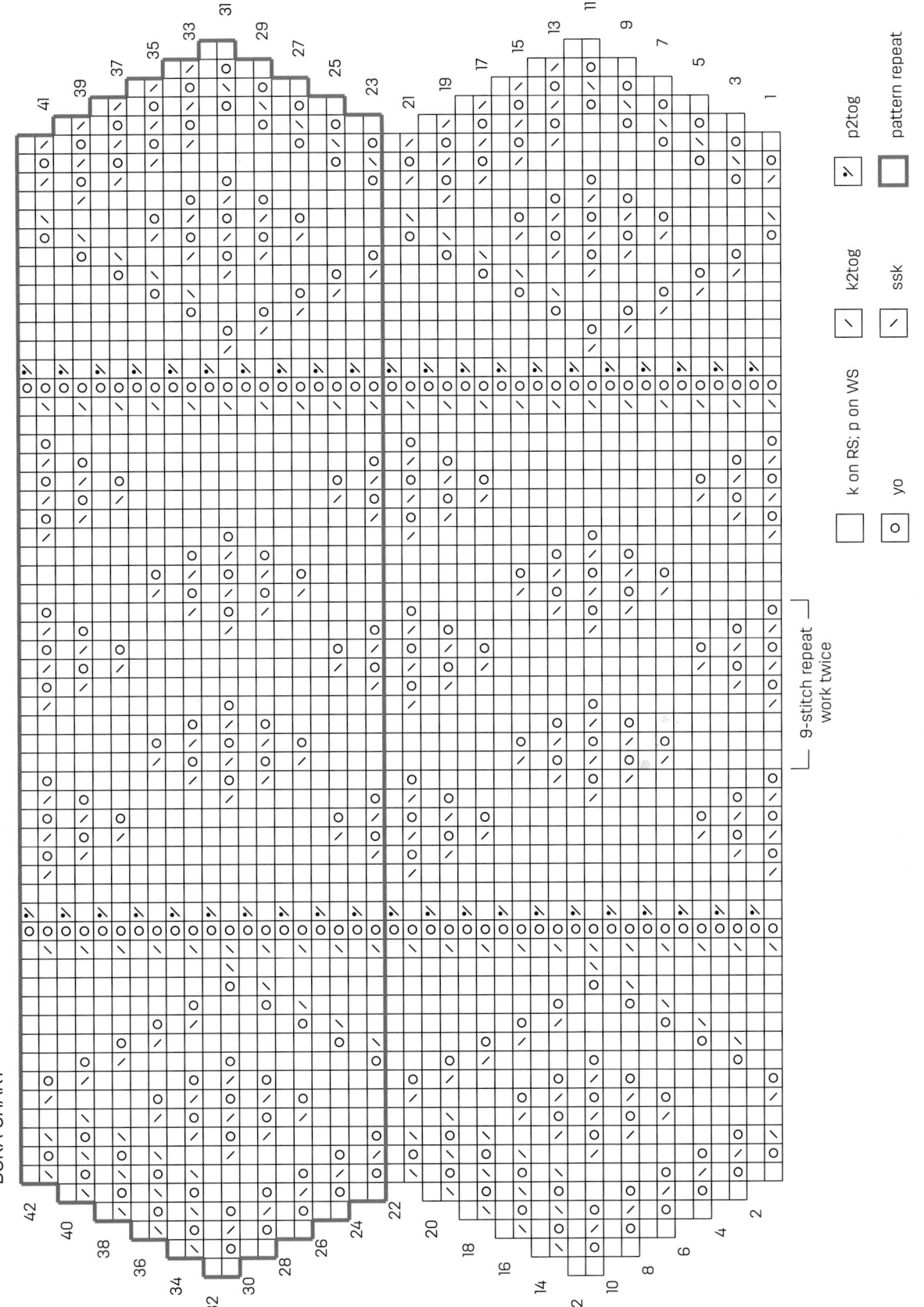

9-stitch repeat work twice

Legend:

	k2tog		p2tog
	ssk		pattern repeat
	yo		k on RS; p on WS

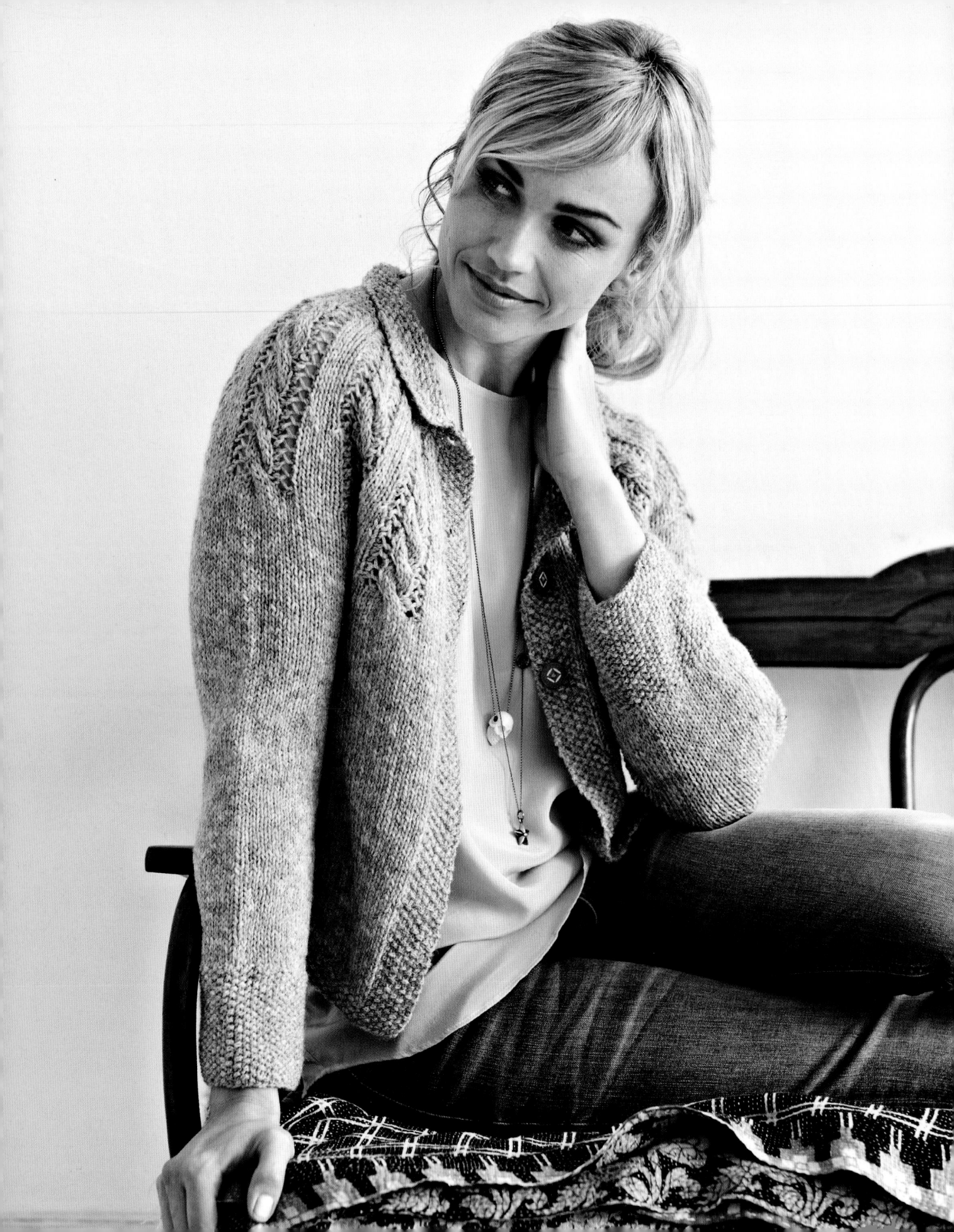

agnes

round-yoke cardigan

The open lace pattern between the cables on the yoke results from working the pattern on both the right and wrong sides. You can also make this cardigan without the collar. All you have to do instead is knit four rows after the top buttonhole and then bind off.

FINISHED SIZE		S	M	L	XL
Bust with about 1" (2.5 cm) overlap	in	35¼	39	41½	44¼
	cm	89.5	99	105.5	112.5
Total length	in	19¼	19½	20¼	20¼
	cm	49	49.5	51.5	51.5

YARN
Aran weight (#4 Medium).

Shown here: BC Garn Semilla Cablé (100% organic wool; 158 yd [145 m]/50 g): light gray #101, 7 (7, 8, 9) balls.

NEEDLES
Sizes U.S. 8 and 10 (5 and 6 mm): set of 5 dpn and 32" (80 cm) circular (cir).

Adjust needle size if necessary to obtain the correct gauge.

NOTIONS
3 buttons ¾" (19 mm) diameter; markers; tapestry needle.

GAUGE
18 sts and 25 rows = 4" (10 cm) in St st on larger needles.

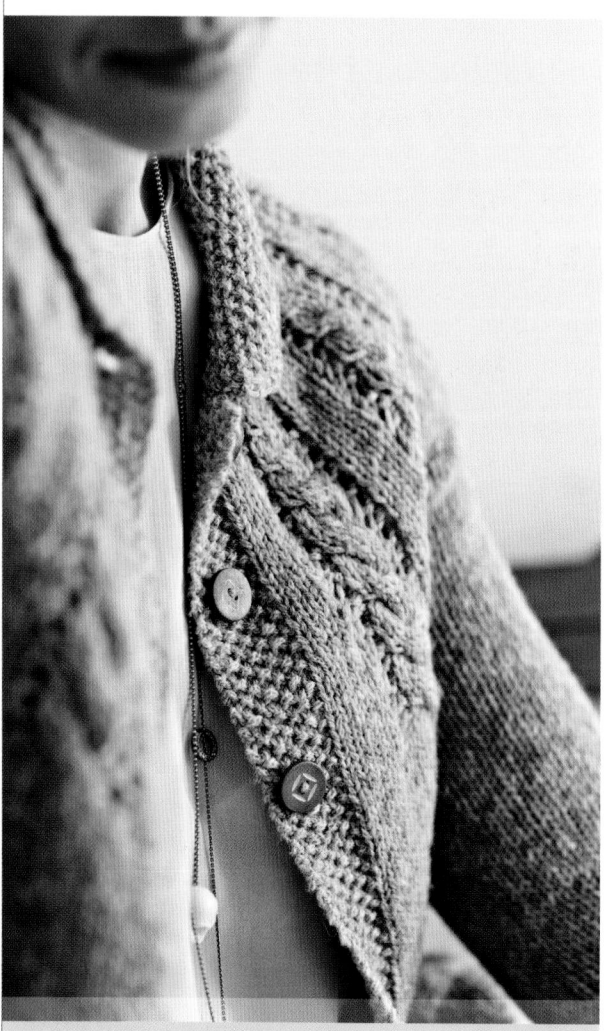

back and front

With smaller cir needle, CO 159 (175, 187, 199) sts. Do not join.

Work 7 rows in seed st.

Change to larger cir needle. Cont in St st and seed st as follows:

ROW 1: (RS) Work 7 sts in seed st as established, knit to last 7 sts, work rem 7 sts in seed st as established.

ROW 2: Work 7 sts in seed st as established, purl to last 7 sts, work rem 7 sts in seed st as established.

Cont in established patt until piece measures 10¼" (26 cm) from CO edge, ending with a WS row.

DIVIDE FOR THE ARMHOLES

NEXT ROW: (RS) Work 39 (43, 46, 49) sts in established patt for right front, BO 5 sts for armhole, work 71 (79, 85, 91) sts for back, BO 5 sts for armhole, work to end of row for left front—149 (165, 177, 189) sts rem; 39 (43, 46, 49) sts for each front, and 71 (79, 85, 91) sts for back. Set piece aside.

sleeves (make 2)

With smaller dpn, CO 52 (54, 56, 58) sts. Place marker (pm) and join for working in rnds, being careful not to twist sts.

Work in seed st for 3½" (9 cm).

Change to larger dpn.

Cont in St st until piece measures 7¾ (6, 4¾, 4¾)" (19.5 [15, 12, 12] cm) from CO edge.

NEXT (INC) RND: K1, M1, knit to last st, M1, k1—2 sts inc'd.

Rep inc rnd every 24 (18, 14, 14) rnds 1 (2, 3, 3) more time(s)—56 (60, 64, 66) sts. Cont even until

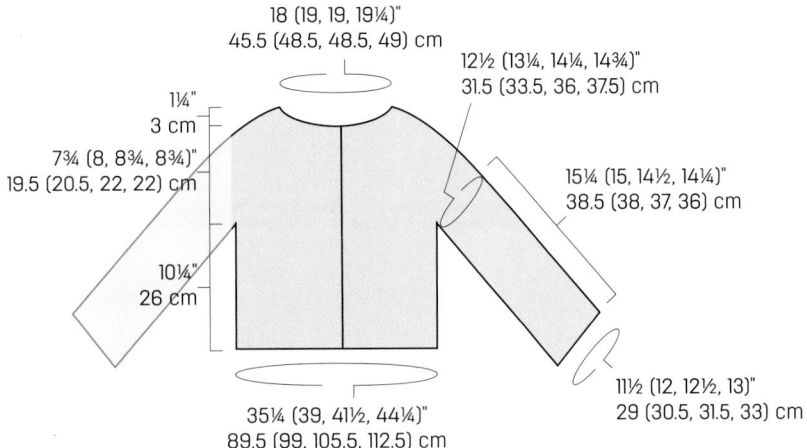

18 (19, 19, 19¼)"
45.5 (48.5, 48.5, 49) cm

12½ (13¼, 14¼, 14¾)"
31.5 (33.5, 36, 37.5) cm

1¼"
3 cm

7¾ (8, 8¾, 8¾)"
19.5 (20.5, 22, 22) cm

15¼ (15, 14½, 14¼)"
38.5 (38, 37, 36) cm

10¼"
26 cm

11½ (12, 12½, 13)"
29 (30.5, 31.5, 33) cm

35¼ (39, 41½, 44¼)"
89.5 (99, 105.5, 112.5) cm

piece measures 15¼ (15, 14½, 14¼)" (38.5 [38, 37, 36] cm) from CO edge, ending last rnd 2 sts before end of rnd.

BO 5 sts—51 (55, 59, 61) sts rem. Set piece aside.

yoke

With larger cir needle and WS facing, work 39 (43, 46, 49) sts for left front in established patt, with WS of first sleeve facing, p51 (55, 59, 61), p71 (79, 85, 91) back sts, with WS of second sleeve facing, p51 (55, 59, 61), then work rem 39 (42, 46, 49) sts of right front—251 (275, 295, 311) sts.

NEXT (SET-UP) ROW: (RS) Work to last 3 sts of right front, ssk, k1, pm, k1, k2tog, knit to last 3 sts of right sleeve, ssk, k1, pm, k1, k2tog, knit to last 3 sts of back, ssk, k1, pm, k1, k2tog, knit to last 3 sts of left sleeve, ssk, k1, pm, k1, k2tog, work to end of row—243 (267, 287, 303) sts rem.

NEXT ROW: *Work in established patt to marker, slm; rep from * 3 more times, then work to end of row.

NEXT (DEC) ROW: (RS) *Work to 3 sts before marker, ssk, k1, sm, k1, k2tog; rep from * 3 more times, then work to end of row—8 sts dec'd.

Rep last 2 rows 2 (3, 5, 5) more times—219 (235, 239, 255) sts rem.

Work 1 WS row even.

NEXT (SET-UP) ROW: (RS) Work Row 1 over first 7 sts at right side of chart, 18-st rep 11 (12, 12, 13) times, and at same time, dec (inc, dec, dec) 1 (1, 3, 1) st(s) evenly across, then work 13 sts at left side of chart—218 (236, 236, 254) sts rem.

Work Rows 2-40 of chart as established—104 (112, 112, 120) sts rem.

Change to smaller size cir needle.

Size S only

NEXT (DEC) ROW: (RS) Work 7 sts in established patt, *p2tog, k1, p1, k2tog, p1, k1; rep from * 10 more times, p2tog, work to end of row—81 sts rem.

Sizes M (L) only

NEXT (DEC) ROW: (RS) (K1, p1) 5 times, *k1, p2tog, k1, p1, k2tog; rep from * 12 more times, p1, k2tog, p1, work to end of row—85 (85) sts rem.

Size XL only

NEXT (DEC) ROW: (RS) (K1, p1) 6 times, *k2tog, p1; rep from * 32 more times, (k1, p1) to last st, k1—87 sts rem.

All sizes

Work 1 WS row even in seed st as established.

NEXT (BUTTONHOLE) ROW: (RS) K1, p1, k1, BO 2 sts for buttonhole, work to end of row—79 (83, 83, 85) sts.

Work 1 WS row and CO 2 sts over buttonhole gap—81 (85, 85, 87) sts.

cardigan without collar

Work 1 row even. BO in patt.

cardigan with collar

Work 1 row even.

BO 4 sts at the beg of next 2 rows—73 (77, 77, 79) sts rem.

Change to larger cir needle.

Cont in seed st and inc 1 st at each end of every RS row twice—77 (81, 81, 83) sts.

Work 1 WS row even.

NEXT (INC) ROW: (RS) K1, M1, work 20 (21, 21, 21) sts in established patt, M2, work 37 (39, 39, 41) sts, M2, work to last st, M1, k1—83 (87, 87, 89) sts.

Work 5 rows even.

NEXT (DEC) ROW: (RS) K2tog, work to last 2 sts, k2tog—2 sts dec'd.

Rep dec row every RS row 2 more times, then every row 3 times—71 (75, 75, 77) sts rem.

BO in patt.

finishing

Weave in ends. Sew underarm seams. Block to finished measurements.

Sew buttons to left front opposite buttonholes. If desired, fold cuff to RS and sew loosely in place at underarm.

AGNES CHART

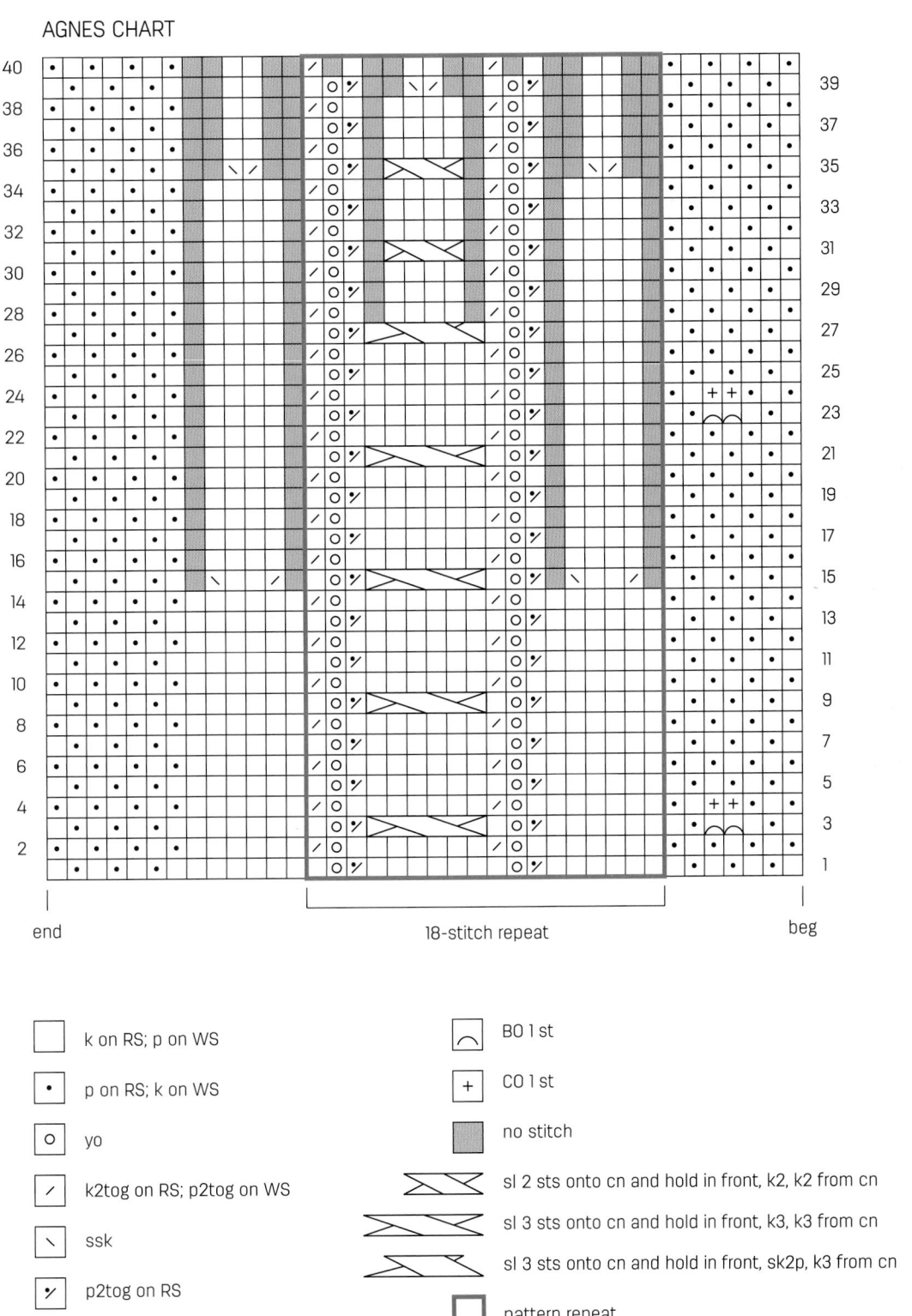

k on RS; p on WS		BO 1 st
· p on RS; k on WS		+ CO 1 st
o yo		no stitch
⁄ k2tog on RS; p2tog on WS		sl 2 sts onto cn and hold in front, k2, k2 from cn
＼ ssk		sl 3 sts onto cn and hold in front, k3, k3 from cn
⅝ p2tog on RS		sl 3 sts onto cn and hold in front, sk2p, k3 from cn
		pattern repeat

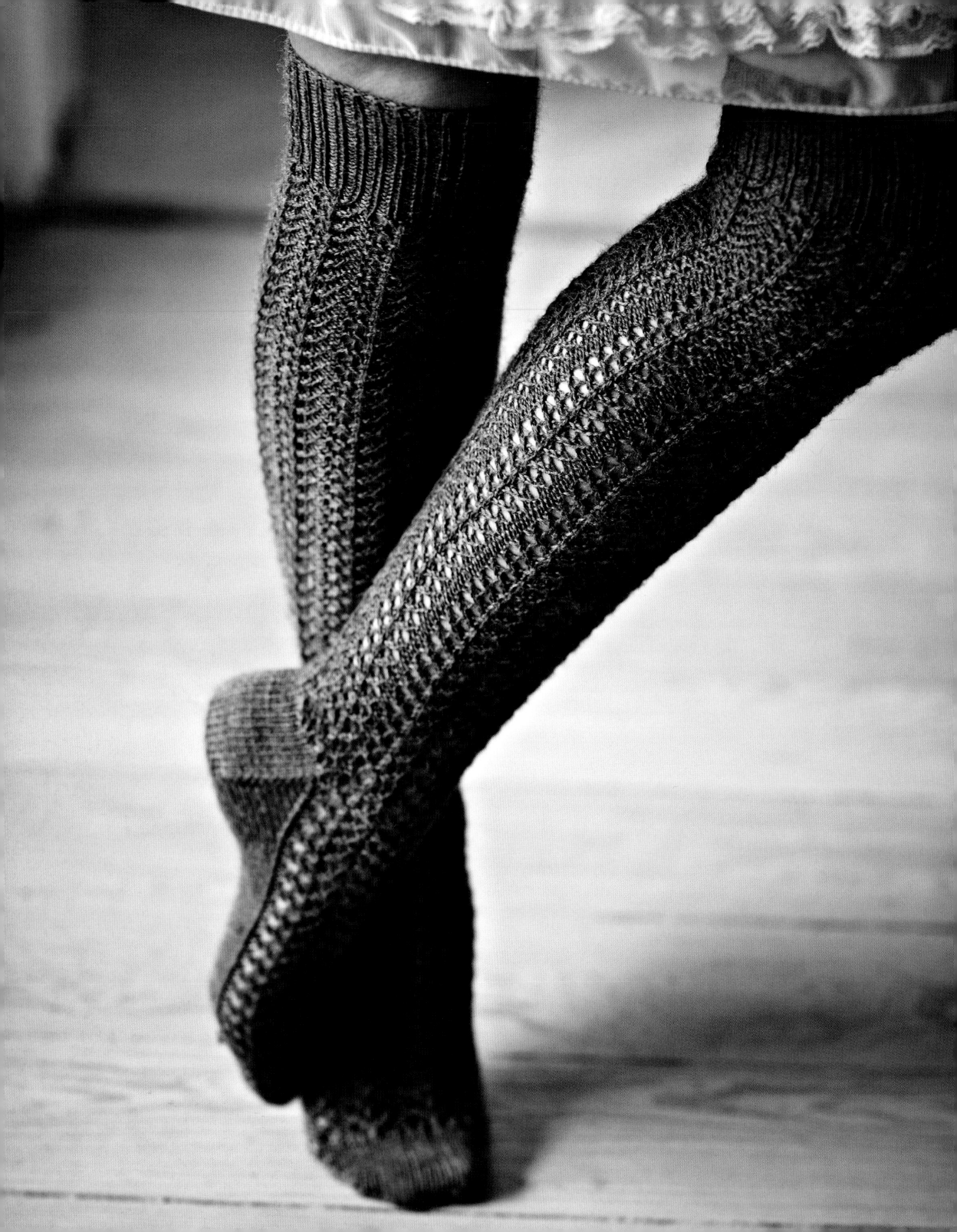

julia

knee stockings

Lift your skirt just a bit to reveal these luxurious handknitted stockings. The shaping of the area over the calf looks like a lace insert.

FINISHED SIZE
6¾" (17 cm) foot circumference.
8¼" (21 cm) leg circumference.
20¼" (51.5 cm) long.

YARN
Fingering weight (#1 Super Fine).

Shown here: Filcolana Arwetta Classic (80% merino wool, 20% nylon; 229 yd [210 m]/50 g): gray-blue heather #726, 3 balls.

NEEDLES
Size U.S. 1.5 (2.5 mm): set of 5 dpn.

Adjust needle size if necessary to obtain the correct gauge.

NOTIONS
Marker; tapestry needle.

GAUGE
34 sts and 44 rnds = 4" (10 cm) in lace patt; 32 sts and 44 rnds = 4" (10 cm) in St st.

stitch guide

LACE PATTERN *(multiple of 7 sts)*
RND 1: *P1, yo, ssk, k1, k2tog, yo, p1; rep from *.
RNDS 2 AND 4: *P1, k5, p1; rep from *.
RND 3: *P1, k1, yo, s2kp, yo, k1, p1; rep from *.
Rep Rnds 1–4 for patt.

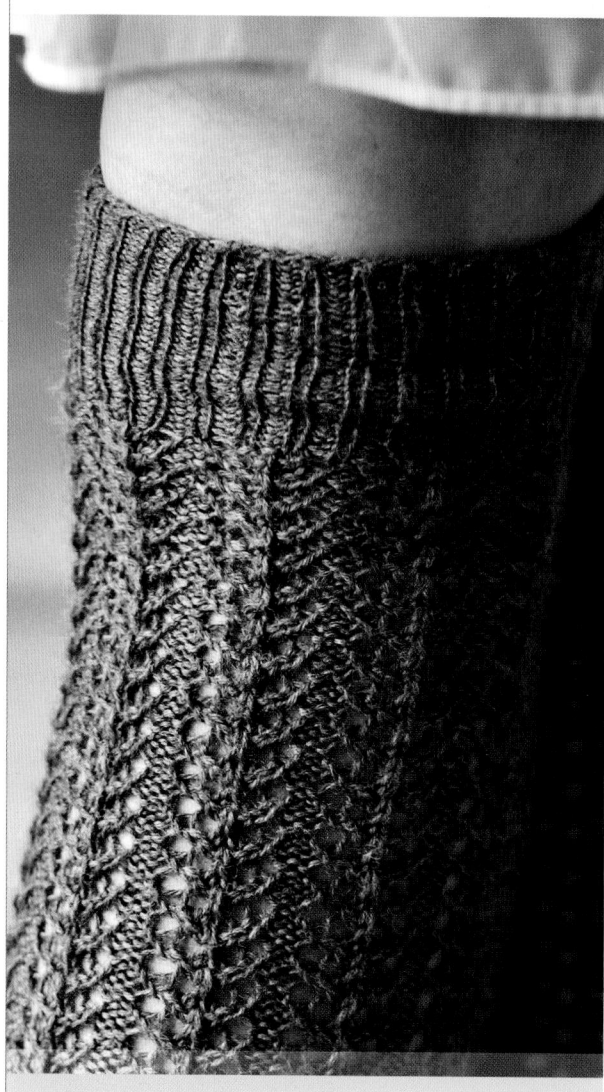

leg

CO 70 sts. Distribute sts evenly over 4 dpn. Place marker (pm) and join for working in rnds, being careful not to twist sts.

Work in k1, p1 rib for 3¼" (8.5 cm). Rearrange sts over dpn with 21 sts each on Needles 1 and 4, and 14 sts each on Needles 2 and 3.

NEXT RND: P1, *k5, p2; rep from * to last 6 sts, k5, p1.

Cont in lace patt until piece measures 9¾" (25 cm) from CO edge, ending with patt Rnd 4.

SHAPE LEG
Work Rnds 5-44 of Lace chart—56 sts rem; 14 sts on each needle.

Cont even in established patt until piece measures about 17" (43 cm) from CO edge, ending with patt Rnd 4.

heel flap and heel turn

Using Needle 4, k14 from Needle 1, turn, leaving 28 sts on Needles 2 and 3 on hold for instep— 28 sts rem.

Work back and forth in St st for 24 rows, ending with a WS row; heel flap should measure about 2¼" (5.5 cm).

ROW 1: K16, ssk, k1, turn.

ROW 2: Sl 1, p5, p2tog, p1, turn.

ROW 3: Sl 1, k6, ssk, k1, turn.

ROW 4: Sl 1, p7, p2tog, p1, turn.

ROW 5: Sl 1, k8, ssk, k1, turn.

ROW 6: Sl 1, p9, p2tog, p1, turn.

ROW 7: Sl 1, k10, ssk, k1, turn.

ROW 8: Sl 1, p11, p2tog, p1, turn.

JULIA CHART

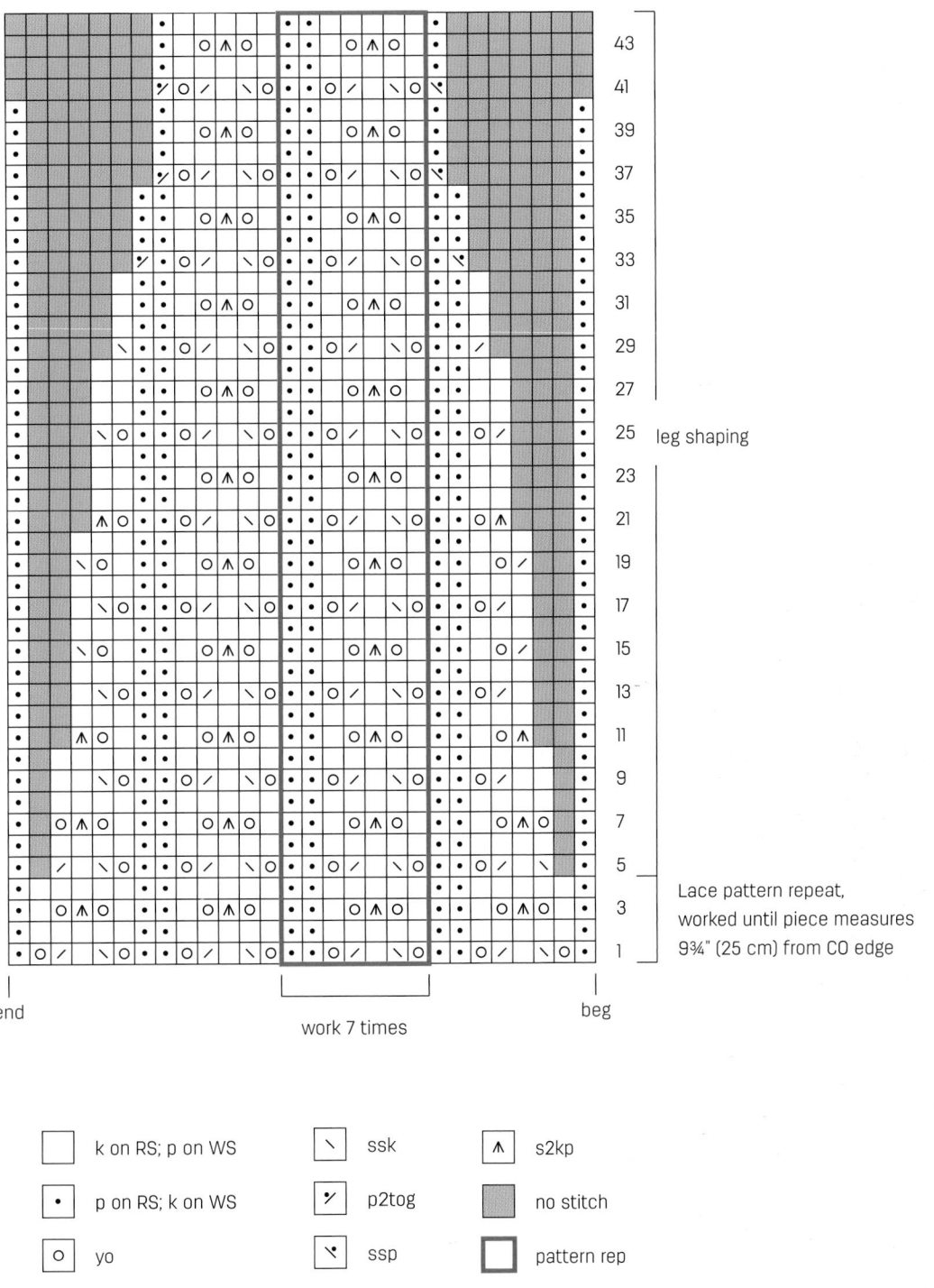

leg shaping

Lace pattern repeat,
worked until piece measures
9¾" (25 cm) from CO edge

end

work 7 times

beg

	k on RS; p on WS		ssk		s2kp
	p on RS; k on WS		p2tog		no stitch
	yo		ssp		pattern rep
	k2tog				

ROW 9: Sl 1, k12, ssk, k1, turn.

ROW 10: Sl 1, p13, p2tog, p1, turn.

ROW 11: Sl 1, k14, ssk, turn.

ROW 12: Sl 1, p14, p2tog, turn—16 sts rem.

gusset and foot

NEXT ROW: (RS) K8 heel sts, pick up 12 edge loops along side of heel, then with Needle 4, pick up 12 edge loops along rem side of heel, join with Needles 2 and 3 for working in rnds again—68 sts; 20 each on Needles 1 and 4, and 14 sts each on Needles 2 and 3.

RND 1: K8, (k1 tbl) 12 times, work next 28 sts in established patt, (k1 tbl) 12 times, knit to end of rnd.

RND 2: Needle 1, knit to last 2 sts, k2tog; Needles 2 and 3, work in established patt; Needle 4, ssk, knit to end of rnd—2 sts dec'd.

RND 3: Work even in established patt.

Rep Rnds 2 and 3 four more times, then rep Rnd 2 once more—56 sts rem; 14 sts on each needle.

Cont even until foot measures 7-8¼" (18-21 cm), or 1½" (3.8 cm) short of desired length from heel.

toe

NEXT RND: Knit.

NEXT (DEC) RND: Needle 1, knit to last 3 sts, ssk, k1; Needle 2, k1, k2tog, knit to end; Needle 3, knit to last 3 sts, ssk, k1; Needle 4, k1, k2tog, knit to end of rnd—4 sts dec'd.

Rep last 2 rnds 5 more times, then rep dec rnd every rnd 3 times—20 sts rem; 5 sts on each needle.

Place all the instep sts on one dpn and the sole sts on second dpn. Graft toe closed using Kitchener st, or turn the sock WS out and join sts using a three-needle BO (for both, see Glossary, pages 11 and 13 respectively).

Make second stocking same as first.

finishing

Weave in ends.

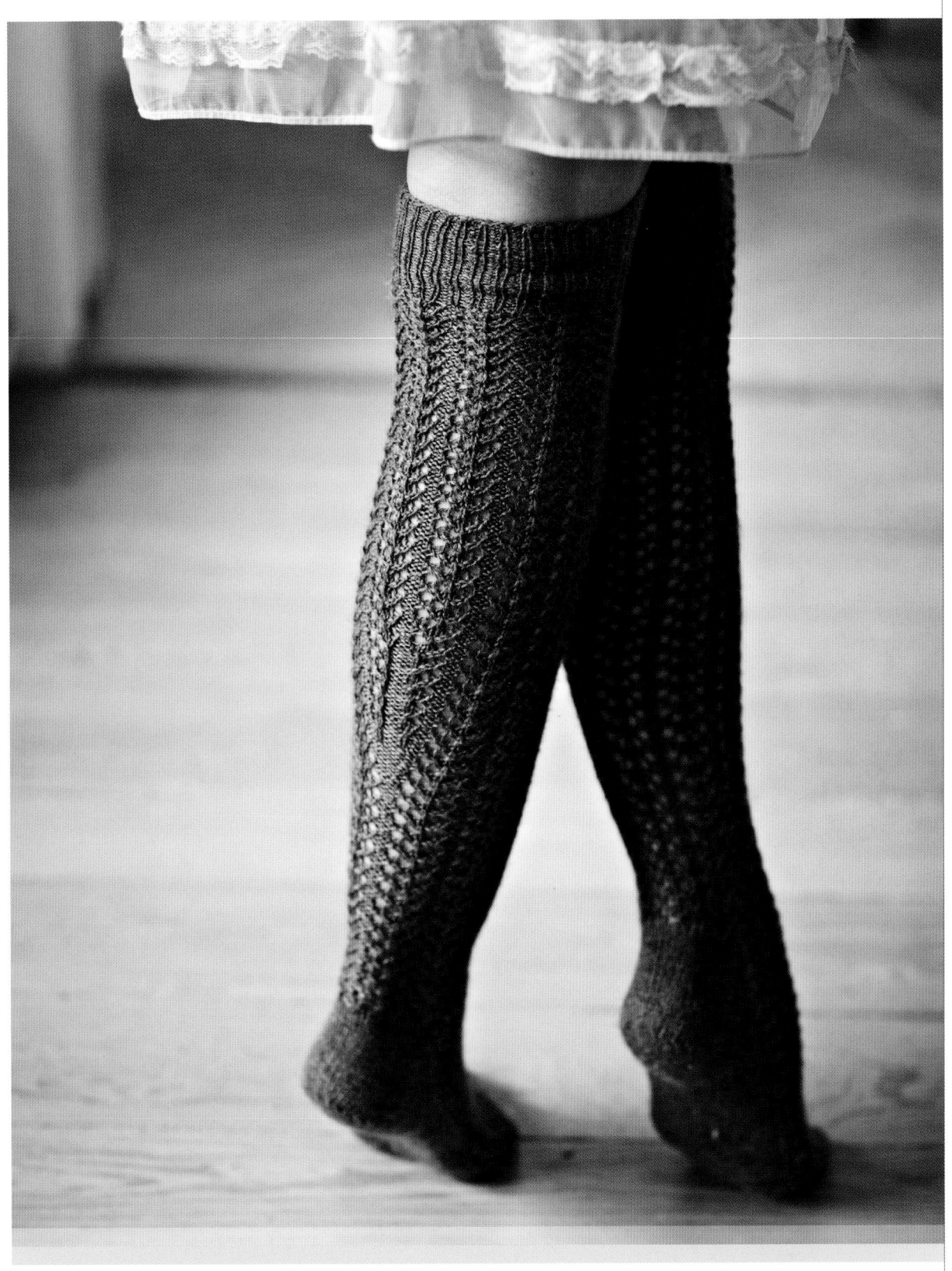

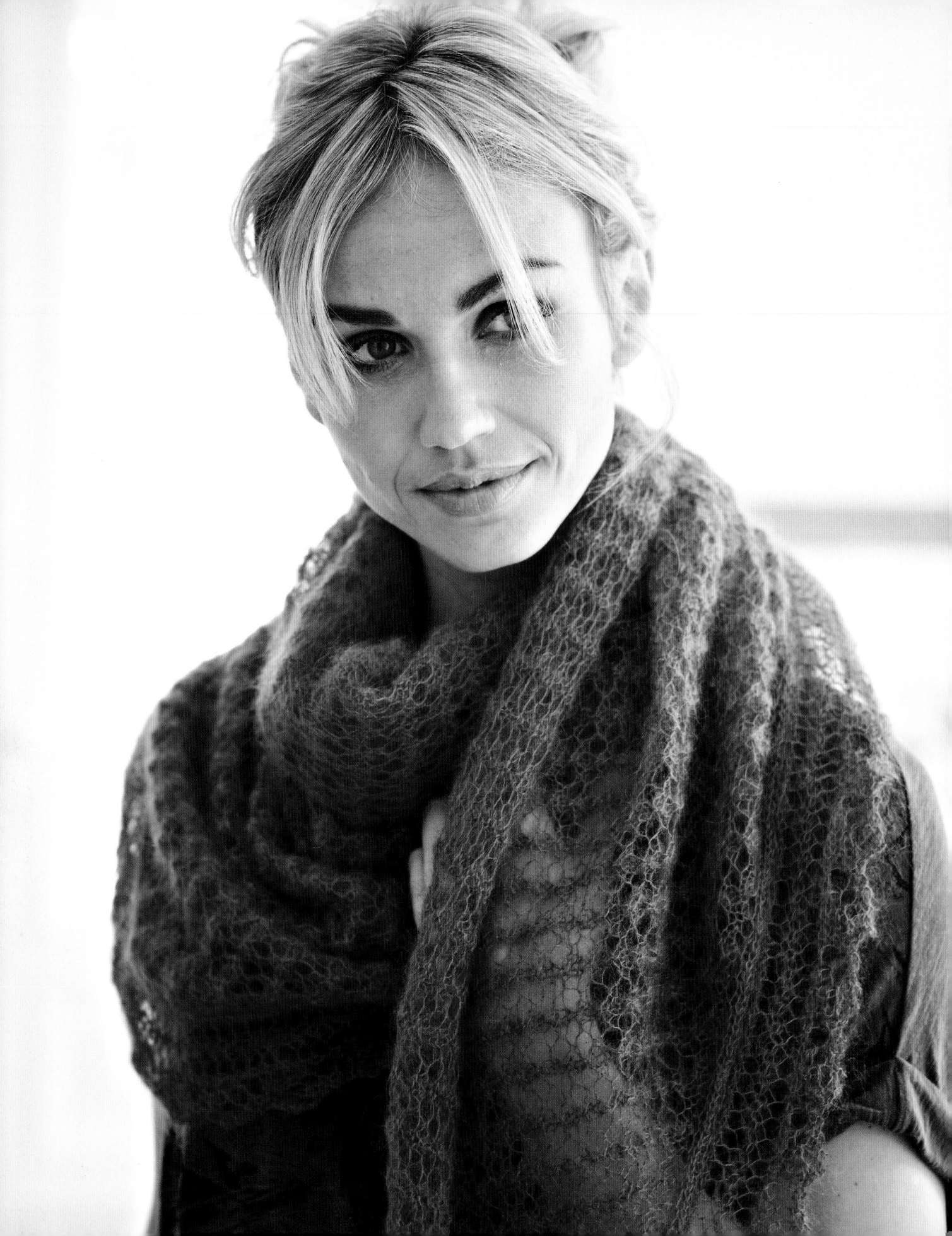

silk

triangular lace shawl

If you follow the instructions to the letter, this large shawl
will cover your neck and shoulders more than adequately,
but since you begin at the bottom tip of the shawl, you
can make it as large as you like—just keep on keeping on!
The lace edging is worked separately and then sewn on.

FINISHED SIZE
About 74¾" (190 cm) wide and 35"
(89 cm) long, including edging.

YARN
Laceweight (#0 Lace).

Shown here: Permin Angel (70%
kid mohair, 30% silk; 229 yd
[210 m]/25 g): redwood #17, 4 balls.

NEEDLES
Size U.S. 6 (4 mm): 32" (80 cm)
circular (cir) and double-pointed
(dpn).

*Adjust needle size if necessary to
obtain the correct gauge.*

NOTIONS
Tapestry needle.

GAUGE
15 sts and 31 rows = 4" (10 cm) in
lace pattern.

NOTE
A circular needle is used to
accommodate the large number
of stitches. Work back and forth.

shawl

With cir needle, CO 7 sts.

Work Rows 1–26 of Shawl chart, rep Rows 15–26 nineteen more times, then rep Rows 15 and 16 once more—263 sts. Add additional patt reps across the row as the number of sts inc. Piece should measure about 33" (84 cm) long at center.

BO loosely as follows: *BO 3, yo, pass last st bound-off over yo; rep from * to end of row.

lace edging

With dpn, CO 10 sts. Rep Rows 1–8 of Edging chart until edging fits along lower edges of shawl and around CO edge without pulling, ending with a complete rep. BO all sts.

finishing

Weave in ends. With RS facing, sew edging to sides of shawl, easing around CO edge, using mattress st (see Glossary, page 12).

Block to finished measurements.

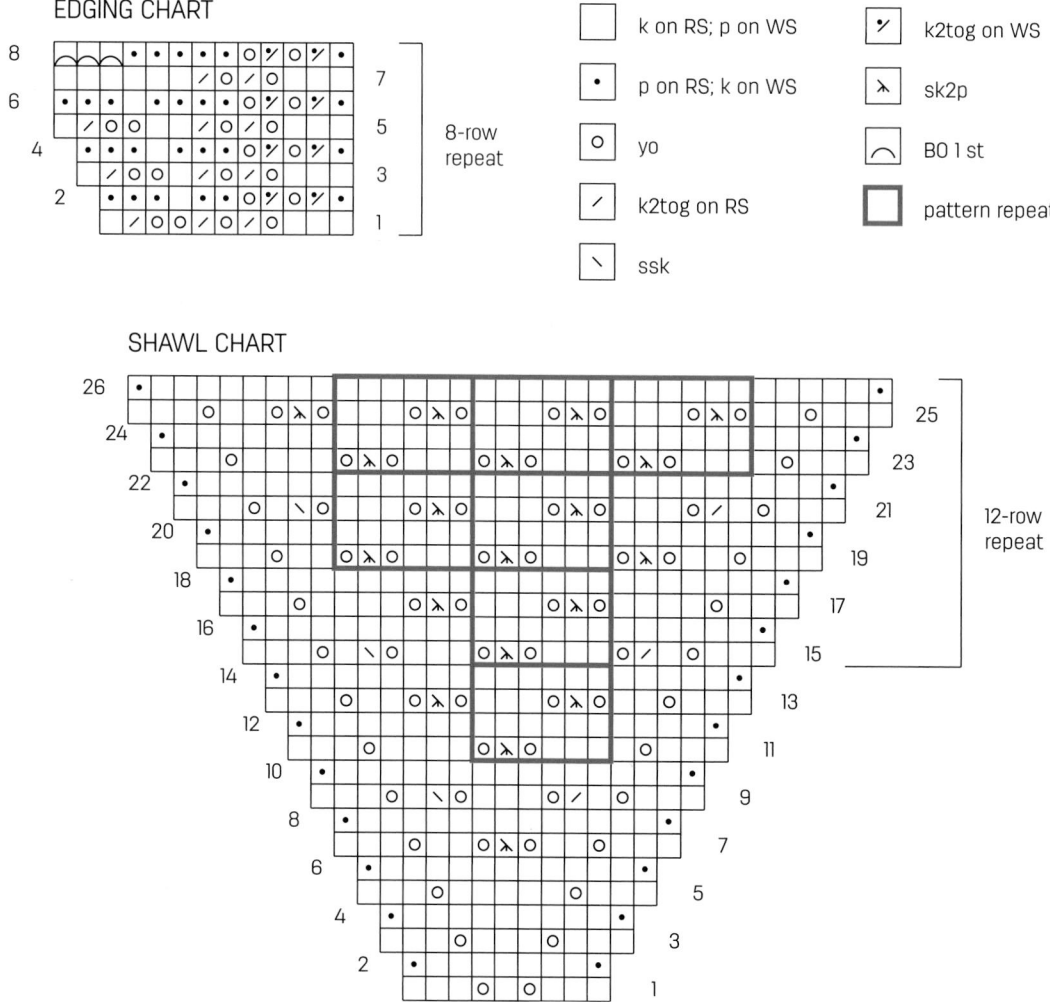

EDGING CHART

8-row repeat

	k on RS; p on WS
•	p on RS; k on WS
o	yo
/	k2tog on RS
\	ssk
⟍	k2tog on WS
⅄	sk2p
⌒	BO 1 st
	pattern repeat

SHAWL CHART

12-row repeat

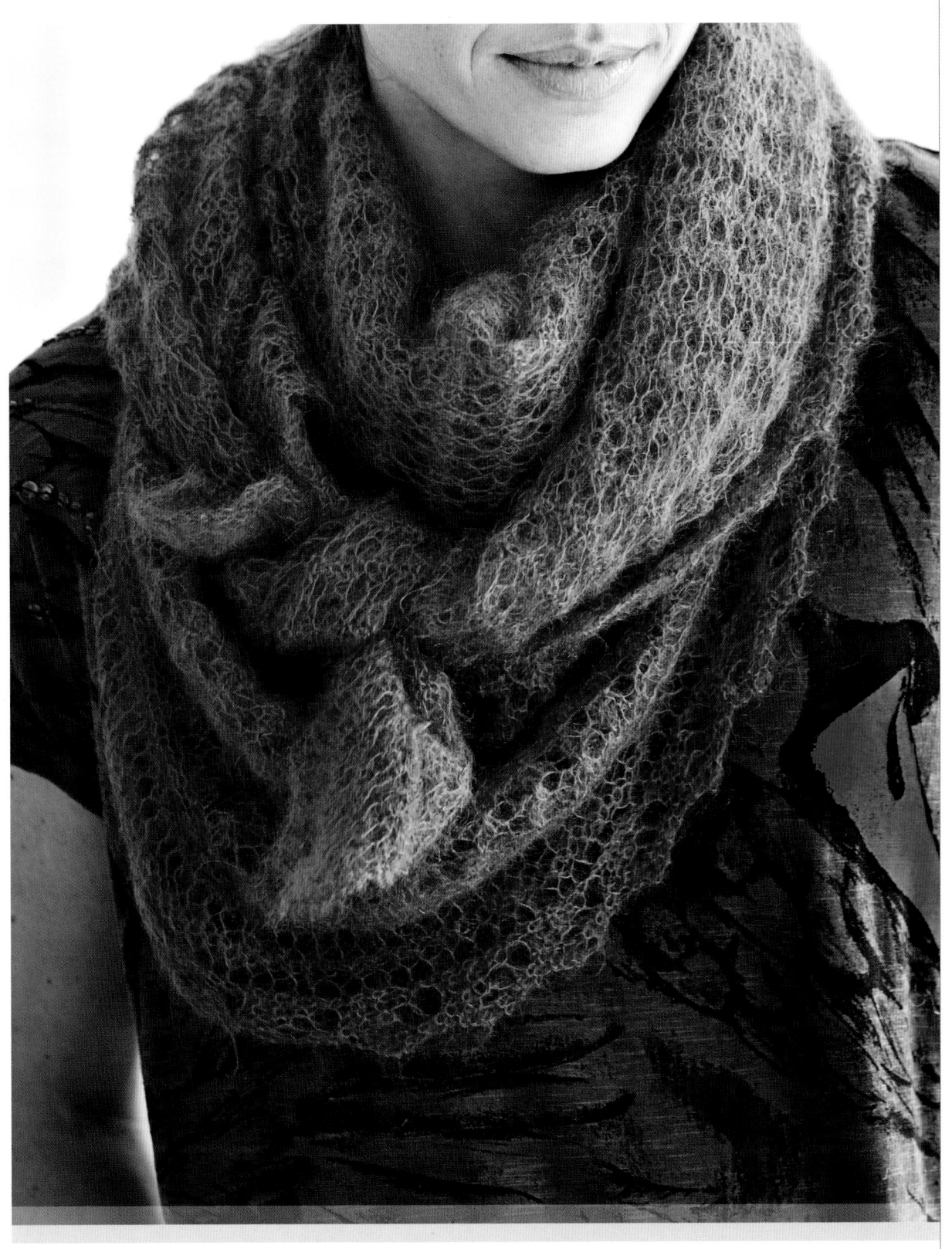

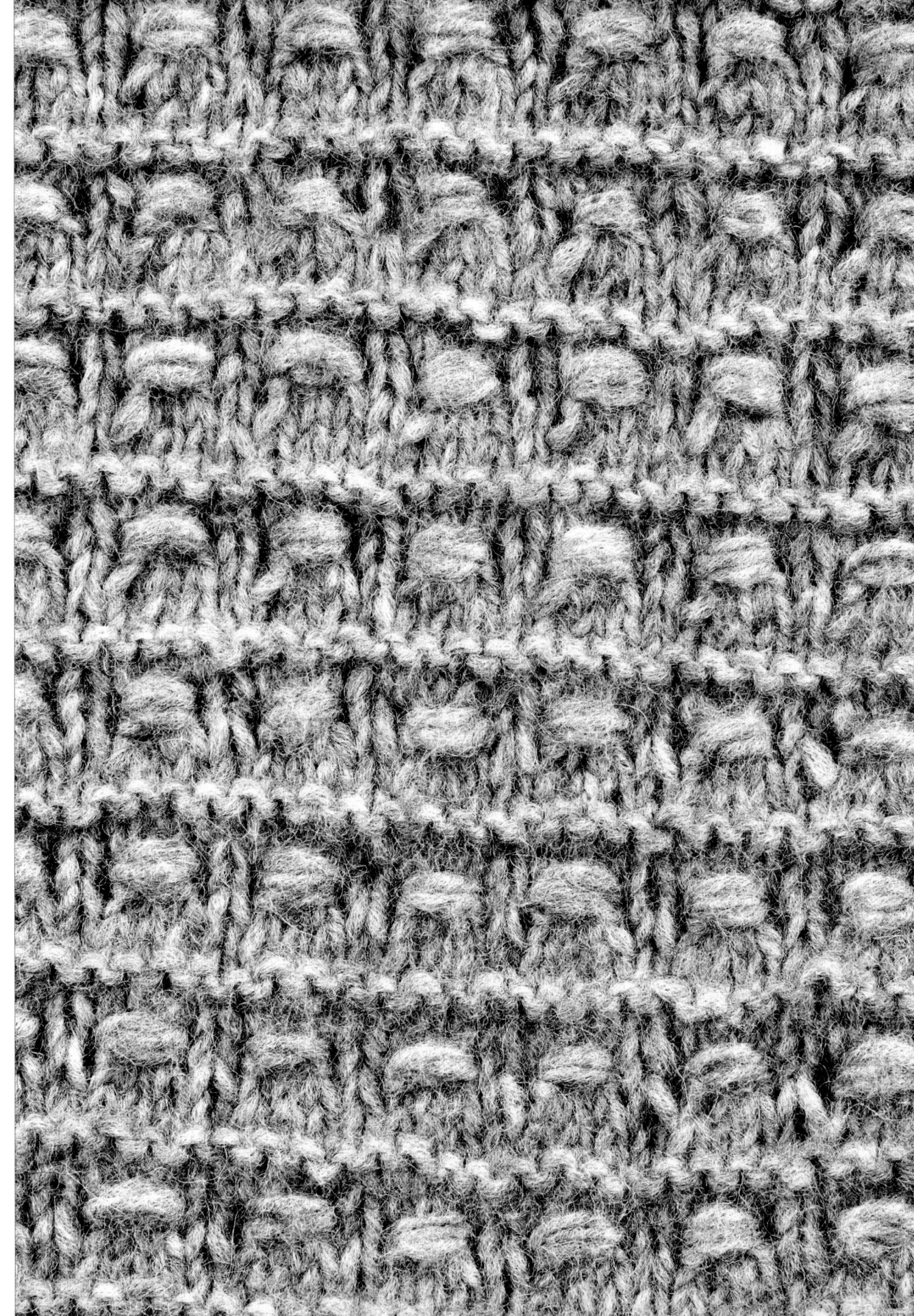

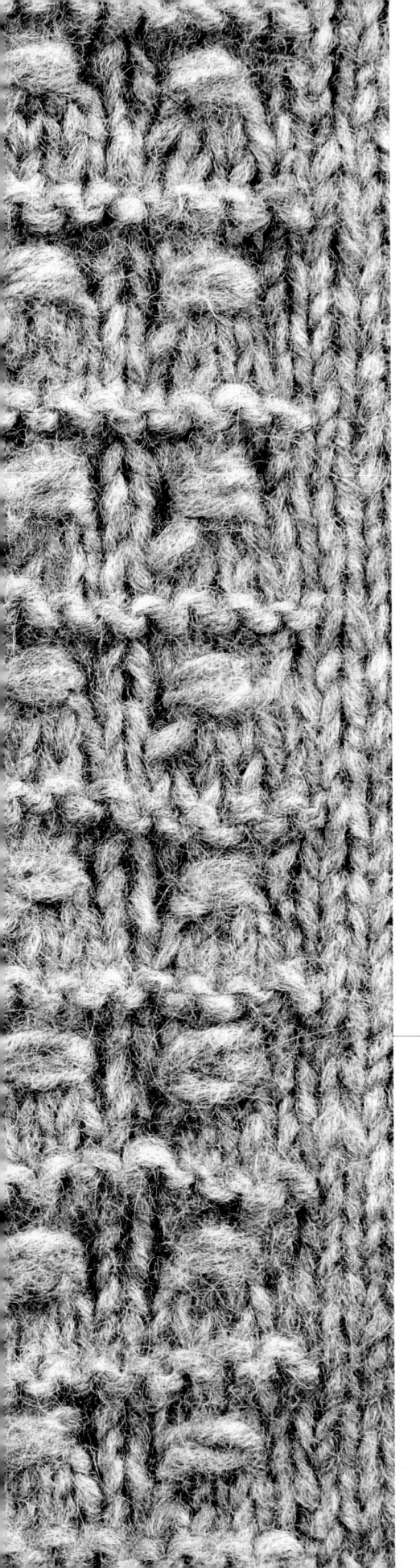

Bobbles

As a general rule, bobbles are worked by increasing
several stitches into one stitch, knitting a couple
of rows over these stitches, and then joining the
bobble by knitting stitches together until one stitch
remains. In the detail photo shown here of the Ella
poncho on page 66, however, the bobbles are worked
a completely different way—the yarn is wrapped
several times around a group of three stitches. Both
types of bobbles provide a wonderful structure for
the knitted fabric.

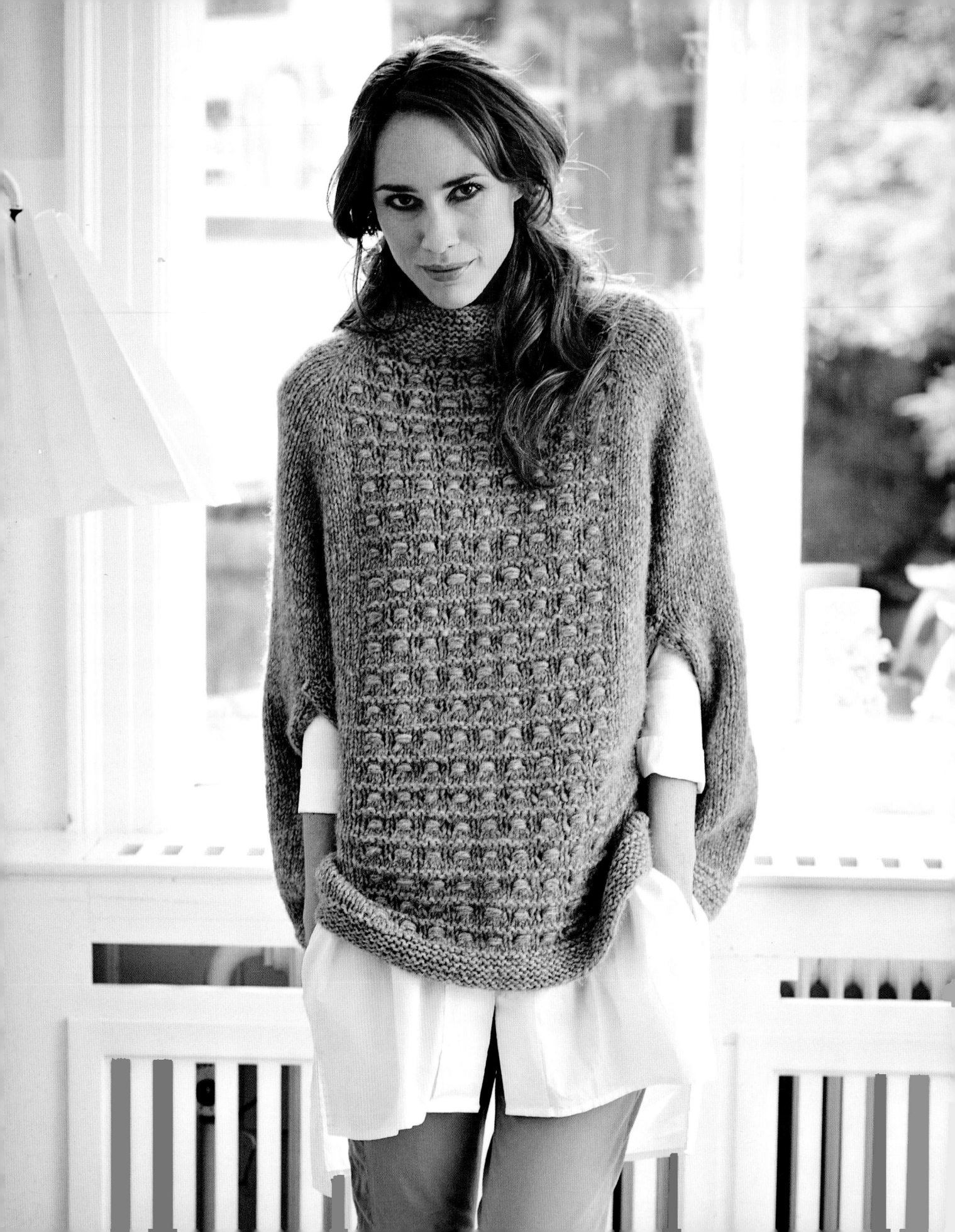

ella

poncho with wrapped stitches

This poncho fits well over the shoulders and has slits you can put your arms through if you want freedom of movement. The poncho is worked from the top down, making it easy to adjust the total length.

FINISHED SIZE		S	M	L	XL
Total length including neckband	in	27¾	27¾	28¼	28¼
	cm	70.5	70.5	72	72
Circumference of lower edge	in	54¾	57¼	60½	62¾
	cm	139	145.5	153.5	159.5

YARN
Chunky weight (#5 Bulky).

Shown here: Gepard Puno (68% baby alpaca, 22% nylon, 10% merino wool; 120 yd [110 m]/50 g): gray #1311, 7 (8, 8, 9) balls.

NEEDLES
Sizes U.S. 10 and 10¾ (6 and 7 mm): 16 and 32" (40 and 80 cm) circular (cir).
Adjust needle size if necessary to obtain the correct gauge.

NOTIONS
Markers; cable needle (cn); tapestry needle.

GAUGE
14 sts and 21 = 4" (10 cm) in St st on larger needles.

stitch guide

WRAPPED STITCHES (BOBBLE)

Slip 3 sts to cn and hold in front, (wrap yarn across back of cn to front at left side, then to back at right side of cn) 3 times, place sts from cn on right-hand needle, and cont to knit.

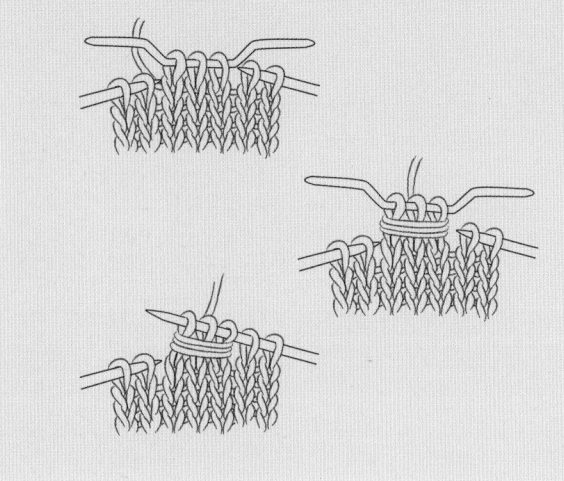

poncho

With short smaller cir needle, CO 64 (64, 68, 68) sts. Place marker (pm) and join for working in rnds, being careful not to twist sts.

Work in garter st in the round (alternate knit 1 rnd, purl 1 rnd) until piece measures 2¼" (5.5 cm) from CO edge, ending with a purl rnd.

Change to short larger cir needle.

NEXT (SET-UP) RND: K1, pm, k27 for back, pm, k1, pm, k3 for left shoulder, pm, k1, pm, k27 (27, 31, 31) for front, pm, k1, pm, k3 for right shoulder.

Note: Change to long larger cir needle when there are too many sts to work comfortably on shorter needle.

RND 1: *K1, slm, M1R, knit to next marker, M1L, slm; rep from * 3 more times—8 sts inc'd.

RND 2: Knit.

RND 3: *K1, slm, knit to next marker, slm; rep from * once more, k1, slm, (k1, bobble) 7 (7, 8, 8) times, (k1, slm) twice, knit to end of rnd.

RND 4: Rep Rnd 1—8 sts inc'd.

RND 5: Knit.

RND 6: *K1, slm, knit to next marker, slm; rep from * once more, k1, slm, p31 (31, 35, 35), slm, k1, slm, knit to end of rnd.

RND 7: Rep Rnd 1—8 sts inc'd.

RND 8: Knit.

RND 9: *K1, slm, knit to next marker, slm; rep from * once more, k1, slm, (k1, bobble) 8 (8, 9, 9) times, k1, slm, k1, slm, knit to end of rnd.

RND 10: Rep Rnd 1—8 sts inc'd.

RND 11: Knit.

RND 12: *K1, slm, knit to next marker, slm; rep from * once more, k1, slm, p35 (35, 39, 39), slm, k1, slm, knit to end of rnd.

RND 13: Rep Rnd 1—8 sts inc'd.

RND 14: Knit.

RND 15: *K1, slm, knit to next m, slm; rep from * once more, k1, slm, (k1, bobble) 9 (9, 10, 10) times, (k1, slm, k1) twice, knit to end of rnd.

RND 16: Rep Rnd 1—8 sts inc'd.

RND 17: Knit.

RND 18: *K1, slm, knit to next marker, slm; rep from * once more, k1, slm, k1, p37 (37, 41, 41), (k1, slm) twice, knit to end of rnd.

Rep Rnds 13–18 five (five, six, six) more times, then rep inc rnd 0 (1, 0, 1) more time(s)—192 (200, 212, 220) sts; 59 (61, 63, 65) sts for back, 59 (61, 67, 69) sts for front, 35 (37, 39, 41) sts for each shoulder, and 4 raglan sts. Work new sts in St st. Remove all markers except the beg-of-rnd marker.

Cont even until piece measures 12½ (12½, 13, 13)" (31.5 [31.5, 33, 33] cm) from neckband, ending with a plain knit rnd. Cut yarn.

side slits

Sl last 30 (32, 35, 37) sts from tip of the right needle to tip of the left needle, sl next 69 (71, 75, 77) sts to short larger cir needle, leave rem 123 (129, 137, 143) sts on hold on longer needle. Join yarn to beg with a RS row. Work even for 4¾" (12 cm), ending with a WS row. Cut yarn and leave sts on hold on shorter needle.

Rejoin yarn to longer needle to beg with a RS row. Work even in St st (knit RS rows, purl WS row) for 4¾" (12 cm), ending with a WS row.

NEXT (JOINING) ROW: (RS) K123 (129, 137, 143), work sts from short cir needle in next patt row, k30 (32, 35, 37), pm for beg of rnd.

Cont even until piece measures 24 (24, 24½, 24½)" (61 [61, 62, 62] cm) from neckband, ending with a knit rnd after a bobble rnd.

Change to long smaller cir needle. Beg with a purl rnd, work 11 rnds in garter st. BO loosely knitwise.

side-slit edging

With short smaller cir needle and RS facing, pick up and k23 sts along front edge of side slit. Knit 5 rows. BO knitwise.

With short smaller cir needle and RS facing, pick up and k23 sts along back edge of same side slit. Knit 1 row. BO knitwise. Sew ends of wide edging on RS to cover slit, and ends of narrow edging on WS under upper band. Work edgings on other side of poncho same way.

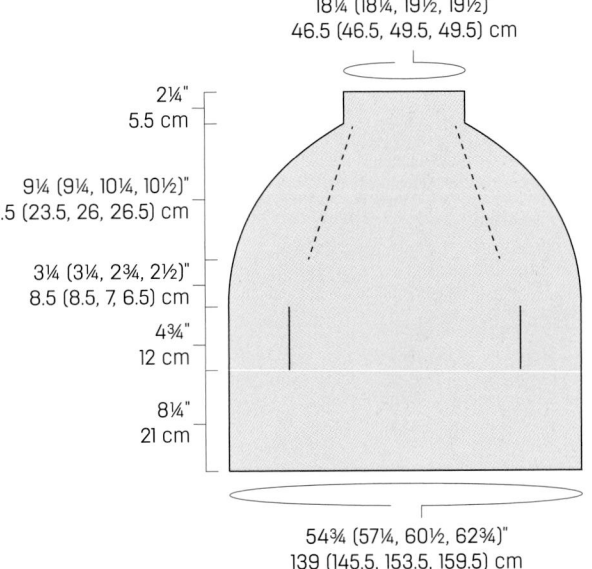

18¼ (18¼, 19½, 19½)"
46.5 (46.5, 49.5, 49.5) cm

2¼"
5.5 cm

9¼ (9¼, 10¼, 10½)"
23.5 (23.5, 26, 26.5) cm

3¼ (3¼, 2¾, 2½)"
8.5 (8.5, 7, 6.5) cm

4¾"
12 cm

8¼"
21 cm

54¾ (57¼, 60½, 62¾)"
139 (145.5, 153.5, 159.5) cm

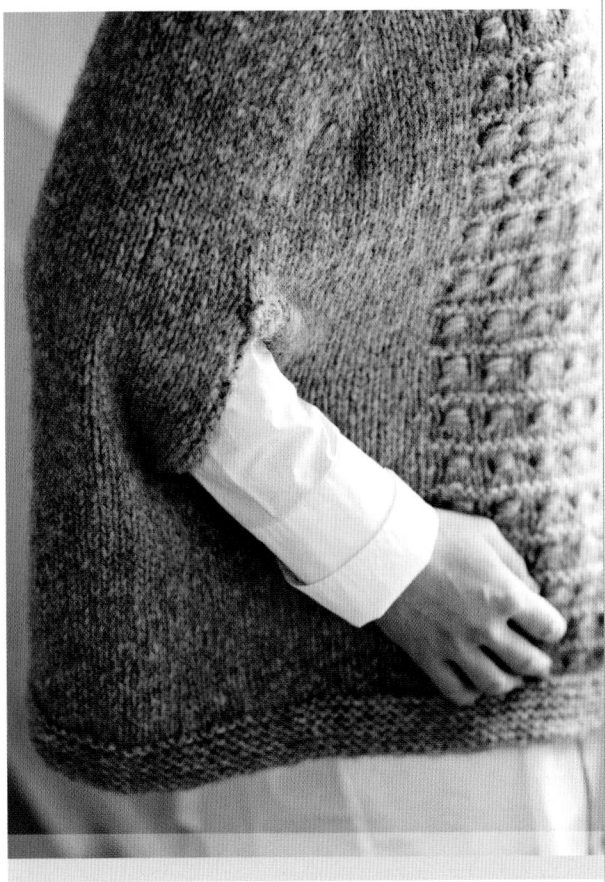

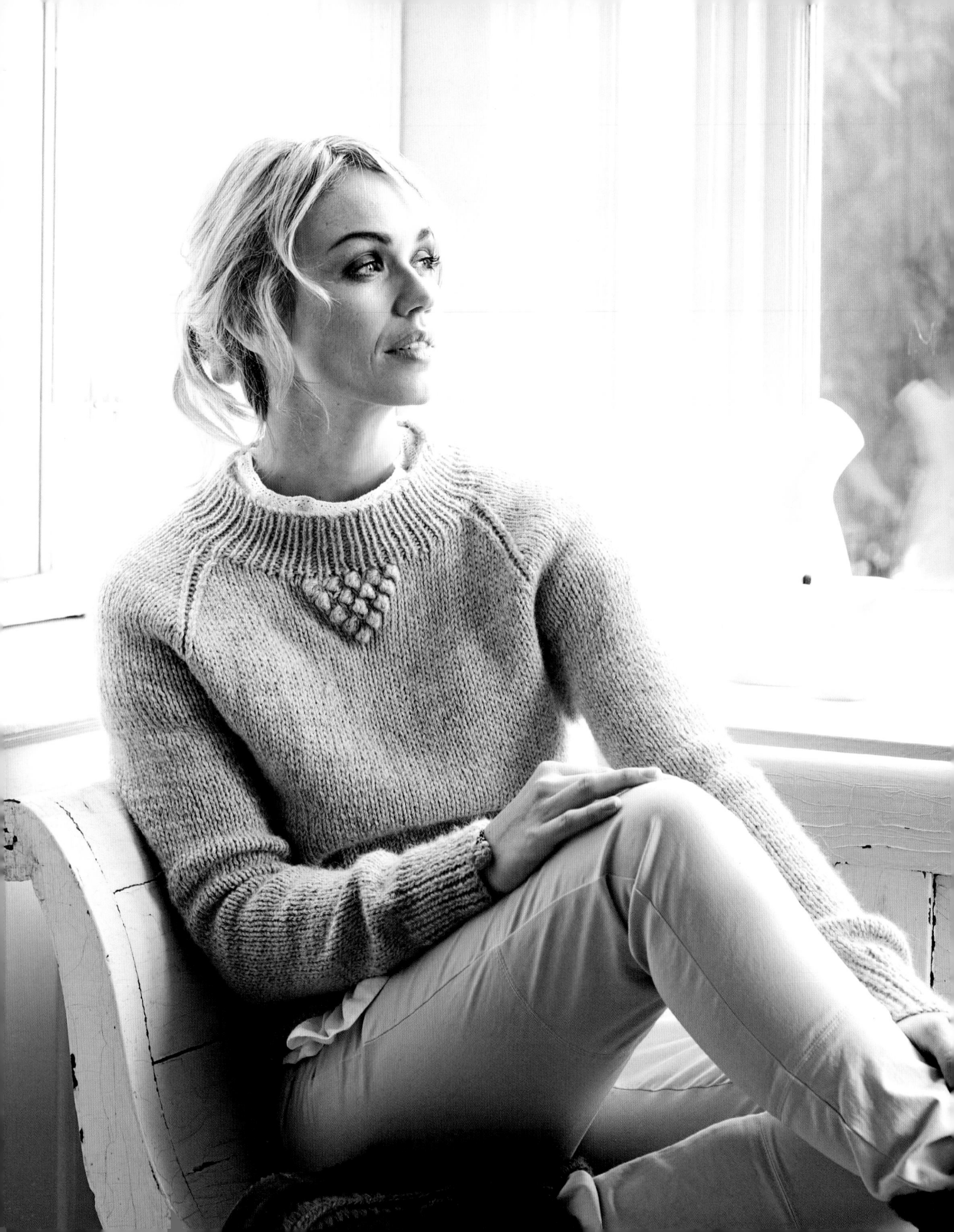

betsy

raglan cardigan with bobbles

Knit an updated classic with the softest alpaca and cashmere yarn.

FINISHED SIZE		S	M	L	XL
Bust	in	34½	37¼	41¼	45
	cm	87.5	94.5	105	114.5
Total length	in	23¾	24	24¼	24½
	cm	60.5	61	61.5	62

YARN
Aran weight (#4 Medium).

Shown here: Sandnes Garn Cashmere Alpaca (84% baby alpaca, 16% cashmere; 74 yd [68 m]/50 g): gray #1042, 12 (13, 14, 15) balls.

NEEDLES
Sizes U.S. 8 and 9 (5 and 5.5 mm): 16 and 32" (40 and 80 cm) circular (cir).

Adjust needle size if necessary to obtain the correct gauge.

NOTIONS
Markers; stitch holders; tapestry needle.

GAUGE
16½ sts and 23 rows = 4" (10 cm) in St st on larger needles.

NOTE
The weight of the yarn may cause the garment to stretch a little, so hold the pieces vertically when you take measurements.

stitch guide

BOBBLE

([K1, p1] twice, k1) into same st. Turn, p5. Turn, sl 3 sts tog (as if to k3tog), k2tog, psso—1 st rem.

CARDIGAN

back

With smaller size cir needle, CO 78 (84, 92, 100) sts. Work back and forth.

Beg with a WS row and work in k1, p1 rib for 4" (10 cm), end with a WS row.

Change to larger cir needle.

NEXT (DEC) ROW: (RS) K12 (13, 15, 15), *k2tog, k11 (12, 13, 15); rep from * 3 more times, k2tog, knit to end of row—73 (79, 87, 95) sts rem.

Cont even in St st until piece measures 6" (15 cm) from CO edge, ending with a WS row.

SHAPE WAIST

NEXT (DEC) ROW: (RS) K2, k2tog, knit to last 4 sts, ssk, k2—2 sts dec'd.

Rep dec row every 8 rows 2 more times—67 (73, 81, 89) sts rem.

Cont even until piece measures 11" (28 cm) from CO edge, ending with a WS row.

NEXT (INC) ROW: (RS) K1, M1, knit to last st, M1, k1—2 sts inc'd.

Rep inc row every 8 rows 2 more times—73 (79, 87, 95) sts.

Cont even until piece measures 15¼" (39 cm) from CO edge, ending with a WS row.

BO 5 (6, 7, 8) sts at beg of next 2 rows—63 (67, 73, 79) sts rem. Place rem sts on holder.

front

Work front same as for back.

sleeves (make 2)

With smaller cir needle, CO 38 (40, 40, 42) sts. Work back and forth.

Beg with a WS row and work in k1, p1 rib for 3¼" (8.5 cm), ending with a WS row.

Change to larger cir needle.

Cont in St st until sleeve measures 4¾, (4¾, 4¾, 3½)" (12 [12, 12, 9] cm) from CO edge, ending with a WS row.

NEXT (INC) ROW: (RS) K1, M1, knit to last st, M1, k1—2 sts inc'd.

Rep inc row every 8 (8, 6, 6) rows 7 (8, 10, 11) more times—54 (58, 62, 66) sts.

Cont even until piece measures 18 (17¾, 17¼, 17)" (45.5 [45, 44, 43] cm) from CO, ending with a WS row.

BO 5 (6, 7, 8) sts at beg of next 2 rows—44 (46, 48, 50) sts rem. Place rem sts on holder.

yoke

With RS facing, place sts for pieces on longer, larger cir needle in this order: back, left sleeve, front, right sleeve—214 (226, 242, 258) sts. Join for working in rnds.

NEXT (SET-UP) RND: Sl last st from right needle to left needle, *k2tog, k61 (65, 71, 77), pm, k2tog,

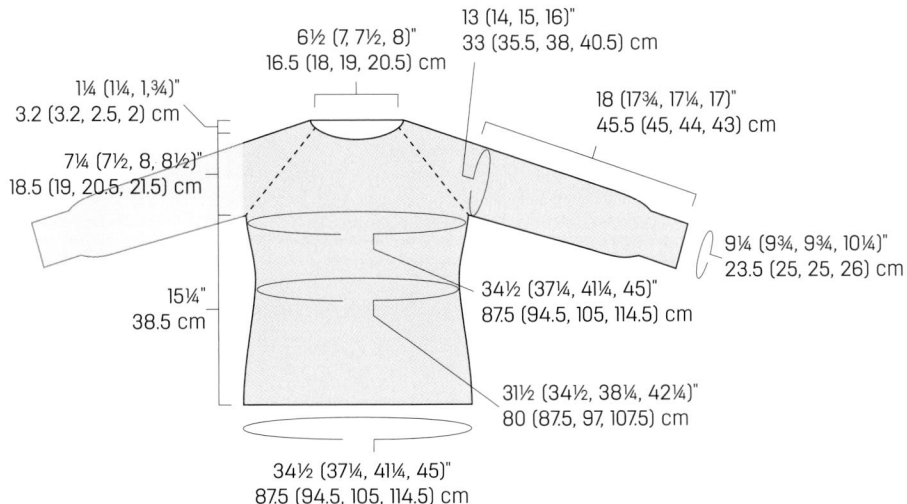

Measurements (on schematic):

6½ (7, 7½, 8)"
16.5 (18, 19, 20.5) cm

13 (14, 15, 16)"
33 (35.5, 38, 40.5) cm

1¼ (1¼, 1,¾)"
3.2 (3.2, 2.5, 2) cm

18 (17¾, 17¼, 17)"
45.5 (45, 44, 43) cm

7¼ (7½, 8, 8½)"
18.5 (19, 20.5, 21.5) cm

9¼ (9¾, 9¾, 10¼)"
23.5 (25, 25, 26) cm

15¼"
38.5 cm

34½ (37¼, 41¼, 45)"
87.5 (94.5, 105, 114.5) cm

31½ (34½, 38¼, 42¼)"
80 (87.5, 97, 107.5) cm

34½ (37¼, 41¼, 45)"
87.5 (94.5, 105, 114.5) cm

k42 (44, 46, 48), pm; rep from * once more—210 (222, 238, 254) sts rem; 61 (65, 71, 77) sts each for front and back, 42 (44, 46, 48) sts for each sleeve, and 4 raglan sts. The last marker placed is the beg-of-rnd marker; rnds beg at right edge of back.

NEXT (DEC) RND: *P1, ssk, knit to 2 sts before next marker, k2tog, slm; rep from * 3 more times—8 sts dec'd.

NEXT 2 RNDS: *P1, knit to next marker, slm; rep from * 3 more times.

Rep last 3 rnds 6 (6, 5, 4) more times, then rep dec rnd once more. Rep dec rnd every other rnd 9 (10, 13, 16) times, and change to short larger cir needle when there are too few sts to work comfortably on longer cir needle. At the same time, when 9 (10, 12, 14) raglan dec rnds have been worked, yoke should measure about 4¾ (5¼, 5¾, 6¼)" (12 [13.5, 14.5, 16] cm)—138 (142, 142, 142) sts rem; 43 (45, 47, 49) sts each for front and back, 24 (24, 22, 20) sts for each sleeve, and 4 raglan sts.

BOBBLE RND 1: (P1, knit to marker, slm) twice, p1, k21 (22, 23, 24), make bobble, k21 (22, 23, 24), slm, p1, knit to marker, slm.

Rep dec rnd—8 sts dec'd.

BOBBLE RND 2: (P1, knit to marker, slm) twice, p1, k19 (20, 21, 22), make bobble, k1, make bobble, k19 (20, 21, 22), slm, p1, knit to marker, slm.

Rep dec rnd—8 sts dec'd.

BOBBLE RND 3: (P1, knit to marker, slm) twice, p1, k17 (18, 19, 20), (make bobble, k1) twice, make bobble, k17 (18, 19, 20), slm, p1, knit to marker, slm.

Rep dec rnd—8 sts dec'd.

BOBBLE RND 4: (P1, knit to marker, slm) twice, p1, k15 (16, 17, 18), (make bobble, k1) 3 times, make bobble, k15 (16, 17, 18), slm, p1, knit to marker, slm.

Rep dec rnd—8 sts dec'd.

BOBBLE RND 5: (P1, knit to marker, slm) twice, p1, k13 (14, 15, 16), (make bobble, k1) 4 times, make bobble, k13 (14, 15, 16), slm, p1, knit to marker, slm.

Rep dec rnd—98 (102, 102, 102) sts rem; 33 (35, 37, 39) sts each for front and back, 14 (14, 12, 10) sts for each sleeve, and 4 raglan sts.

Work 1 rnd even.

SHAPE NECK

NEXT RND: (P1, ssk, knit to 2 sts before marker, k2tog, slm) twice, p1, ssk, k23 (24, 26, 27), place last 17 (17, 19, 19) sts from tip of right needle onto holder for neck, knit to 2 sts before marker, k2tog, slm, p1, ssk, knit to last 2 sts, k2tog—73 (77, 75, 75) sts rem; 31 (33, 35, 37) sts for back, 7 (8, 8, 9) sts for each side of front, 12 (12, 10, 8) sts for each sleeve, and 4 raglan sts.

Cut yarn. Shift last 21 (22, 20, 19) sts from tip of right needle to tip of left needle; needle tips are at gap at front neck. Join yarn to work a WS row.

NEXT ROW: (WS) BO 3 sts, knit the knit sts and purl the purl sts to end of row.

NEXT ROW: (RS) BO 3 sts, *knit to 2 sts before marker, k2tog, slm, p1, ssk; rep from * 3 more times, knit to end of row—59 (63, 61, 61) sts rem; 29 (31, 33, 35) sts rem for back, 3 (4, 4, 5) sts for each side of front, 10 (10, 8, 6) sts for each sleeve, and 4 raglan sts.

NEXT ROW: BO 3 sts, work to end of row.

Size S only

NEXT ROW: (RS) BO 3 sts and remove raglan marker (1 st on right needle tip), *ssk, knit to 2 sts before next marker, k2tog, remove marker, p1; rep from * 2 more times—47 sts rem; 27 sts for back, 0 sts for each front, 8 sts for each sleeve, and 4 raglan sts.

Sizes M/L only

NEXT ROW: (RS) BO 3 sts (1 st on right needle tip), *remove marker, p1, k1, ssk, knit to 2 sts before next marker, k2tog; rep from * 2 more times, remove marker, p1—51 (49) sts rem; 29 (31) sts for back, 1 st for each front, 8 (6) sts for each sleeve, and 4 raglan sts.

Size XL only

NEXT ROW: (RS) BO 3 sts, sl last st back on left needle tip, pass next st over first st, sl st back to right needle tip, *remove marker, p1, ssk, knit to 2 sts before next marker, k2tog; rep from * twice more, remove marker, p2tog—47 sts rem; 33 sts for back, 1 st for each front, 4 sts for each sleeve, and 4 raglan sts.

neckband

Change to short smaller cir needle. With RS facing, knit rem sts, pick up and k10 (10, 10, 11) sts along the left neck edge, knit 17 (17, 19, 19) held neck sts, pick up and k10 (10, 10, 11) sts along right neck edge—84 (88, 88, 88) sts. Pm for beg of rnd and join for working in rnds. Work in k1, p1 rib for 2" (5 cm). BO all sts loosely in rib.

finishing

Weave in ends. Block to finished measurements.

Sew the sleeve and side seams. Sew underarm seams.

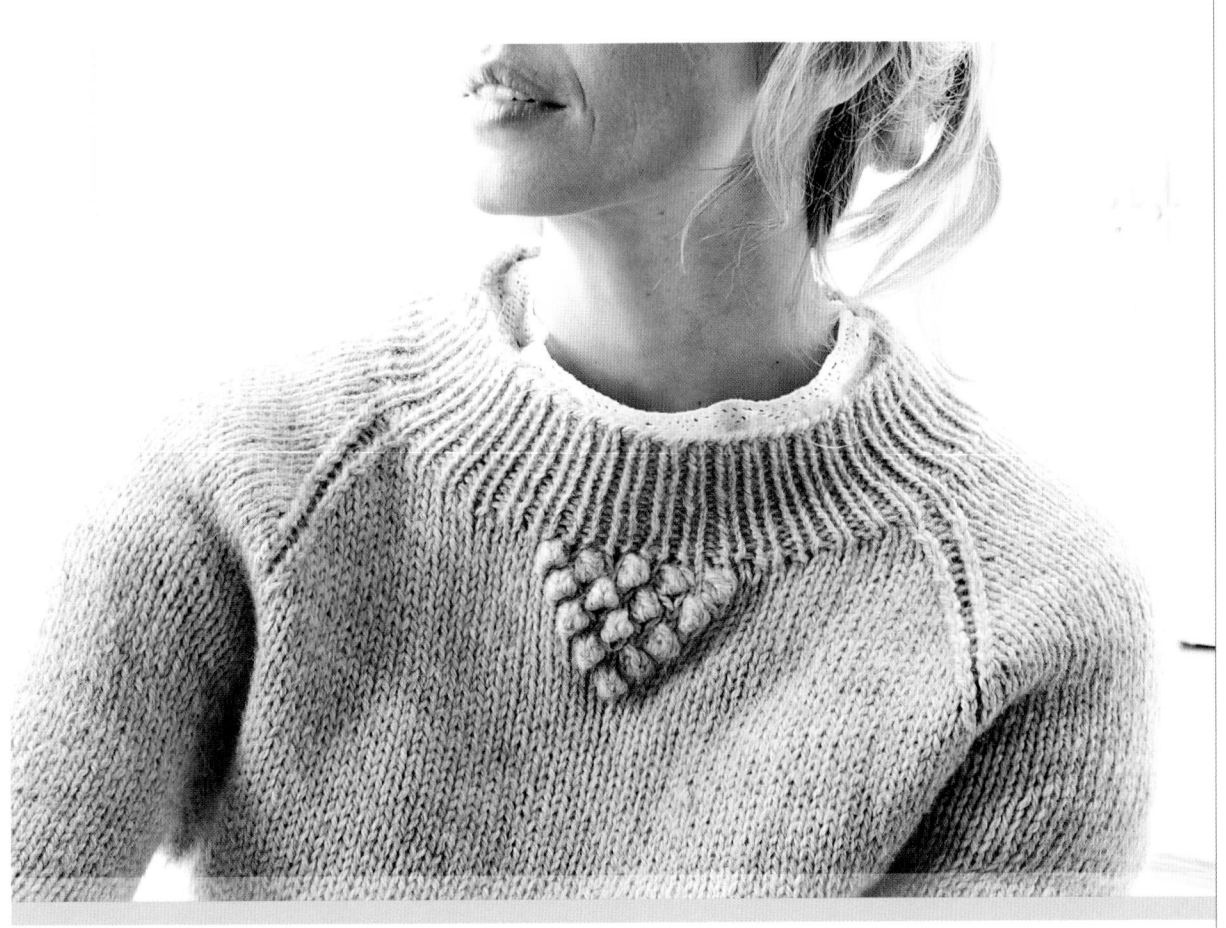

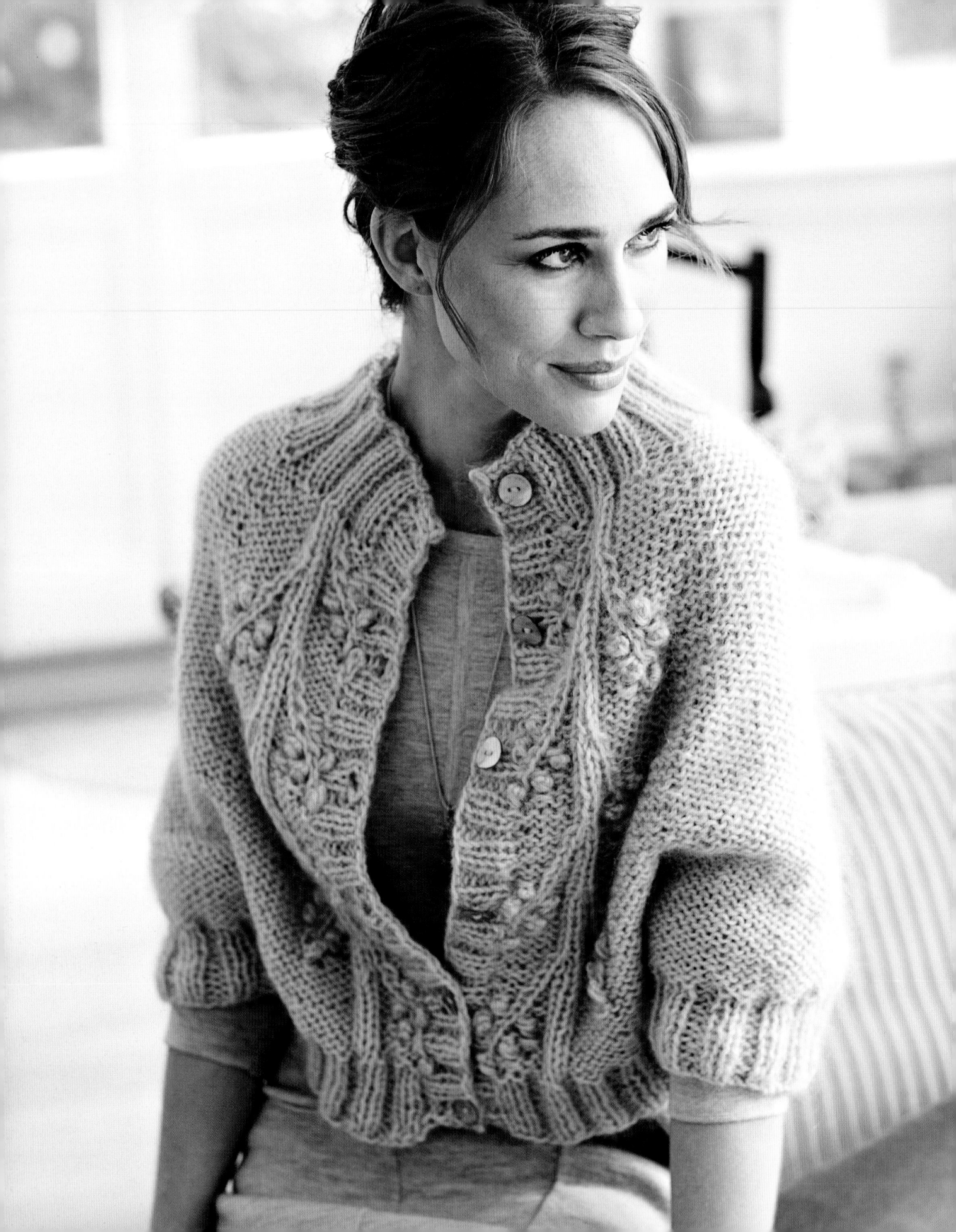

clara

short sweater with vine motifs

You're sitting pretty in this bolero-style cardigan with a swag of berries embellishing the front. The cardigan is knitted from the top down in a light wool and mohair yarn. Deep raglan shaping gives a somewhat oversized fit.

FINISHED SIZE		S	M	L	XL
Bust	in	33½	34¾	37¼	38½
	cm	85	88.5	94.5	98
Total length not including neckband	in	18	18¾	19¼	20¼
	cm	45.5	47.5	49	51.5

YARN
Worsted weight (#4 Medium).

Shown here: Onion Mohair+Wool (50% mohair, 50% wool; 145 yd [133 m]/50 g): light blue #306, 6 (7, 8, 8) balls.

NEEDLES
Sizes U.S. 10¾ and 11 (7 and 8 mm): 32" (80 cm) circular (cir).

Adjust needle size if necessary to obtain the correct gauge.

NOTIONS
6 buttons ¾" (20 mm); markers; holders or waste yarn; tapestry needle.

GAUGE
13 sts and 17½ = 4" (10 cm) in St st with yarn held double on larger needles.

NOTES
This sweater is worked back and forth from the top down.

Raglan increases are worked on wrong-side (knit) rows.

stitch guide

PATTERN LEFT AND RIGHT
See charts.

RAGLAN INCREASE
M1: With left needle tip, lift the strand between the last knitted stitch and the first stitch on the left needle from front to back, then knit the lifted loop through the back.

sweater

The sweater is worked from the top down.

With smaller cir needle and yarn held double, CO 72 sts.

ROW 1: (WS) K1, p2, (k2, p2) across to last st, k1.

Always knitting the first st and last st of every row, work in established rib patt for 2¾" (7 cm), end with a RS row.

Change to larger cir needle.

SET-UP ROW: (WS) K12 sts for right front, place marker (pm), k2, pm, k10 sts for sleeve, pm, k2, pm, k20 sts for back, pm, k2, pm, k10 sts for sleeve, pm, k2, pm, k12 sts for left front.

Cont in pattern and raglan shaping as follows:

ROW 1: (RS) Work Row 1 of chart A over first 12 sts, slm, purl to last 12 sts, slipping markers as you come to them, work Row 1 of chart B over rem 12 sts.

ROW 2: Work Row 2 of chart B over first 12 sts, *M1, slm, k2, slm, M1, knit to next marker; rep from * 2 more times, M1, slm, k2, slm, M1, work Row 2 of chart A over rem 12 sts—8 sts inc'd.

ROW 3: Work Row 3 of chart A over first 13 sts, purl to last 13 sts, work Row 3 of chart B over rem 13 sts.

ROW 4: Work Row 4 of chart B over first 13 sts, *M1, slm, k2, slm, M1, knit to next marker; rep from * 2 more times, M1, slm, k2, slm, M1, work Row 4 of chart A over rem 13 sts—8 sts inc'd.

Cont through Row 32 of charts A and B, then rep Rows 17-32 throughout.

At the same time, cont raglan inc every WS row 2 (2, 3, 3) more times, then every 4 rows 12 (13, 14, 15) times—200 (208, 224, 232) sts; 28 (29, 31, 32) sts for each front, 42 (44, 48, 50) sts for each sleeve, 52 (54, 58, 60) sts for back, and 8 raglan sts. Work new sts in reverse St st.

Work 6 (6, 2, 2) rows even, end with a RS row.

DIVIDE BODY AND SLEEVES

NEXT ROW: (RS) Removing raglan markers, work 28 (29, 31, 32) sts in established patt, BO 2 raglan sts, work 42 (44, 48, 50) sleeve sts, BO 2 raglan sts, k52 (54, 58, 60) back sts, BO 2 raglan sts, work 42 (44, 48, 50) sleeve sts, BO 2 raglan sts, work to end—192 (200, 216, 224) sts rem.

NEXT ROW: Work 28 (29, 31, 32) front sts, place 42 (44, 48, 50) sleeve sts on holder or waste yarn, CO 2 sts, work 52 (54, 58, 60) back sts, place 42 (44, 48, 50) sleeve sts on holder or waste yarn, CO 2 sts, work rem 28 (29, 31, 32) sts—112 (116, 124, 128) sts.

back and front

NEXT ROW: (RS) K1 (edge st), k2, *p2, k2; rep from * to last st, k1 (edge st).

NEXT ROW: K1 (edge st), p2, *k2, p2; rep from * to last st, k1 (edge st).

Cont in established patt until rib measures 2" (5 cm). BO loosely in rib.

CHART A (LEFT FRONT)

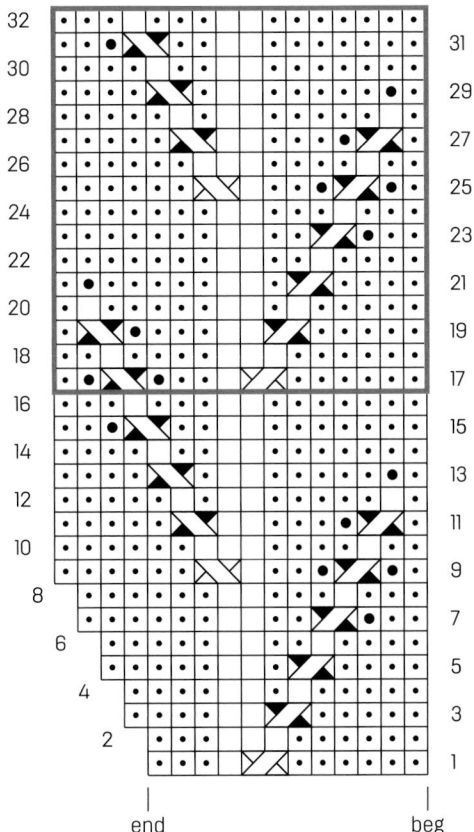

end · · · · · · · · beg

CHART B (RIGHT FRONT)

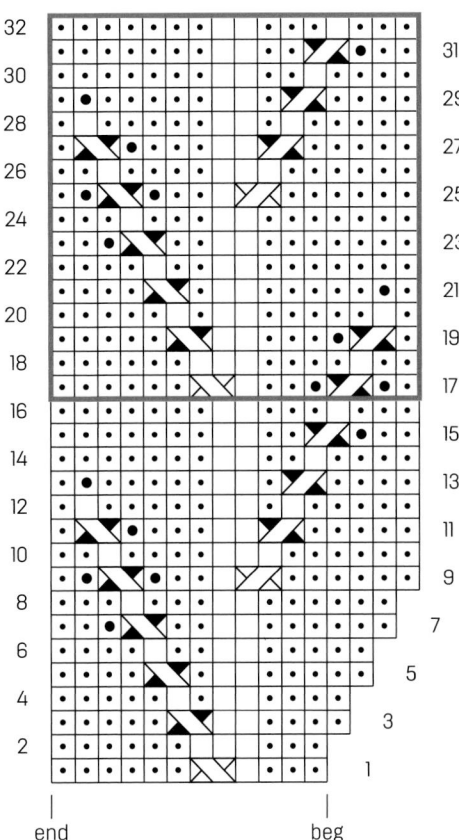

end · · · · · · · · beg

sleeves (make 2)

With WS facing, return held 42 (44, 48, 50) sleeve sts to larger cir needle, join yarn and CO 2 (1, 1, 2) st(s), knit to end, CO 2 (1, 1, 2) st(s)—46 (46, 50, 54) sts.

NEXT ROW: (RS) K2, *p2, k2; rep from * to end of row.

NEXT ROW: P2, *k2, p2; rep from * to end of row.

Cont in established patt until sleeve measures 2" (5 cm). BO loosely in rib.

☐ k on RS; p on WS

· p on RS; k on WS

● bobble: [(k1, k1tbl) twice, k1] in same st, turn; p5, turn; k5, turn; p2tog, p1, p2tog, turn; k3tog

⤫ sl 1 st onto cn and hold in back, k1, k1 from cn

⤫ sl 1 st onto cn and hold in back, k1, p1 from cn

⤫ sl 1 st onto cn and hold in front, k1, k1 from cn

⤫ sl 1 st onto cn and hold in front, p1, k1 from cn

☐ pattern repeat

finishing and edgings

Weave in ends. Sew sleeve and underarm seams. Block to finished measurements.

BUTTONBAND

With smaller cir needle and RS facing, pick up and k62 (62, 66, 66) sts along left front edge (at a rate of about 3 sts for every 4 rows). Along the ribbed edges, pick up sts between the edge st and next st, along the rest of the front edge without edge sts, pick up sts in the outermost st or as close to the outer edge as possible. The closer the picked-up sts are to the outer edge, the less likely the front band will have a tendency to roll, which is exactly what it would do along reverse St st.

NEXT ROW: (WS) P2, *k2, p2; rep from * to end of row.

NEXT ROW: (RS) *K2, p2; rep from * to last 2 sts, k2.

Work 3 more rows in established rib patt. BO all in rib.

BUTTONHOLE BAND

Pick up and k62 (62, 66, 66) sts along right front edge same as for buttonband, and work 2 rows in rib patt.

NEXT (BUTTONHOLE) ROW: (WS) P2, *BO 1 st, work in patt until there are 10 (10, 11, 11) sts on the tip of the right needle after buttonhole, BO 1 st, work in patt until there are 11 sts on the tip of the right needle after buttonhole; rep from * once more, BO 1 st, work in patt to last 3 sts, BO 1 st, work rem st.

NEXT ROW: (RS) K2, *CO 1 st over gap, work to next buttonhole; rep from * 4 more times, CO 1 st over gap, k2.

Work 1 row in established rib patt.

BO all sts in patt.

Sew buttons to buttonband opposite buttonholes.

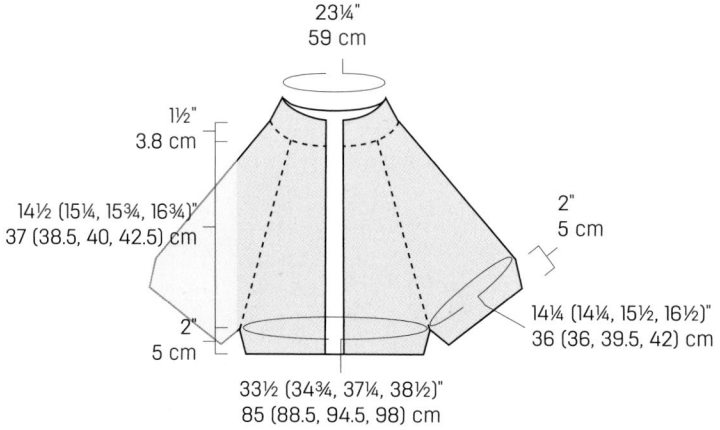

23¼"
59 cm

1½"
3.8 cm

14½ (15¼, 15¾, 16¾)"
37 (38.5, 40, 42.5) cm

2"
5 cm

2"
5 cm

14¼ (14¼, 15½, 16½)"
36 (36, 39.5, 42) cm

33½ (34¾, 37¼, 38½)"
85 (88.5, 94.5, 98) cm

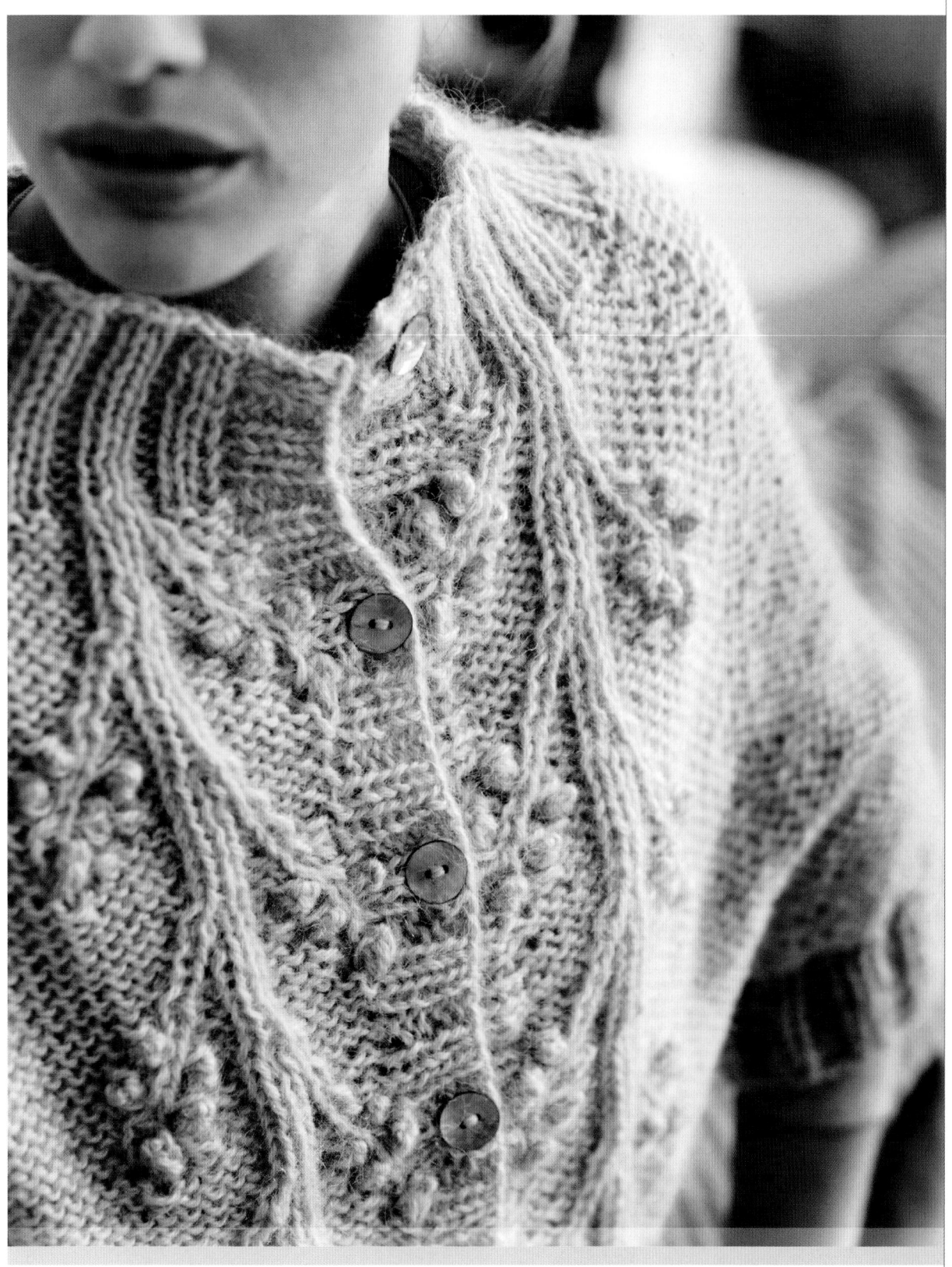

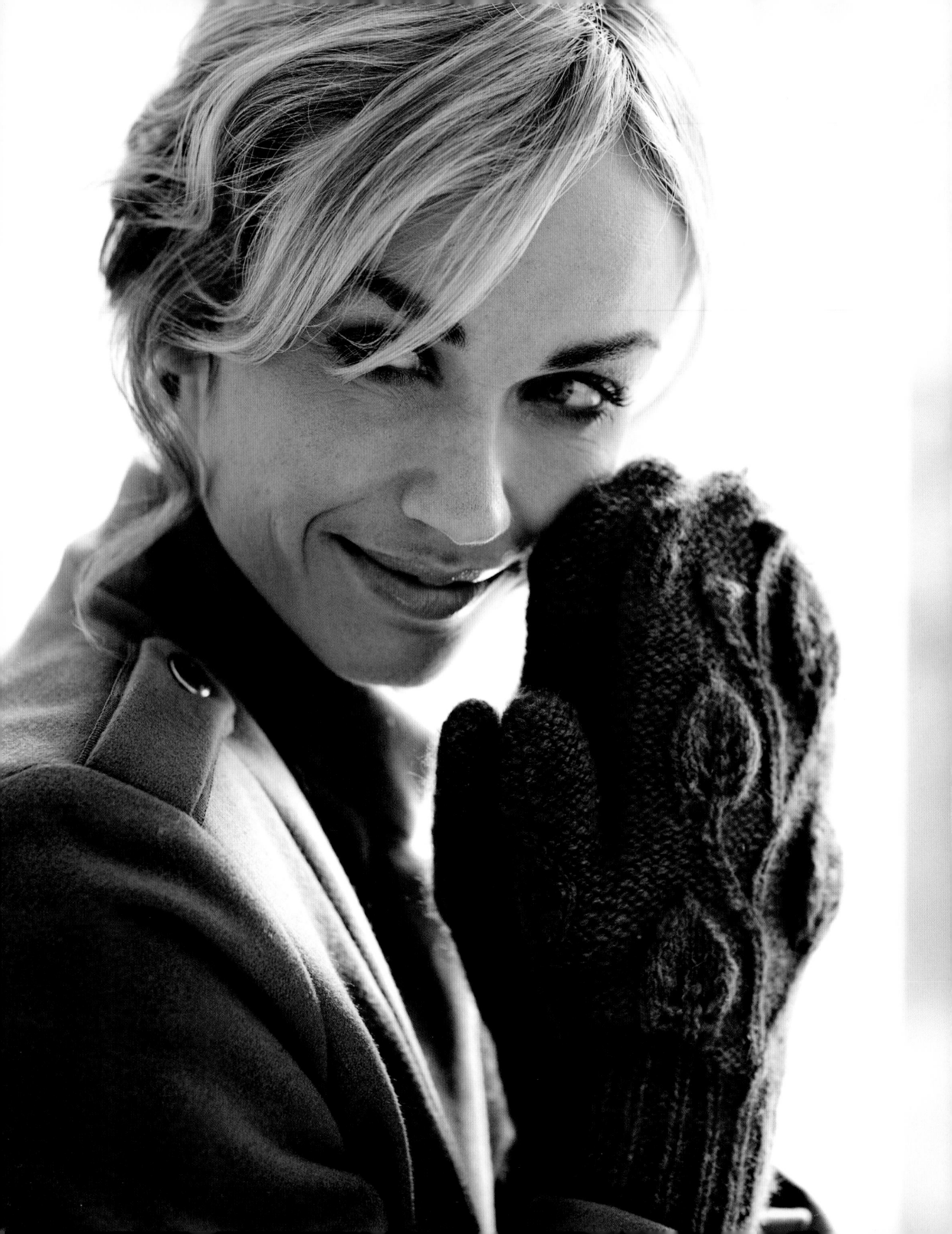

nora

leaf-pattern mittens

A leaf pattern covers the back of the hand,
and this motif repeated in the thumb
gusset, which is also shaped with a leaf.

FINISHED SIZE
6½" (16.5 cm) hand circumference
and 10½" (26.5 cm) long.

YARN
DK weight (#3 Light). (See Notes
on next page.)

Shown here: Choose any one of
these yarns.

Sandnes Garn Alpaca (100%
baby alpaca; 120 yd [110 m]/50 g):
petroleum blue #6554, 2 balls.

Rowan Felted Tweed DK (50%
merino wool, 25% alpaca, 25%
viscose; 191 yd [175 m]/50 g): gray-
purple #179, 2 balls.

Qiviut Musk Ox (100% musk ox,
2 ply; 219 yd [200 m]/50 g):
natural brown, 1 ball.

Laceweight (#0 Lace).

Isager Spinni (100% wool, single
ply; 330 yd [305 m]/50 g): ochre
#3, 2 balls.

NEEDLES
For the Sandnes Alpaca mittens,
size U.S. 4 (3.5 mm): set of 5 dpn.

For the others, sizes U.S. 2.5 and 6
(3 and 4 mm): set of 5 dpn.

*Adjust needle size if necessary to
obtain the correct gauge.*

NOTIONS
Markers; cable needle (cn);
tapestry needle.

GAUGE
24½ sts and 34½ rnds = 4" (10 cm)
in St st on larger needles.

stitch guide

BOBBLE

([K1, p1] twice, k1) in same st—5 sts. Turn. P5, turn. K5, turn. K2tog, k1, k2tog, turn. P3tog—1 st rem.

left mitten

With smaller dpn, CO 45 sts. Distribute sts evenly over 4 dpn. Place marker (pm) and join for working in rnds, being careful not to twist sts.

RND 1: *P2, k1; rep from * around.

Rep Rnd 1 until rib measures about 4" (10 cm).

NEXT (DEC) RND: P2, k1, p2tog, k1, p2tog, work in established rib patt to last 3 sts, p2tog, k1—42 sts rem.

Change to larger dpn.

Work Rnds 1-10 of Left mitten chart (page 88).

THUMB GUSSET

RND 11: Work in established patt to last 4 sts, pm, work Row 1 of Thumbs chart (page 87) over next 3 sts, pm, then work last st of Left mitten chart—50 sts.

RND 12: Work in established patt to marker, slm, work Row 2 of Thumbs chart to next marker, slm, work to end of rnd.

Cont as established through Rnd 22 of Left mitten chart—58 sts.

RND 23: Work to thumb gusset marker, remove marker, place 13 thumb sts on holder for thumb, CO 3 sts over gap, remove marker, work in established patt to end of rnd—46 sts.

Cont through Rnd 49, ending last rnd 1 st before end of rnd, sl next st to tip of right needle, remove beg-of-rnd marker, sl last st back to left needle tip, pm for new beg of rnd (make sure that the length is correct by referring to the third Note in the box at left about trying on the mitten)—41 sts rem.

SHAPE TOP

RND 50: S2kp, p8, k1, p3, k3, p3, s2kp, purl to last st, sl next st to right needle tip, remove beg-of-rnd marker, sl last st back to left needle tip, pm for new beg of rnd—37 sts rem.

RND 51: S2kp, p7, sl 1 st onto cn and hold in front, p1, k1 from cn, p2, s2kp, p2, s2kp, purl to last st, sl next st to right needle tip, remove beg-of-rnd marker, sl last st back to left needle tip, pm for new beg of rnd—31 sts rem.

RND 52: S2kp, p7, k1, p4, s2kp, purl to last st, sl next st to right needle tip, remove beg-of-rnd marker, sl last st back to left needle tip, pm for new beg of rnd—27 sts rem.

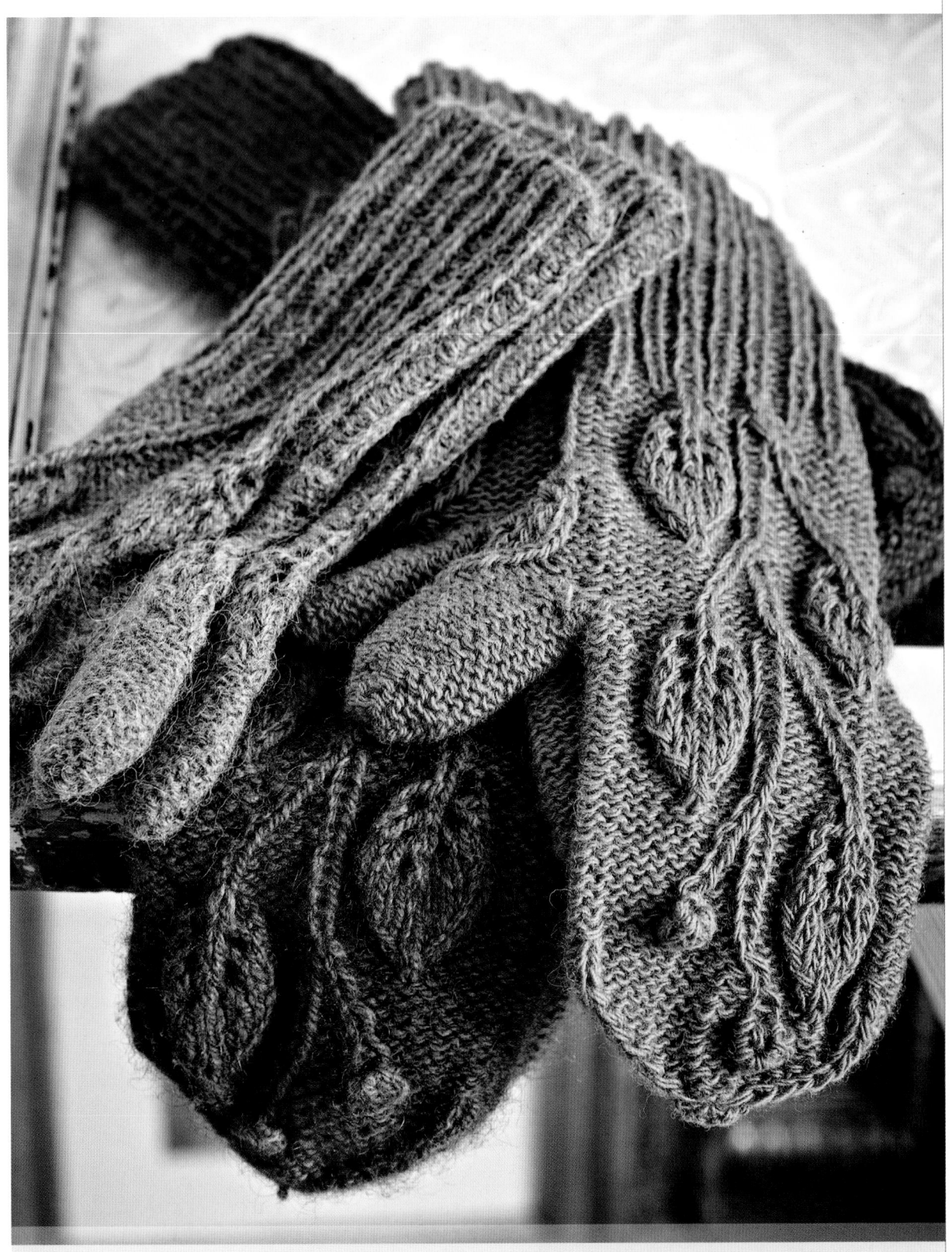

RND 53: S2kp, p6, make bobble (see Stitch Guide), p3, s2kp, purl to last st, sl next st to right needle tip, remove beg-of-rnd marker, sl last st back to left needle tip, pm for new beg of rnd—23 sts rem.

RND 54: S2kp, p8, s2kp, purl to last st, sl next st to right needle tip, remove beg-of-rnd marker, sl last st back to left needle tip, pm for new beg of rnd—19 sts rem.

RND 55: S2kp, p6, s2kp, purl to last st, sl next st to right needle tip, remove beg-of-rnd marker, sl last st back to left needle tip, pm for new beg of rnd—15 sts rem.

RND 56: S2kp, p4, s2kp, purl to end of rnd—12 sts rem.

Arrange sts with 6 sts each on 2 dpn. Graft top of mitten closed using Kitchener stitch (see Glossary, page 11).

THUMB

With RS facing and using larger dpn, place 13 held thumb gusset sts on 2 dpn, join yarn, and with third dpn, pick up and k5 sts along CO edge above gap—18 sts. Pm and join for working in rnds.

NEXT RND: Work Rnd 13 of Thumbs chart over first 13 sts, p5.

Work 4 more rnds as established. Cont in rev St st (purl every rnd) until thumb measures about ½" (1.3 cm) short of desired length.

NEXT (DEC) RND: *P2tog, p1; rep from * around—12 sts rem.

Purl 2 rnds even.

NEXT (DEC) RND: *P2tog; rep from * around—6 sts rem.

Cut yarn, leaving a tail 8" (20.5 cm) long. Thread tail through rem sts, pull tight to close hole, fasten off on WS.

right mitten

With smaller dpn, CO 45 sts. Distribute sts evenly over 4 dpn. Pm and join for working in rnds, being careful not to twist sts.

RND 1: *K1, p2; rep from * around.

Rep Rnd 1 until rib measures about 4" (10 cm).

NEXT (DEC) RND: K1, p2tog, work in established rib patt to last 8 sts, p2tog, k1, p2tog, k1, p2—42 sts rem.

Change to larger dpn.

Work Rnds 1-10 of Right mitten chart.

THUMB GUSSET

RND 11: P1, pm, work Row 1 of Thumbs chart over next 3 sts, pm, then work in established patt to end of rnd—50 sts.

RND 12: P1, slm, work Row 2 of Thumbs chart to next marker, slm, work to end of rnd.

Cont as established through Rnd 22 of Right mitten chart—58 sts.

RND 23: P1, remove marker, place 13 thumb sts on holder for thumb, CO 3 sts over gap, remove marker, work in established patt to end of rnd—46 sts.

Cont through Rnd 48.

RND 49: Work rnd in established patt to end of rnd, remove beg-of-rnd marker, sl 1 to right needle tip, pm for new beg of rnd—42 sts rem.

SHAPE TOP

RND 50: P18, s2kp, p3, k3, p3, k1, p8, s2kp, remove beg-of-rnd marker, sl 1 to right needle tip, pm for new beg of rnd—38 sts rem.

RND 51: P16, s2kp, p2, s2kp, p2, sl 1 st onto cn and hold in back, k1, p1 from cn, p7, s2kp, remove beg-of-rnd marker, sl 1 to right needle tip, pm for new beg of rnd—32 sts rem.

RND 52: P14, s2kp, p4, k1, p7, s2kp, remove beg-of-rnd marker, sl 1 to right needle tip, pm for new beg of rnd—28 sts rem.

RND 53: P12, s2kp, p3, make bobble, p6, s2kp, remove beg-of-rnd marker, sl 1 to right needle tip, pm for new beg of rnd—24 sts rem.

RND 54: P10, s2kp, p8, s2kp, remove beg-of-rnd marker, sl 1 to right needle tip, pm for new beg of rnd—20 sts rem.

RND 55: P8, s2kp, p6, s2kp, remove beg-of-rnd marker, sl 1 to right needle tip, pm for new beg of rnd—16 sts rem.

RND 56: P6, s2kp, p4, s2kp—12 sts rem.

Complete right mitten same as left mitten.

finishing

Weave in ends.

THUMBS

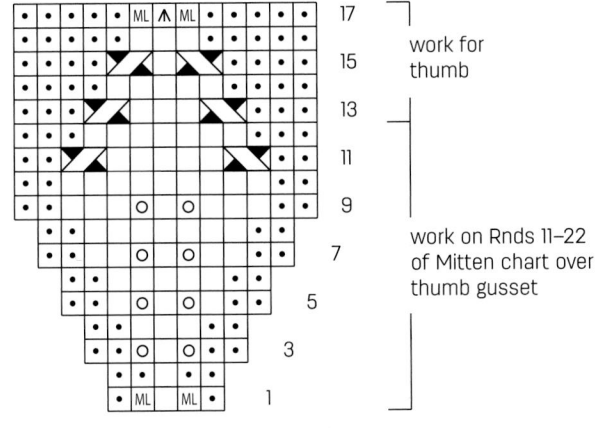

work for thumb

work on Rnds 11–22 of Mitten chart over thumb gusset

□	k on RS; p on WS
•	p on RS; k on WS
o	yo
/	k2tog
\	ssk
⌄	p2tog
∧	s2kp
ML	M1L
•	bobble
⢳⟋	sl 1 st onto cn and hold in back, k1, k1 from cn
⟍⢳	sl 1 st onto cn and hold in front, k1, k1 from cn
◤⟋	sl 1 st onto cn and hold in back, k1, p1 from cn
⟍◢	sl 1 st onto cn and hold in front, p1, k1 from cn

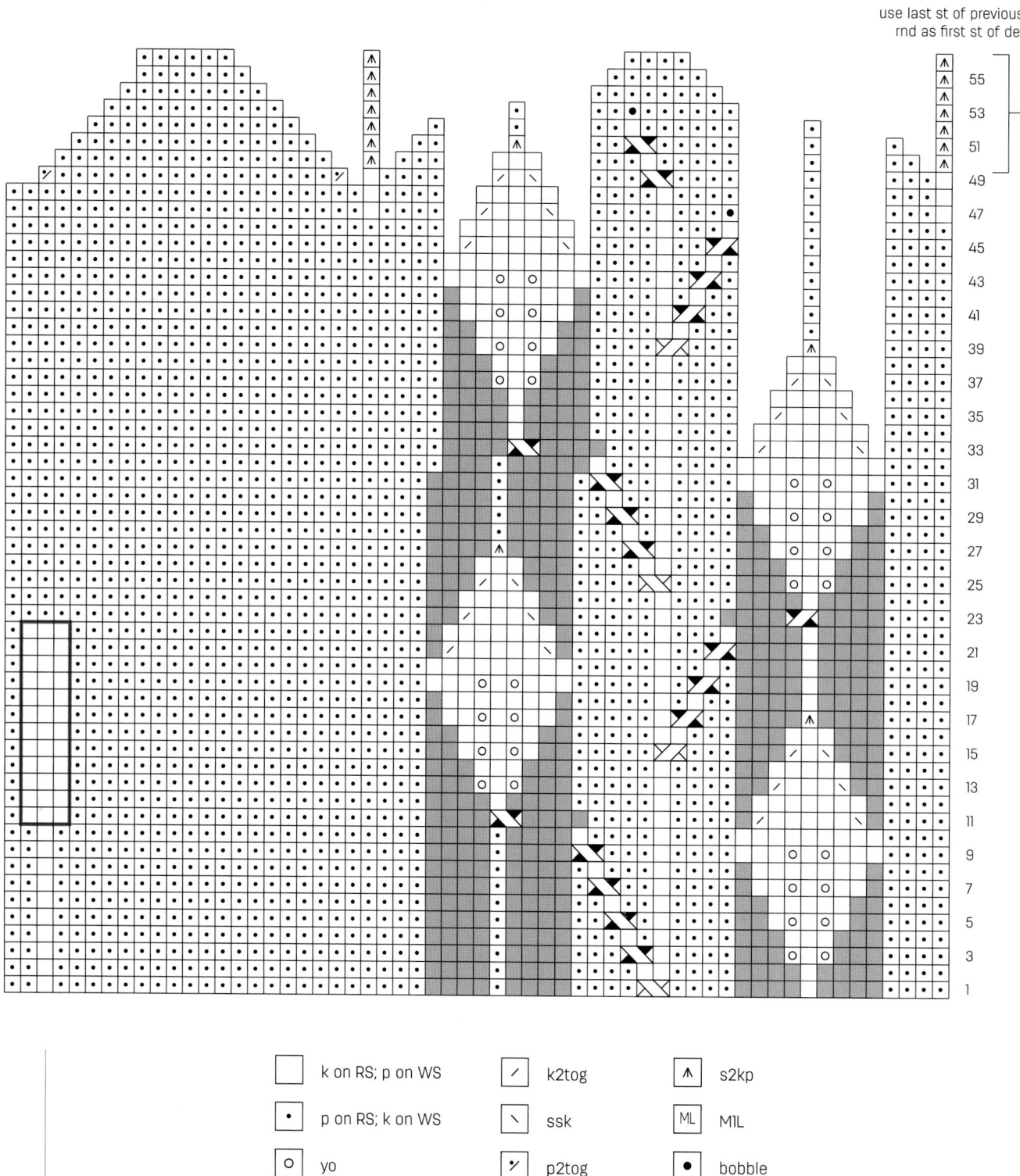

use last st of previous
rnd as first st of dec

	k on RS; p on WS	/	k2tog	∧	s2kp
•	p on RS; k on WS	\	ssk	ML	M1L
o	yo	⟋	p2tog	●	bobble

RIGHT MITTEN

use first st of next
rnd as last st of dec

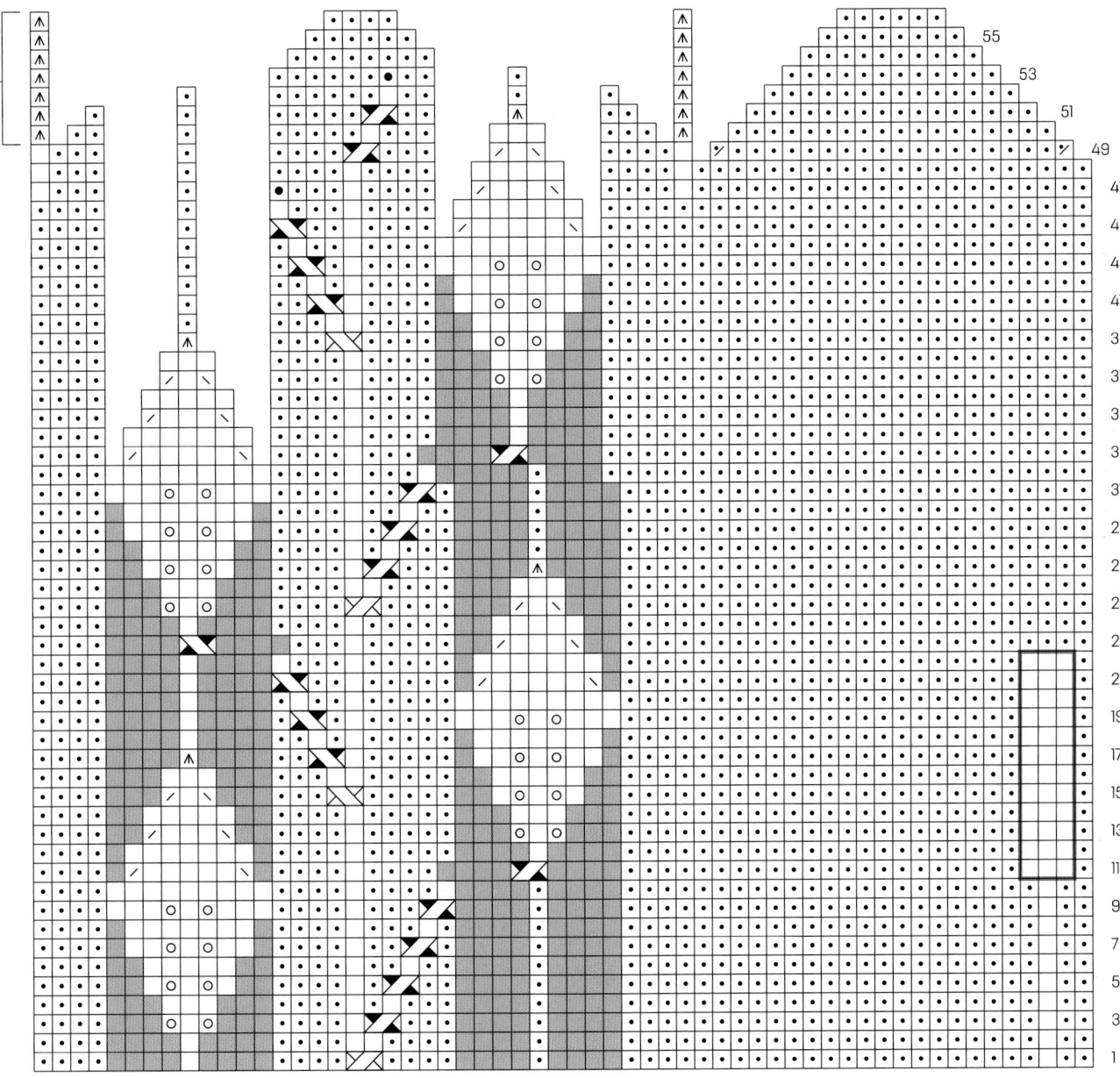

55
53
51
49
47
45
43
41
39
37
35
33
31
29
27
25
23
21
19
17
15
13
11
9
7
5
3
1

⊬⊼		sl 1 st onto cn and hold in back, k1, k1 from cn
⊠⊻		sl 1 st onto cn and hold in front, k1, k1 from cn
◥◣		sl 1 st onto cn and hold in back, k1, p1 from cn
◢◤		sl 1 st onto cn and hold in front, p1, k1 from cn

▨ no stitch

▢ thumb gusset

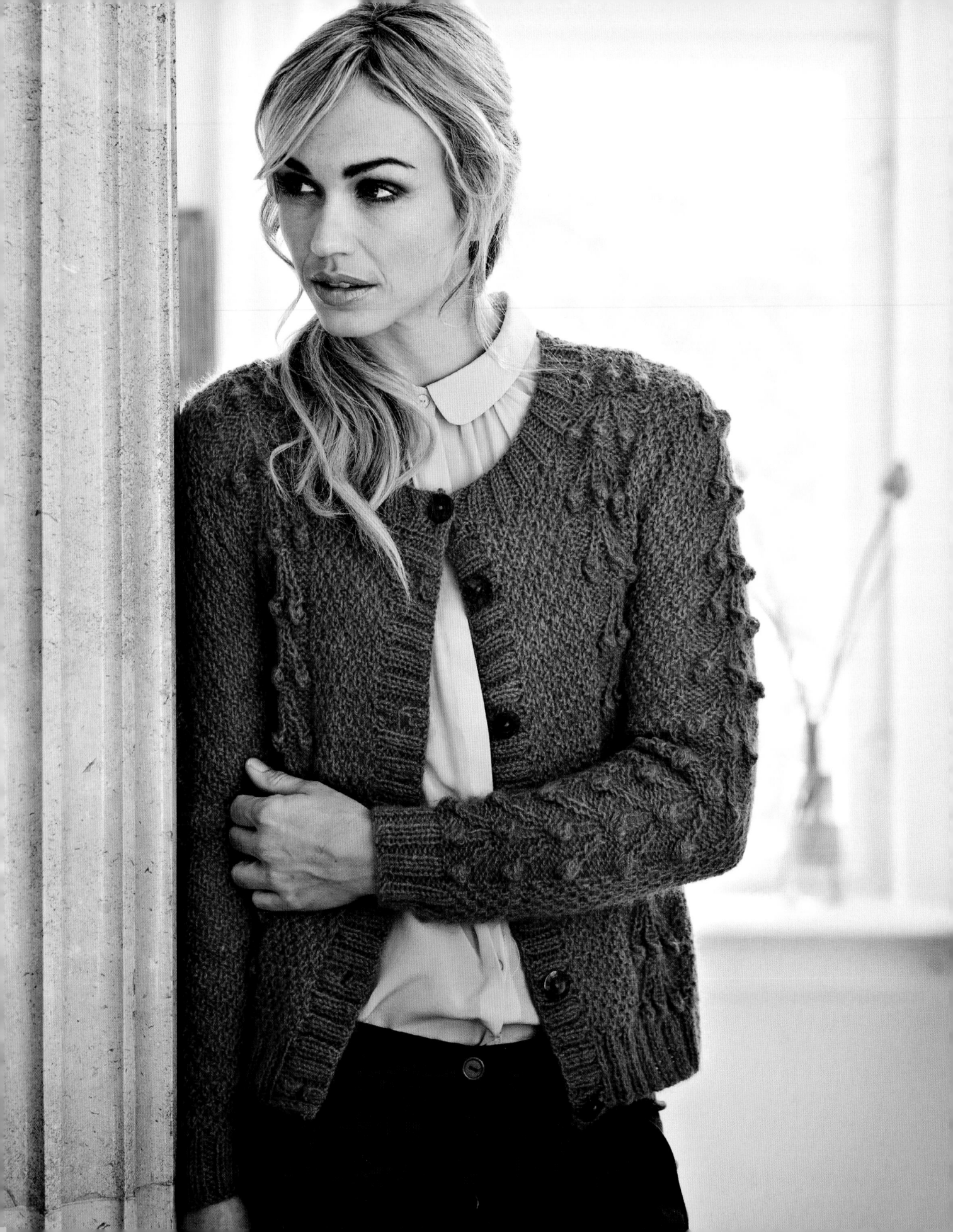

leise

seed stitches and bobbles

The vertical motifs on the fronts and sleeves punctuate
the lovely silhouette of this cardigan. The sweater is
worked with a combination of two light yarns—organic
wool and kid mohair—so it's practically weightless.

FINISHED SIZE		S	M	L	XL
Bust	in	34¼	37½	41	43¾
	cm	87	95	104	111
Total length	in	22¼	22¾	23	23½
	cm	56.5	58	58.5	59.5

YARN
Fingering weight (#2 Super Fine).

Shown here: BC Garn Semilla
Fino (100% organic wool; 262 yd
[240 m]/50 g): #115, 4 (4, 5, 5) balls.

Laceweight (#0 Lace).

BC Yarn Kid Mohair (70% super kid
mohair, 30% polyamide; 246 yd
[225 m]/25 g): #12, 4 (4, 5, 5) balls.

NEEDLES
Sizes U.S. 8 and 10 (5 and 6 mm):
straight.

*Adjust needle size if necessary to
obtain the correct gauge.*

NOTIONS
Stitch holders; tapestry needle;
6 buttons ¾" (20 mm) diameter.

GAUGE
18 sts and 22 rows = 4" (10 cm)
in moss st on larger needles.

NOTE
The sweater is worked with
1 strand of each yarn held tog
throughout.

stitch guide

MOSS STITCH
ROW 1: *K1, p1; rep from * across.
ROW 2: Knit the knit sts and purl the purl sts.
ROW 3: *P1, k1; rep from * across.
ROW 4: Knit the knit sts and purl the purl sts.
Repeat Rows 1–4 for patt.

back

With smaller needles and 1 strand of each yarn held tog, CO 78 (86, 94, 102) sts.

SET-UP ROW: (WS) K1 (edge st), p1, k2, (p2, k2) to last 2 sts, p1, k1 (edge st).

NEXT ROW: K1 (edge st), k1, (p2, k2) to last 4 sts, p2, k1, k1 (edge st).

Cont in established rib patt until piece measures 2¼" (5.5 cm), ending with a WS row, and inc 1 (dec 1, dec 1, dec 3) st(s) evenly spaced across last row—79 (85, 93, 99) sts rem.

Change to larger needles. Cont in moss st, keeping edge sts in garter st (knit every row) until piece measures 4" (10 cm) from CO edge, ending with a WS row.

SHAPE WAIST

NEXT (DEC) ROW: (RS) K1, k2tog (or p2tog to maintain patt), work in established patt to last 3 sts, k2tog (or p2tog to maintain patt), k1—2 sts dec'd.

Work 7 rows even.

Rep last 8 rows once, then rep dec row once more—73 (79, 87, 93) sts rem.

Work even until piece measures 10¼ (10¼, 10¾, 10¾)" (26 [26, 27.5, 27.5] cm) from CO edge, ending with a WS row.

NEXT (INC) ROW: (RS) K1, M1, work in established patt to last st, M1, k1—2 sts inc'd.

Work 5 rows even.

Rep last 6 rows once, then rep inc row once more—79 (85, 93, 99) sts.

Work even until piece measures 14½" (37 cm) from CO edge, ending with a WS row.

SHAPE ARMHOLES

BO 3 (4, 4, 4) sts at beg of next 2 rows, 2 sts at beg of next 2 (2, 4, 4) rows. Dec 1 st each end every RS row 3 (3, 2, 3) times—63 (67, 73, 77) sts rem.

Cont even until armhole measures 7 (7½, 7¾, 8¼)" (18 [19, 19.5, 21] cm), ending with a WS row.

SHAPE NECK AND SHOULDERS

NEXT ROW: (RS) Work 18 (20, 22, 24) sts in established patt, join a second pair of yarns and BO center 27 (27, 29, 29) sts for neck, then work to end of row—18 (20, 22, 24) sts rem each for each shoulder. Work both sides at same time with separate balls of yarn.

BO 9 (10, 11, 12) sts at beg of next 4 rows.

left front

With smaller needles and 1 strand of each yarn held tog, CO 39 (43, 47, 51) sts.

SET-UP ROW: (WS) K1 (edge st), (p2, k2) to last 2 sts, p1, k1 (edge st).

NEXT ROW: (RS) K1 (edge st), k1, (p2, k2) to last st, k1 (edge st).

Cont in established rib patt until piece measures 2¼" (5.5 cm), ending with a WS row, dec 0 (1, 1, 2) st(s) evenly across last row—39 (42, 46, 49) sts rem.

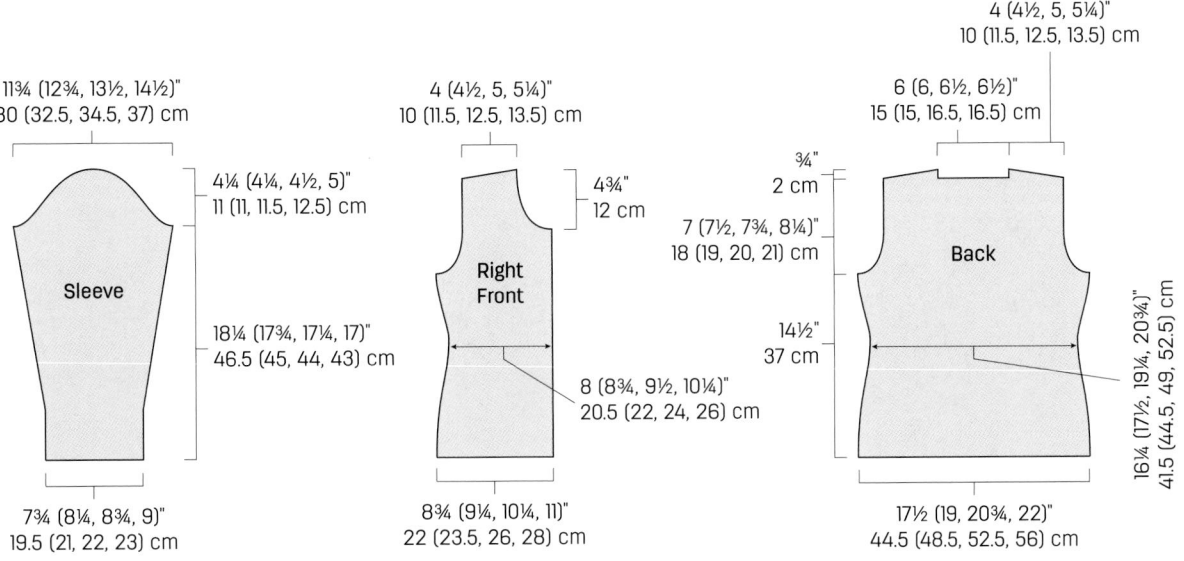

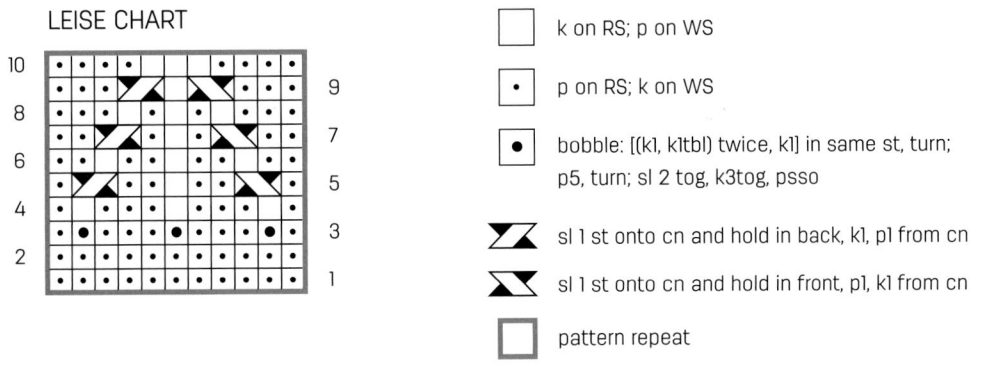

LEISE CHART

k on RS; p on WS

• p on RS; k on WS

⊙ bobble: [(k1, k1tbl) twice, k1] in same st, turn; p5, turn; sl 2 tog, k3tog, psso

sl 1 st onto cn and hold in back, k1, p1 from cn

sl 1 st onto cn and hold in front, p1, k1 from cn

pattern repeat

Change to larger needles.

SET-UP ROW: (RS) K1 (edge st), work Row 1 of moss st over next 13 (15, 18, 20) sts, work Row 1 of chart over next 11 sts, work Row 1 of moss st to last st, k1 (edge st).

Cont edge sts in garter st until piece measures 4" (10 cm) from CO edge, ending with a WS row.

SHAPE WAIST

NEXT (DEC) ROW: (RS) K1, k2tog (or p2tog to maintain patt), work in established patt to end of row—1 st dec'd.

Work 7 rows even.

Rep last 8 rows once, then rep dec row once more—36 (39, 43, 46) sts rem.

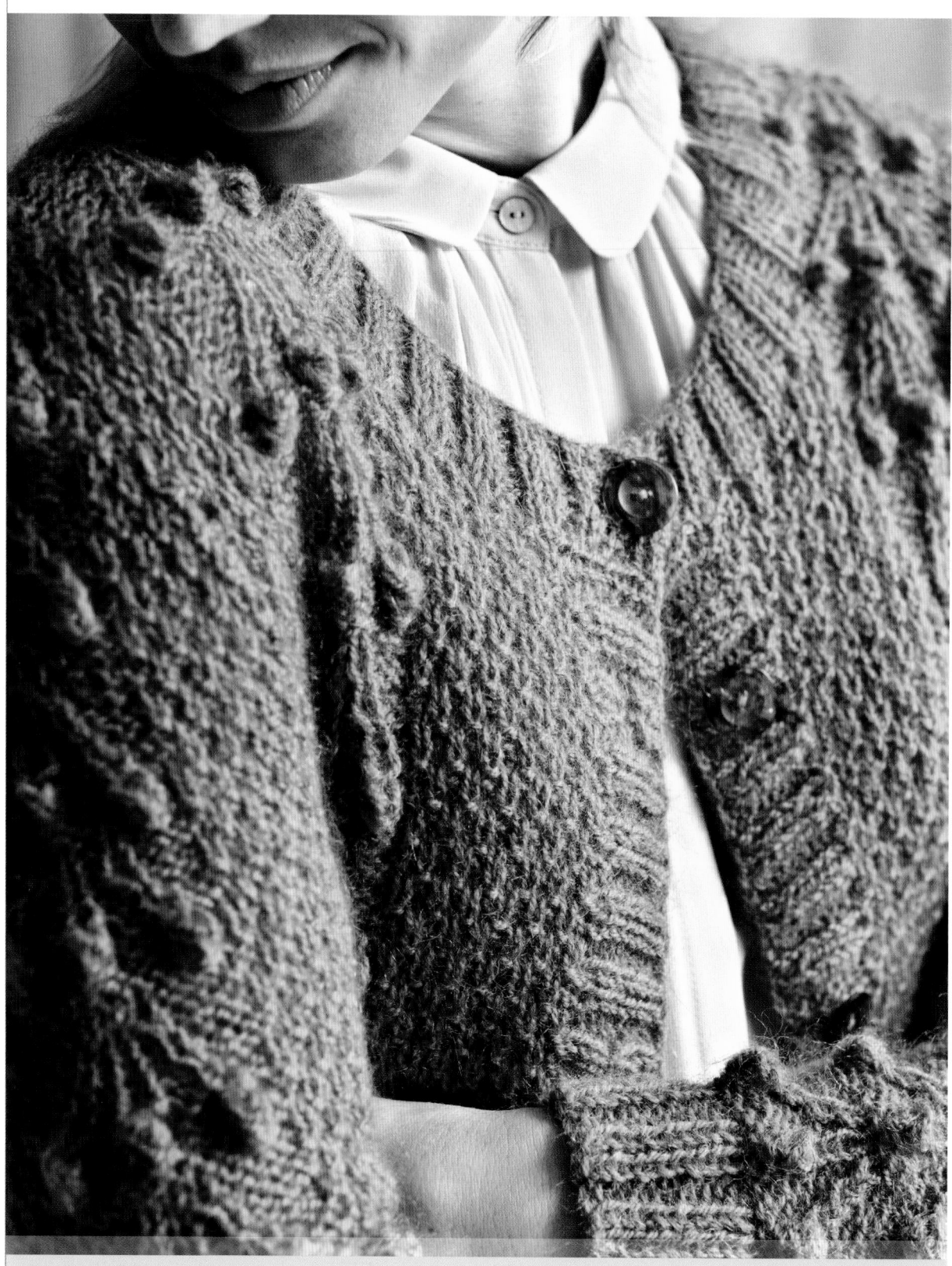

perfectly feminine knits

Work even until piece measures 10¼ (10¼, 10¾, 10¾)" (26 [26, 27.5, 27.5] cm) from CO edge, ending with a WS row.

NEXT (INC) ROW: (RS) K1, M1, work in established patt to end of row—1 st inc'd.

Work 5 rows even.

Rep last 6 rows once, then rep inc row once more—39 (42, 46, 49) sts.

Work even until piece measures 14½" (37 cm) from CO edge, ending with a WS row.

SHAPE ARMHOLE

BO at beg of RS rows 3 (4, 4, 4) sts once, 2 sts 1 (1, 2, 2) time(s), then 1 st 3 (3, 2, 3) times—31 (33, 36, 38) sts rem.

Cont even until armhole measures 3 (3½, 3¾, 4¼)" (7.5 [9, 9.5, 11] cm), ending with a WS row.

SHAPE NECK

NEXT ROW: (RS) Work in established patt to last 6 (6, 7, 7) sts, place rem sts on holder for neck—25 (27, 29, 31) sts rem.

BO at beg of WS rows 3 sts once, 2 sts once, then 1 st twice—18 (20, 22, 24) sts rem.

Cont even until armhole measures 7 (7½, 7¾, 8¼)" (18 [19, 19.5, 21] cm), ending with a WS row.

SHAPE SHOULDER

BO 9 (10, 11, 12) sts at beg of next 2 RS rows.

right front

With smaller needles and 1 strand of each yarn held tog, CO 39 (43, 47, 51) sts.

SET-UP ROW: (WS) K1 (edge st), p1, (k2, p2) to last st, k1 (edge st).

NEXT ROW: (RS) K1 (edge st), (k2, p2) to last 2 sts, k1, k1 (edge st).

Cont in established rib patt until piece measures 2¼" (5.5 cm), ending with a WS row, dec 0 (1, 1, 2) st(s) evenly across last row—39 (42, 46, 49) sts rem.

Change to larger needles.

SET-UP ROW: (RS) K1 (edge st), work Row 1 of moss st over next 13 (14, 15, 16) sts, work Row 1 of chart over next 11 sts, work Row 1 of moss st to last st, k1 (edge st).

Cont edge sts in garter st until piece measures 4" (10 cm) from CO edge, ending with a WS row.

SHAPE WAIST

NEXT (DEC) ROW: (RS) Work in established patt to last 3 sts, k2tog (or p2tog to maintain patt) k1—1 st dec'd.

Work 7 rows even.

Rep last 8 rows once, then rep dec row once more—36 (39, 43, 46) sts rem.

Work even until piece measures 10¼ (10¼, 10¾, 10¾)" (26 [26, 27.5, 27.5] cm) from CO edge, ending with a WS row.

NEXT (INC) ROW: (RS) Work in established patt to last st, M1, k1—1 st inc'd.

Work 5 rows even.

Rep last 6 rows once, then rep inc row once more—39 (42, 46, 49) sts.

Work even until piece measures 14½" (37 cm) from CO edge, ending with a RS row.

SHAPE ARMHOLE

BO at beg of WS rows 3 (4, 4, 4) sts once, 2 sts 1 (1, 2, 2) time(s), then 1 st 3 (3, 2, 3) times—31 (33, 36, 38) sts rem.

Cont even until armhole measures 3 (3½, 3¾, 4¼)" (7.5 [9, 9.5, 11] cm), ending with a RS row.

SHAPE NECK

NEXT ROW: (WS) Work in established patt to last 6 (6, 7, 7) sts, place rem sts on holder for neck—25 (27, 29, 31) sts rem.

BO at beg of RS rows 3 sts once, 2 sts once, then 1 st twice—18 (20, 22, 24) sts rem.

Cont even until armhole measures 7 (7½, 7¾, 8¼)" (18 [19, 19.5, 21] cm), ending with a RS row.

SHAPE SHOULDER

BO 9 (10, 11, 12) sts at beg of next 2 WS rows.

sleeves (make 2)

With smaller needles and 1 strand of each yarn held tog, CO 34 (38, 38, 42) sts.

SET-UP ROW: (WS) K1 (edge st), p1, k2, (p2, k2) to last 2 sts, p1, k1 (edge st).

NEXT ROW: K1 (edge st), k1, (p2, k2) to last 4 sts, p2, k1, k1 (edge st).

Cont in established rib patt until piece measures 2¼" (5.5 cm), ending with a WS row, and inc 1 (dec 1, inc 1, dec 1) st evenly spaced across last row—35 (37, 39, 41) sts rem.

Change to larger needles.

SET-UP ROW: (RS) K1 (edge st), work Row 1 of moss st over next 11 (12, 13, 14) sts, work Row 1 of chart over next 11 sts, work Row 1 of moss st to last st, k1 (edge st).

Cont even in established patt until piece measures 4 (4¾, 3½, 2¾)" (10 [12, 9, 7] cm) from CO edge, ending with a WS row.

NEXT (INC) ROW: (RS) K1, M1, work in established patt to last st, M1, k1—2 sts inc'd.

Working inc sts into moss st, work 7 (5, 5, 5) rows even.

Rep last 8 (6, 6, 6) rows 7 (8, 9, 10) times, then rep inc row once more—53 (57, 61, 65) sts.

Cont even until piece measures 18¼ (17¾, 17¼, 17)" (46.5 [45, 44, 43] cm), from CO edge, ending with a WS row.

SHAPE CAP

BO 3 (4, 4, 4) sts at beg of next 2 rows, 2 sts at beg of next 4 rows. Dec 1 st each end every RS row 5 (5, 6, 7) times. BO 2 sts at beg of next 4 rows, 3 sts at beg of next 4 (2, 2, 2) rows, then 4 sts at beg of next 0 (2, 2, 2) rows—9 (9, 11, 13) sts rem.

BO rem sts.

finishing and bands

Sew shoulder seams.

BUTTONBAND

With smaller needles and RS facing, pick up and k99 (99, 103, 103) sts along left front edge.

NEXT ROW: (WS) P2, (k2, p2) to last st, k1 (edge st).

NEXT ROW: (RS) K1 (edge st), (k2, p2) to last 2 sts, k2.

Cont in established rib until buttonband measures 1¼" (3.2 cm). BO all sts in rib.

BUTTONHOLE BAND

With smaller needles and RS facing, pick up and k99 (99, 103, 103) sts along right front edge.

NEXT ROW: (WS) K1 (edge st), p2, (k2, p2) to end of row.

NEXT ROW: (RS) (K2, p2) to last 3 sts, k2, k1 (edge st).

Work 1 more row in established rib.

NEXT (BUTTONHOLE) ROW: (RS) Work 4 sts in established rib, *BO 2 sts for buttonhole, work in rib until 19 (19, 20, 20) sts are on right needle

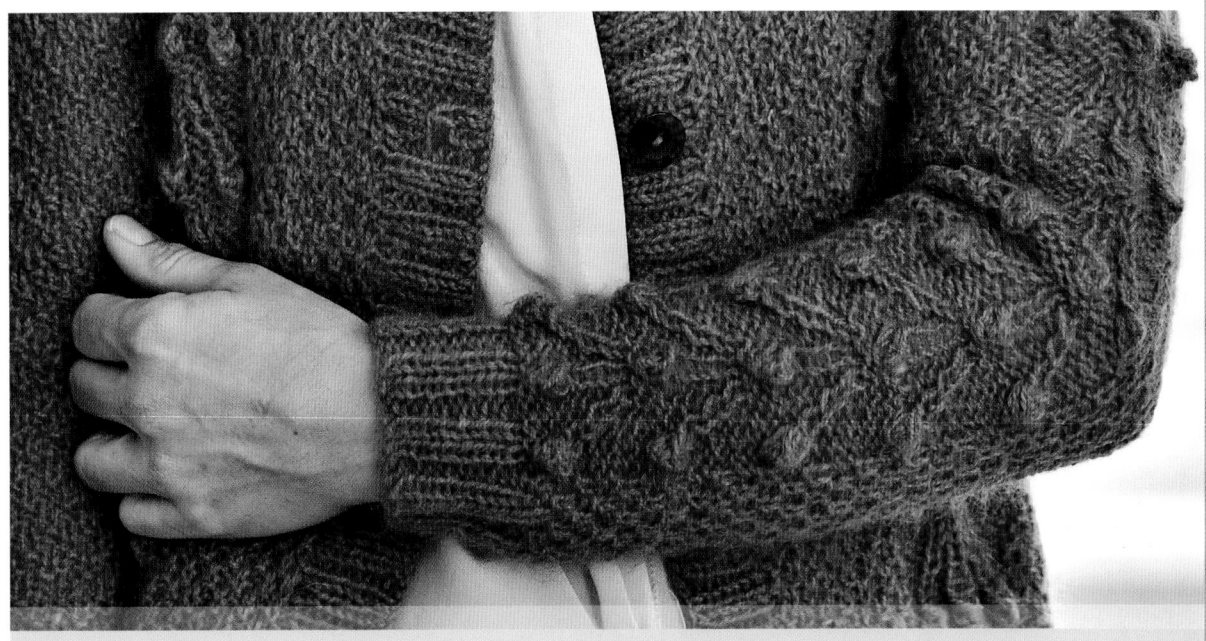

tip after buttonhole gap; rep from * 3 more times, BO 2 sts for buttonhole, work to end of row.

NEXT ROW: *Work in established rib patt to buttonhole, CO 2 sts over gap; rep from * 4 more times, work to end of row.

Cont even until band measures 1¼" (3.2 cm). BO all sts in rib.

NECKBAND
With smaller needles and RS facing, pick up and k6 sts along end of buttonhole band, k6 (6, 7, 7) sts from holder, pick up and k30 sts along right neck, 26 (26, 28, 28) sts along back neck, 30 sts along left neck to held sts, k6 (6, 7, 7) sts from holder, then 6 sts along end of buttonband—110 (110, 114, 114) sts

ROW 1: (WS) P2, (k2, p2) to end of row.

ROW 2: (RS) (K2, p2) to last 2 sts, k2.

Work 1 more row in established rib.

NEXT (BUTTONHOLE) ROW: (RS) Work 3 sts in established rib, BO 2 sts for buttonhole, work to end of row.

NEXT ROW: Work to buttonhole, CO 2 sts over gap, work in rib to end of row.

Cont even until neckband measures 1¼" (3.2 cm). BO all sts in rib.

Weave in ends. Block pieces to finished measurements. Sew in sleeves. Sew sleeve and side seams. Sew buttons to buttonband and end of neckband opposite buttonholes.

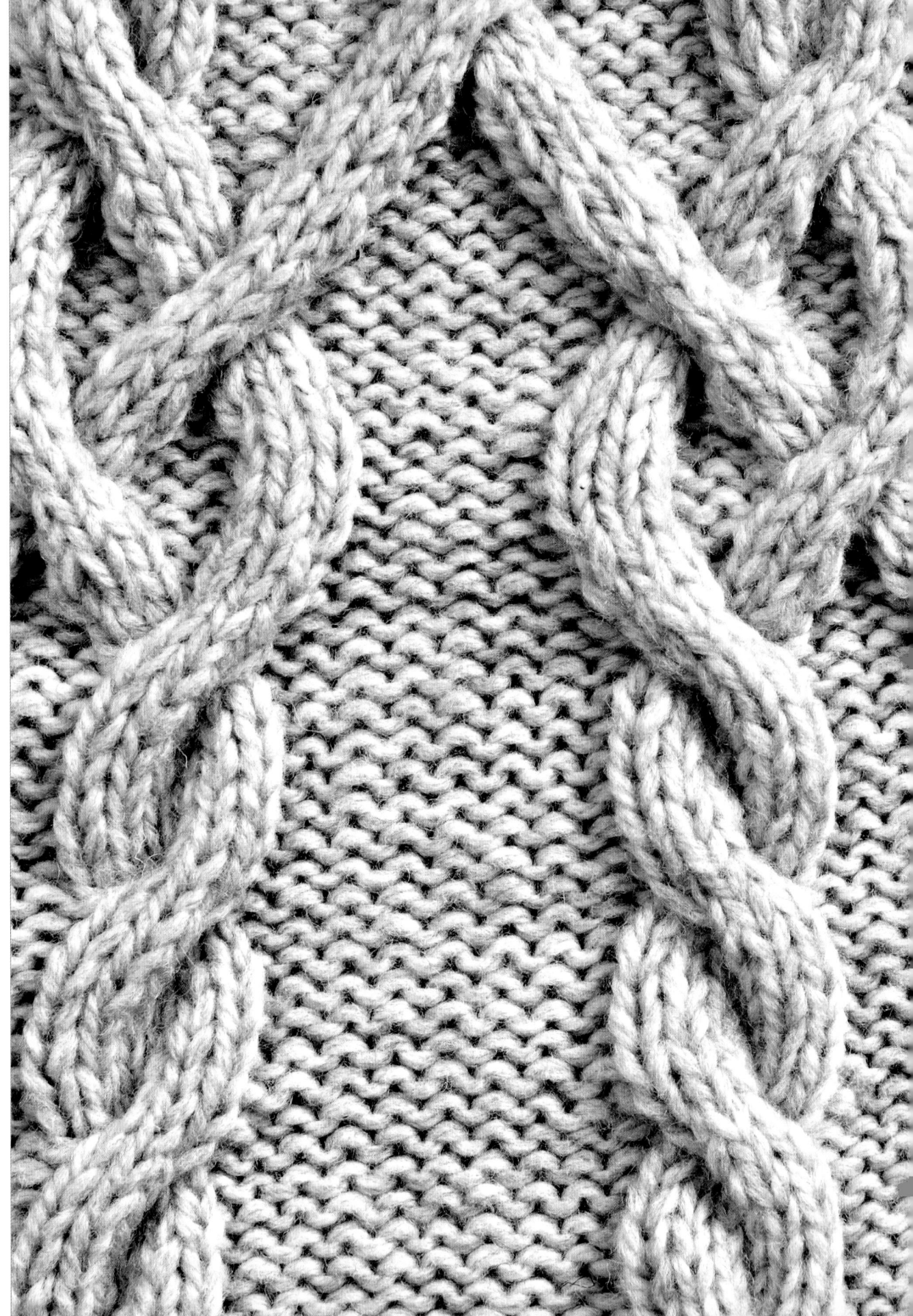

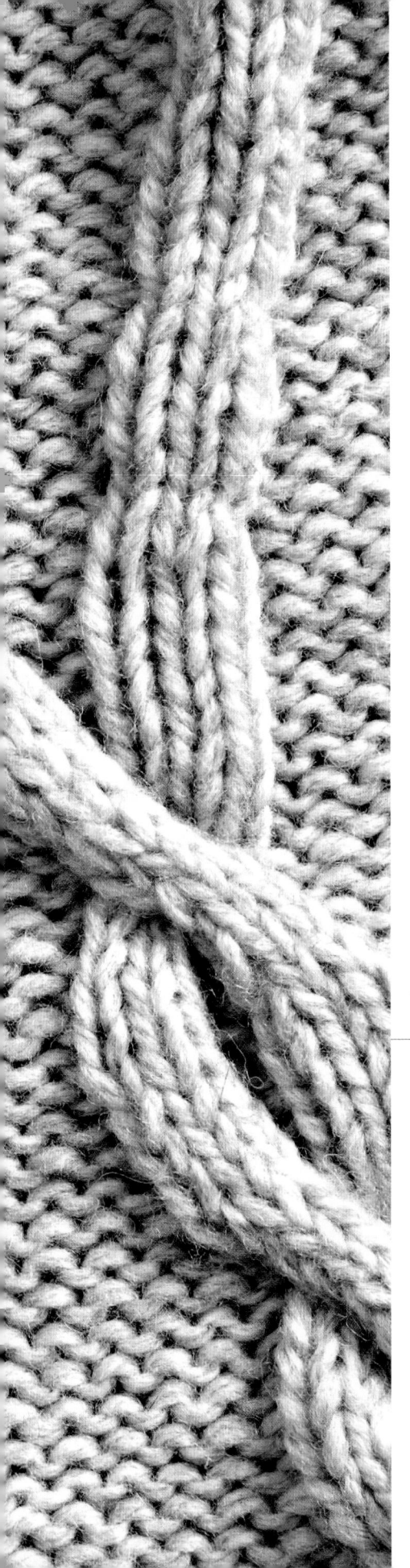

Cables

At their most basic, cables are formed by stitches that change place. In this section, you'll find a classic raglan sweater with Irish roots transformed by nontraditional cable patterns. You can work cables in an allover pattern as on the Naja cap or work cables on a background of reverse stockinette to make them stand out more distinctly.

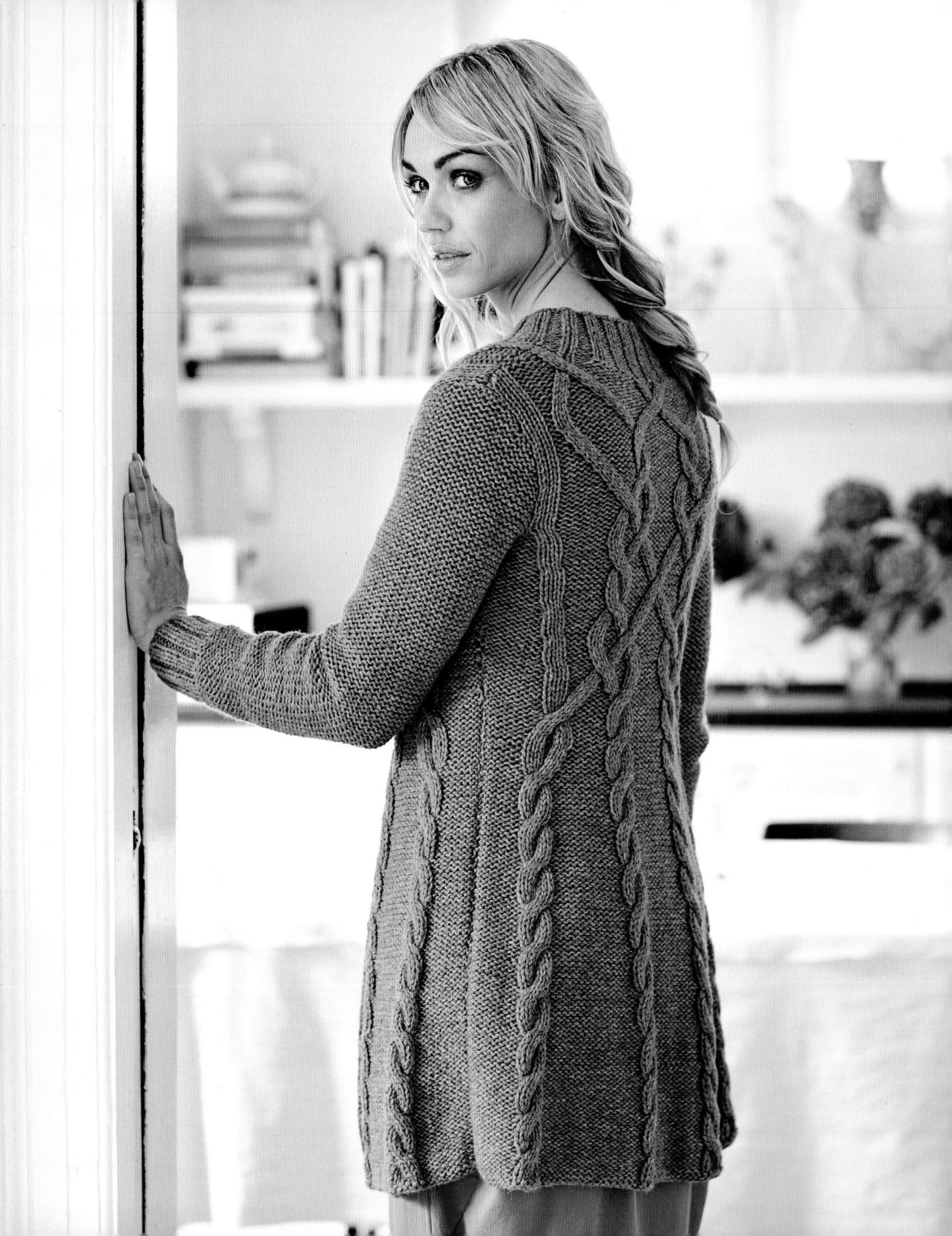

benedicte

pretty shaping with cables

Look at the back of this sweater, which is offered in both a coat length and one that ends at the hip, and it's easy to see how the cables shape the garment. Both versions are worked from the same basic pattern. The only difference is the frequency of decreases on the lower part of the back and front.

FINISHED SIZE		S	M	L	XL
Bust	in	33	37¼	40	43¾
	cm	84	94.5	101.5	111
Total length, sweater	in	24¼	24¾	25	25¼
	cm	61	62	62	63
Total length, coat	in	31	31½	31½	31¾
	cm	78.5	80	80	80.5

YARN

For Hip-Length Sweater
Chunky weight (#5 Bulky).

Shown here: Sandnes Garn Fritidsgarn (100% pure new wool; 76 yd [70 m]/50 g): natural heather #2641, 12 (13, 14, 15) balls.

For Coat
Chunky weight (#5 Bulky).

Shown here: Isager Highland Wool (100% lambswool; 306 yd [280 m]/50 g): curry (A), 8 (9, 9, 10) balls.

Laceweight (#0 Lace).

Isager Alpaca 1 (100% alpaca, 437 yd [400 m]/50 g): #59 (B), 10 (12, 14, 14) balls.

NEEDLES
Sizes U.S. 9 and 10½ (5.5 and 6.5 mm): straight. Size U.S. 9 (5.5 mm): 32" (80 cm) circular (cir).

Adjust needle size if necessary to obtain the correct gauge.

NOTIONS
Stitch holders; markers; cable needle (cn); tapestry needle.

Sweater: 6 buttons ⅞" (22 mm) diameter.

Coat: 8 buttons ⅞" (22 mm) diameter.

GAUGE
Sweater: 14 sts and 19 rows = 4" (10 cm) in St st on larger needles.

Coat: 14 sts and 21 rows = 4" (10 cm) in St st on larger needles with 2 strands each of A and B held tog.

stitch guide

CABLE A (6 STS)
ROWS 1, 3, AND 5: (RS) Knit.
ROWS 2, 4, AND 6: Purl.
ROW 7: Sl 3 sts onto cn and hold in front, k3, k3 from cn.
ROW 8: Purl.
Rep Rows 1–8 for patt.

CABLE B (6 STS)
ROWS 1, 3, AND 5: (RS) Knit.
ROWS 2, 4, AND 6: Purl.
ROW 7: Sl 3 sts onto cn and hold in back, k3, k3 from cn.
ROW 8: Purl.
Rep Rows 1–8 for patt.

HIP-LENGTH SWEATER

back

With larger needles, CO 100 (106, 112, 118) sts.

Knit 1 WS row.

NEXT (SET-UP) ROW: (RS) K1 (edge st), p10 (13, 16, 19), place marker (pm), work (Row 1 of Cable A over 6 sts, pm, p18) twice, work Row 1 of Cable B over 6, sts, pm, p18, pm, work Cable B over 6 sts, pm, p10 (13, 16, 19), k1 (edge st).

NEXT ROW: K1 (edge st), *knit to marker, slm, work Row 2 cable over 6 sts, slm; rep from * 3 more times, knit to last st, k1 (edge st).

Work 5 more rows in established patt.

SHAPE WAIST

NEXT (DEC) ROW: (RS) K1 (edge st), *purl to 2 sts before cable, p2tog, slm, work next row of cable over 6 sts, slm, p2tog; rep from * 3 more times, purl to last st, k1 (edge st)—8 sts dec'd.

Rep dec row every 8 rows 4 more times—60 (66, 72, 78) sts rem, ending with Row 8 of cable patt. Piece should measure about 8¾" (22 cm) from CO edge.

NEXT ROW: (RS) K1 (edge st), p2 (5, 8, 11), slm, work Row 1 of chart over 54 sts and remove next 6 m, slm, p2 (5, 8, 11), k1 (edge st).

Cont in established patt until piece measures 10¾ (10¾, 10¼, 10¼)" (27.5 [27.5, 26, 26] cm), ending with a WS row.

NEXT (INC) ROW: (RS) K1 (edge st), m1p, work to last st in established patt, m1p, k1 (edge st)—2 sts inc'd.

Rep inc row every 6 rows 4 more times—70 (76, 82, 88) sts. Work new sts in rev St st. At the same time, remove rem markers on Row 56.

Sizes M (L, XL) only
NEXT ROW: (RS) Work to 1 st before chart sts, sl 1 st onto cn and hold in back, k3, p1 from cn, work 48 sts in established patt, sl 3 sts onto cn and hold in front, p1, k3 from cn, work to end of row.

Rep last row every 8 rows 1 (3, 5) more time(s) to move 3 knit sts at each end closer to edge, and cont rem inc.

All sizes
Work even until piece measures 16½ (16½, 16¼, 16¼)" (42 [42, 41.5, 41.5] cm) from CO edge, ending with a WS row.

SHAPE ARMHOLES
BO 3 (3, 4, 4) sts at beg of next 2 rows, 2 sts at beg of next 2 rows. Dec 1 st each end every RS row 2 (3, 3, 4) times—56 (60, 64, 68) sts rem.

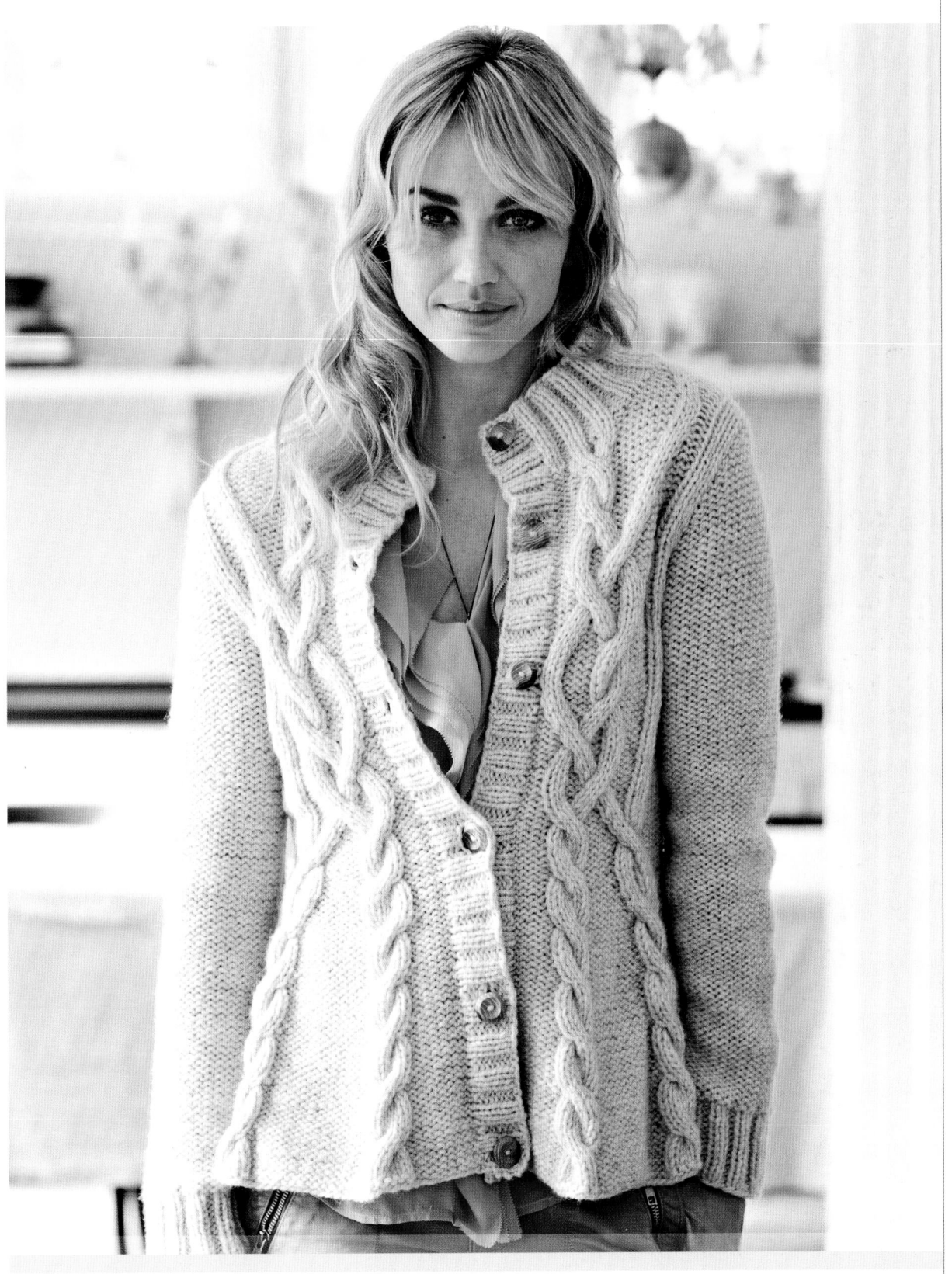

Cont even until armhole measures 7 (7½, 8, 8¼)" (18 [19, 20.5, 21] cm), ending with a WS row. *Note: Not all chart rows may need to be worked before reaching required length.*

SHAPE NECK AND SHOULDERS

NEXT ROW: (RS) BO 6 (7, 8, 9) sts, work in established patt until there are 7 (8, 8, 9) sts on right needle tip, place next 30 (30, 32, 32) sts on holder for neck, join a 2nd ball of yarn and work to end of row. Work both sides at same time with separate balls of yarn.

NEXT ROW: BO 6 (7, 8, 9) sts, work to neck; work to end of row.

BO 7 (8, 8, 9) sts from armhole edge at beg of next 2 rows.

left front

With larger needles, CO 51 (54, 57, 60) sts.

Knit 1 WS row.

NEXT (SET-UP) ROW: (RS) K1 (edge st), p10 (13, 16, 19) sts, pm, work Row 1 of Cable A over 6 sts, pm, p18 sts, pm, work Cable A over 6 sts, pm, p9, k1 (edge st).

NEXT ROW: K1 (edge st), k9, slm, work Row 2 of Cable A over 6 sts, slm, k18, slm, work Cable A over 6 sts, slm, k10 (13, 16, 19) sts, k1 (edge st).

Work 5 more rows in established patt.

SHAPE WAIST

NEXT (DEC) ROW: (RS) K1 (edge st), *purl to 2 sts before cable, p2tog, slm, work next row of Cable A over 6 sts, slm, p2tog; rep from * once more, purl to last st, k1 (edge st)—4 sts dec'd.

Rep dec row every 8 rows 4 more times—31 (34, 37, 40) sts rem, ending with a Row 8 of Cable A patt. Piece should measure about 8¾" (22) cm from CO edge.

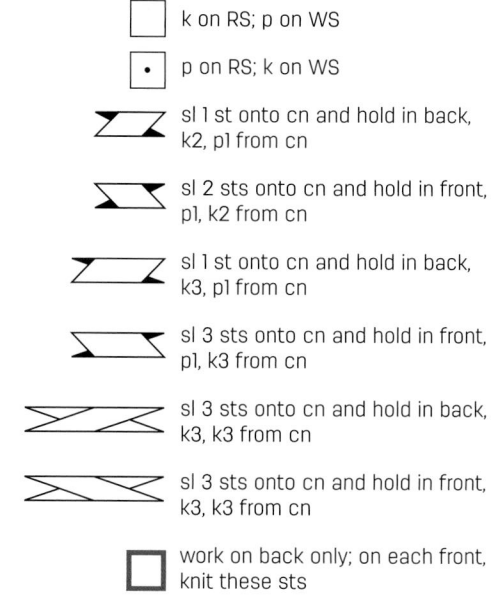

☐ k on RS; p on WS

⦁ p on RS; k on WS

sl 1 st onto cn and hold in back, k2, p1 from cn

sl 2 sts onto cn and hold in front, p1, k2 from cn

sl 1 st onto cn and hold in back, k3, p1 from cn

sl 3 sts onto cn and hold in front, p1, k3 from cn

sl 3 sts onto cn and hold in back, k3, k3 from cn

sl 3 sts onto cn and hold in front, k3, k3 from cn

☐ work on back only; on each front, knit these sts

Note: For sizes M (L, XL) only, beg with Row 57, cont crossing 3 knit sts at right side of chart 1 st to the right 2 (4, 6) more times, and 3 knit sts at left side of chart 1 st to the left 2 (4, 6) more times.

NEXT ROW: (RS) K1 (edge st), p2 (5, 8, 11), sm, beg at right edge of chart and work Row 1 of chart over 27 sts and remove next 2 marker, slm, k1 (edge st).

NEXT ROW: K1 (edge st), slm, beg at center of chart and work Row 2 of chart over 27 sts, slm, k2 (5, 8, 11), k1 (edge st).

Cont in established patt until piece measures 10¾ (10¾, 10¼, 10¼)" (27.5 [27.5, 26, 26] cm from CO edge, ending with a WS row.

NEXT (INC) ROW: (RS) K1 (edge st), m1p, purl to marker, slm, work next row of chart over 27 sts, slm, k1 (edge st)—1 st inc'd.

Rep inc row every 6 rows 4 more times—36 (39, 42, 45) sts. Work new sts in rev St st. At the same time, remove rem markers on Row 56.

BENEDICTE CHART

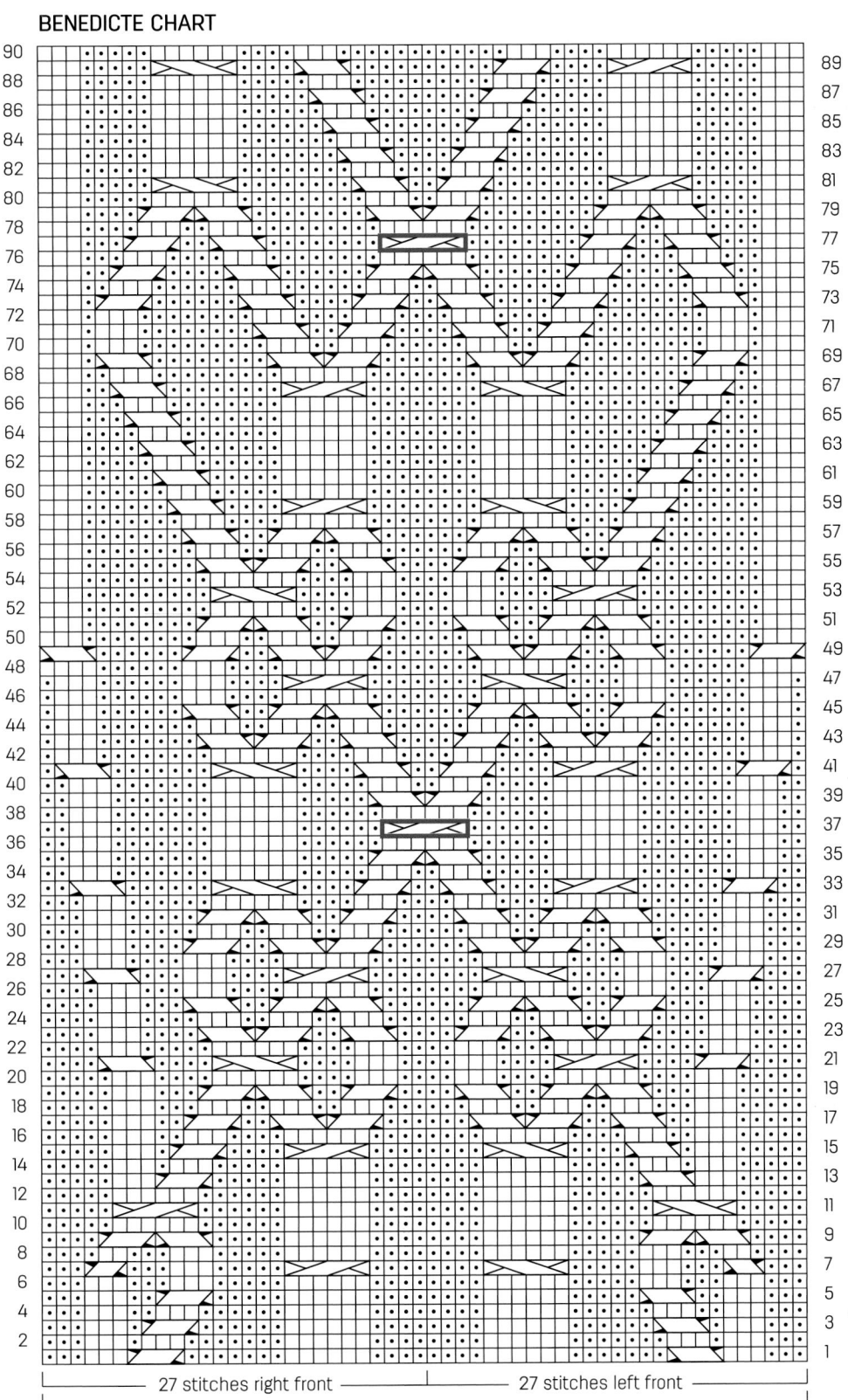

27 stitches right front

27 stitches left front

54 stitches back

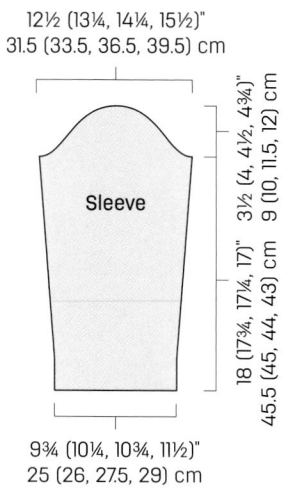

12½ (13¼, 14¼, 15½)"
31.5 (33.5, 36.5, 39.5) cm
Sleeve
3½ (4, 4½, 4¾)"
9 (10, 11.5, 12) cm
18 (17¾, 17¼, 17)"
45.5 (45, 44, 43) cm
9¾ (10¼, 10¾, 11½)"
25 (26, 27.5, 29) cm
2¼ (2¾, 3¼, 3¾)"
5.5 (7, 8.5, 9.5) cm
3"
7.5 cm
Right Front
8½ (9½, 10¼, 11¼)"
21.5 (24, 26, 28.5) cm
7¼ (8, 8¾, 9¾)"
18.5 (20.5, 22, 25) cm
12¾ (13¾, 14½, 15½)"
32.5 (35, 37, 39) cm
8 (8, 8¼, 8¼)"
20.5 (20.5, 21, 21) cm
2¼ (2¾, 3¼, 3¾)"
5.5 (7, 8.5, 9.5) cm
¾"
2 cm
7 (7½, 7¾, 8¼)"
18 (19, 20.5, 21) cm
Back
Short: 16½ (16½, 16¼, 16¼)"
42 (42, 41.5, 41.5) cm
Long: 23¼ (23¼, 22¾, 22¾)"
59 (59, 58, 58) cm
16½ (18¾, 20, 21¾)"
42 (47.5, 51, 55) cm
13¾ (15½, 17¼, 18¾)"
35 (39.5, 44, 47.5) cm
27¾ (29½, 31¼, 32¾)"
70.5 (75, 79.5, 83) cm

Sizes M (L, XL) only

NEXT ROW: (RS) Work to 1 st before chart sts, sl 1 st onto cn and hold in back, k3, p1 from cn, work 24 sts in established patt, work to end of row.

Rep last row every 8 rows 1 (3, 5) more time(s) to move 3 knit sts at right closer to side edge, and cont rem inc.

All sizes

Cont even until piece measures 16½ (16½, 16¼, 16¼)" (42 [42, 41.5, 41.5] cm) from CO edge, ending with a WS row.

SHAPE ARMHOLE

BO at beg of RS rows 3 (3, 4, 4) sts once, 2 sts once. Dec 1 st at beg of RS rows 2 (3, 3, 4) times—29 (31, 33, 35) sts rem.

Cont even until armhole measures 4¾ (5¼, 5¾, 6)" (12 [13.5, 14.5, 15] cm), ending with a RS row.

SHAPE NECK

NEXT ROW: (WS) Work 8 (8, 9, 9) sts and place on holder for neck, work in established patt to end of row—21 (23, 24, 26) sts rem.

BO at beg of WS rows 3 sts once, 2 sts once, then 1 st 3 times—13 (15, 16, 18) sts rem.

Cont even until armhole measures 7 (7½, 8, 8¼)" (18 [19, 20.5, 21] cm), ending with a WS row.

SHAPE SHOULDER

BO at beg of next 2 RS rows 6 (7, 8, 9) sts once, then 7 (8, 8, 9) sts once.

right front

With larger needles, CO 51 (54, 57, 60) sts.

Knit 1 WS row.

NEXT (SET-UP) ROW: (RS) K1 (edge st), p9, pm, work Row 1 of Cable B over 6 sts, pm, p18, pm, work Cable B over 6 sts, pm, p10 (13, 16, 19), k1 (edge st).

NEXT ROW: K1 (edge st), k10 (13, 16, 19), slm, work Row 2 of Cable B over 6 sts, slm, k18, slm, work Cable B over 6 sts, slm, k9, k1 (edge st).

Work 5 more rows in established patt.

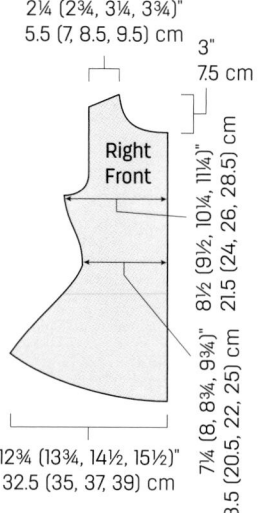

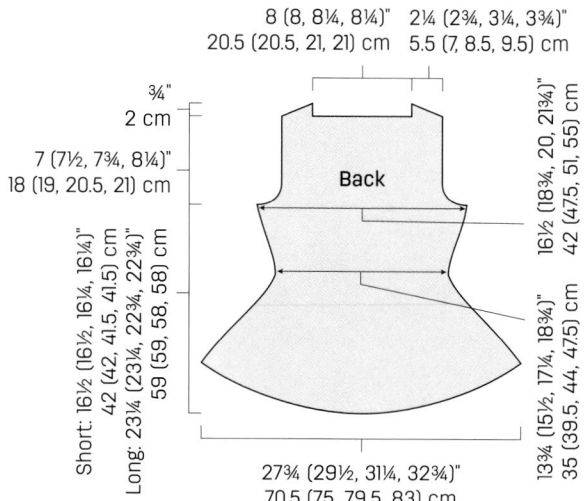

SHAPE WAIST

NEXT (DEC) ROW: (RS) K1 (edge st), *purl to 2 sts before cable, p2tog, slm, work next row of Cable B over 6 sts, slm, p2tog; rep from * once more, purl to last st, k1 (edge st)—4 sts dec'd.

Rep dec row every 8 rows 4 more times—31 (34, 37, 40) sts rem, ending with Row 8 of Cable A patt. Piece should measure about 8¾" (22) cm from CO edge.

NEXT ROW: (RS) K1 (edge st), slm, beg at center of chart and work Row 1 of chart over 27 sts and remove next 2 markers, slm, p2 (5, 8, 11), k1 (edge st).

NEXT ROW: K1 (edge st), k2 (5, 8, 11), slm, beg at left edge of chart and work Row 2 of chart over 27 sts, slm, k1 (edge st).

Cont in established patt until piece measures 10¾ (10¾, 10¼, 10¼)" (27.5 [27.5, 26, 26] cm from CO edge, ending with a WS row.

NEXT (INC) ROW: (RS) K1 (edge st), purl to marker, slm, work next row of chart over 27 sts, slm, m1p, k1 (edge st)—1 st inc'd.

Rep inc row every 6 rows 4 more times—36 (39, 42, 45) sts. Work new sts in rev St st. At the same time, remove rem markers on Row 56.

Sizes M (L, XL) only
NEXT ROW: (RS) Work to last 3 chart sts, sl 3 sts onto cn and hold in front, p1 from cn, k3, work to end of row.

Rep last row every 8 rows 1 (3, 5) more time(s) to move 3 knit sts at left closer to side edge, and cont rem inc.

All sizes
Cont even until piece measures 16½ (16½, 16¼, 16¼)" (42 [42, 41.5, 41.5] cm) from CO edge, ending with a RS row.

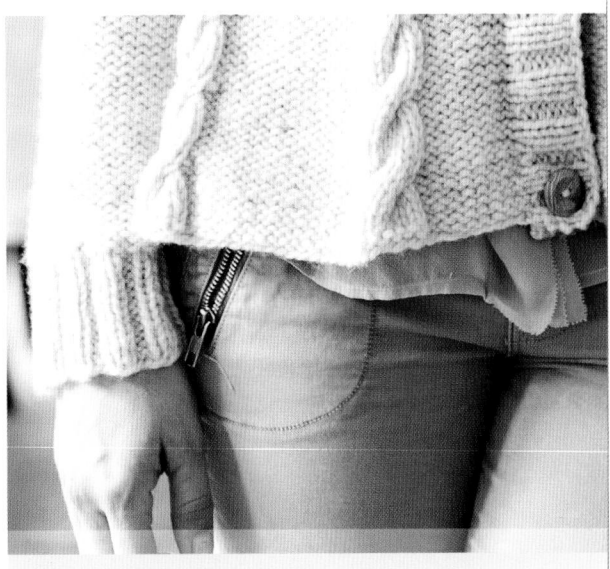

SHAPE ARMHOLE
BO at beg of WS rows 3 (3, 4, 4) sts once, 2 sts once. Dec 1 st at beg of WS rows 2 (3, 3, 4) times—29 (31, 33, 35) sts rem.

Cont even until armhole measures 4¾ (5¼, 5¾, 6)" (12 [13.5, 14.5, 15] cm), ending with a WS row.

SHAPE NECK
NEXT ROW: (RS) Work 8 (8, 9, 9) sts and place on holder for neck, work in established patt to end of row—21 (23, 24, 26) sts rem.

BO at beg of RS rows 3 sts once, 2 sts once, then 1 st 3 times—13 (15, 16, 18) sts rem.

Cont even until armhole measures 7 (7½, 8, 8¼)" (18 [19, 20.5, 21] cm), ending with a RS row.

SHAPE SHOULDER
BO at beg of next 2 WS rows 6 (7, 8, 9) sts once, then 7 (8, 8, 9) sts once.

sleeves (make 2)
With smaller needles, CO 42 (42, 46, 46) sts.

ROW 1: (WS) P2, (k2, p2) to end of row.

ROW 2: (K2, p2) to last 2 sts, k2.

Cont in established rib patt until rib measures 2½" (6.5 cm), ending with a WS row.

Change to larger needles.

NEXT (DEC) ROW: (RS) P6 (5, 5, 7), *p2tog, p2 (4, 3, 4); rep from * 6 (4, 6, 4) more times, p2tog, purl to end of row—34 (36, 38, 40) sts rem.

Cont even in rev St st (purl RS rows, knit WS rows) until piece measures 6" (15 cm) from CO edge, ending with a WS row.

NEXT (INC) ROW: (RS) P1, m1p, purl to last st, m1p, p1—2 sts inc'd.

Rep inc row every 12 (12, 10, 8) rows 4 (4, 5, 6) more times—44 (46, 50, 54) sts.

Cont even until piece measures 18 (17¾, 17¼, 17)" (45.5 [45, 44, 43] cm) from CO edge, ending with a WS row.

SHAPE CAP

BO 3 sts at beg of next 2 rows, 2 sts at beg of next 2 (2, 2, 4) rows. Dec 1 st each end every RS row 5 (6, 7, 7) times. BO 2 sts at beg of next 2 rows, then 3 sts at beg of next 4 rows. BO rem 8 (8, 10, 10) sts.

finishing and edgings

Weave in ends. Block pieces to finished measurements.

Sew shoulder seams.

NECKBAND

With smaller needles and RS facing, knit 8 (8, 9, 9) held sts, pick up and k19 sts along right neck edge, knit 30 (30, 32, 32) held back neck sts, pick up and k19 sts along left neck edge, then knit rem held 8 (8, 9, 9) sts—84 (84, 88, 88) sts.

ROW 1: (WS) K1 (edge st), p2, (k2, p2) to last st, k1 (edge st).

ROW 2: K1 (edge st), (k2, p2) to last 3 sts, k2, k1 (edge st).

Cont in established rib patt until neckband measures 2½" (6.5 cm). BO all sts loosely in rib.

BUTTONBAND

With smaller needles and RS facing, pick up and k98 (102, 102, 106) sts evenly along left front edge (about 3 sts for every 4 rows).

ROW 1: (WS) P2, (k2, p2) to the end.

ROW 2: K2 (p2, k2) to the end.

Cont in established rib patt until buttonband measures 1¼" (3.2 cm). BO all sts loosely in rib. Pm to mark placement of 6 buttonholes along right front edge, with first about ¾" (2 cm) down from neck and last about ¾" (2 cm) up from lower edge, and rem 4 evenly spaced in between.

BUTTONHOLE BAND

With smaller needles and RS facing, pick up and k98 (102, 102, 106) sts evenly along right front edge (about 3 sts for every 4 rows).

ROW 1: (WS) P2, (k2, p2) to the end.

ROW 2: K2 (p2, k2) to the end.

Work 1 more row in established rib patt.

NEXT (BUTTONHOLE) ROW: (RS) *Work in rib patt to marker, BO 2 sts for buttonhole; rep from * 5 more times, work in rib to end of row.

NEXT ROW: Work in established rib patt and CO 2 sts over each gap.

Cont in established rib patt until band measures 1¼" (3.2 cm). BO all sts loosely in rib.

Sew sleeve and side seams. Sew in sleeves. Sew buttons to buttonband opposite buttonholes.

COAT

back

With larger needles and 2 strands each of A and B held tog, CO 100 (106, 112, 118) sts.

Knit 1 WS row.

NEXT (SET-UP) ROW: (RS) K1 (edge st), p10 (13, 16, 19), place marker (pm), work (Row 1 of Cable A over 6 sts, pm, p18) twice, work Row 1 of Cable B over 6 sts, pm, p18, pm, work Cable B over 6 sts, pm, p10 (13, 16, 19), k1 (edge st).

NEXT ROW: K1 (edge st), *knit to marker, slm, work Row 2 cable over 6 sts, slm; rep from * 3 more times, knit to last st, k1 (edge st).

Work 25 more rows in established patt.

SHAPE WAIST

NEXT (DEC) ROW: (RS) K1 (edge st), *purl to 2 sts before cable, p2tog, slm, work next row of cable over 6 sts, slm, p2tog; rep from * 3 more times, purl to last st, k1 (edge st)—8 sts dec'd.

Rep dec row every 8 rows 4 more times—60 (66, 72, 78) sts rem, ending with Row 8 of cable patt. Piece should measure about 11½" (29 cm) from CO edge.

NEXT ROW: (RS) K1 (edge st), p2 (5, 8, 11), slm, work Row 1 of chart over 54 sts and remove next 6 markers, slm, p2 (5, 8, 11), k1 (edge st).

Cont in established patt until piece measures 17¼ (17¼, 17, 17)" (44 [44, 43, 43] cm), ending with a WS row.

NEXT (INC) ROW: (RS) K1 (edge st), m1p, work to last st in established patt, m1p, k1 (edge st)— 2 sts inc'd.

Rep inc row every 6 rows 4 more times—70 (76,

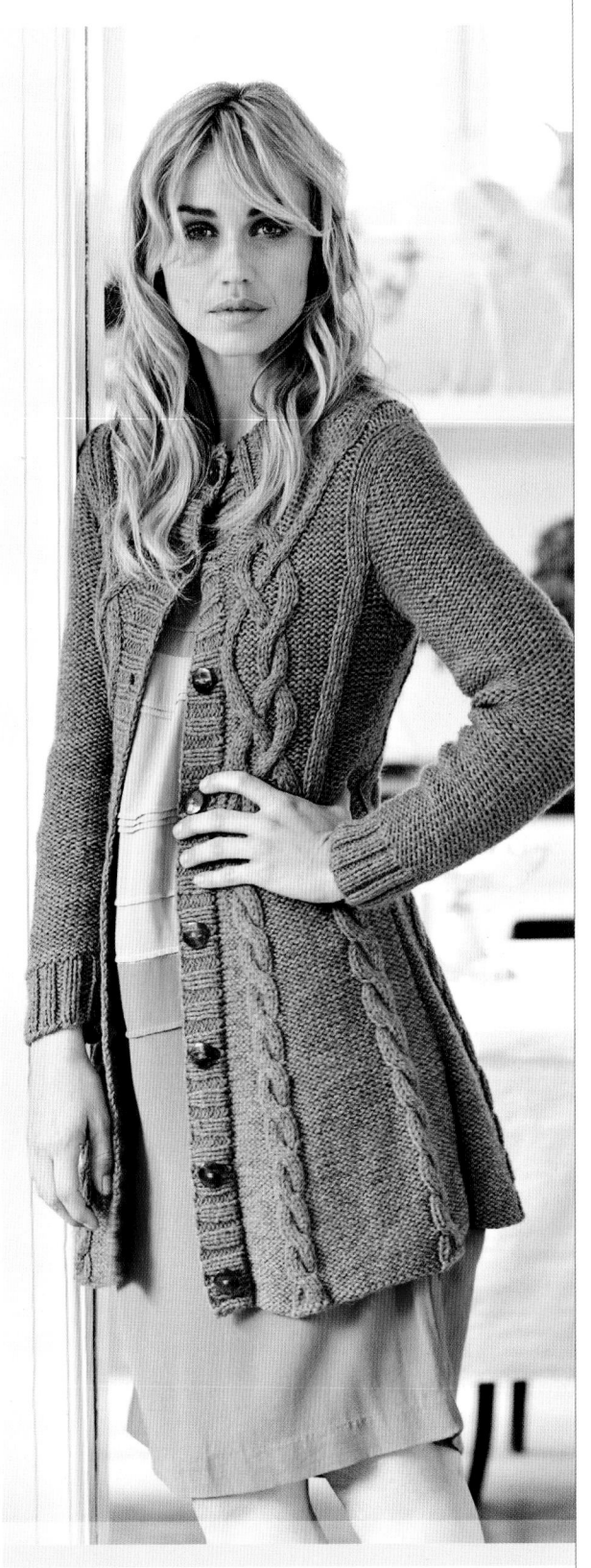

82, 88) sts. Work new sts in rev St st. At the same time, remove rem markers on Row 56.

Sizes M (L, XL) only

NEXT ROW: (RS) Work to 1 st before chart sts, sl 1 st onto cn and hold in back, k3, p1 from cn, work 48 sts in established patt, sl 3 sts onto cn and hold in front, p1, k3 from cn, work to end of row.

Rep last row every 8 rows 1 (3, 5) more time(s) to move 3 knit sts at each end closer to edge, and cont rem inc.

Rep last row every 8 rows 1 (3, 5) more time(s), and cont rem inc.

All sizes

Work even until piece measures 23¼ (23¼, 22¾, 22¾)" (59 [59, 58, 58] cm) from CO edge, ending with a WS row.

SHAPE ARMHOLES

BO 3 (3, 4, 4) sts at beg of next 2 rows, 2 sts at beg of next 2 rows. Dec 1 st each end every RS row 2 (3, 3, 4) times—56 (60, 64, 68) sts rem.

Cont even until armhole measures 7 (7½, 8, 8¼)" (18 [19, 20.5, 21] cm), ending with a WS row. *Note: Not all chart rows may need to be worked before reaching required length.*

SHAPE NECK AND SHOULDERS

NEXT ROW: (RS) BO 6 (7, 8, 9) sts, work in established patt until there are 7 (8, 8, 9) sts on tip of right needle, place next 30 (30, 32, 32) sts on holder for neck, join a 2nd ball of yarn and work to end of row. Work both sides at same time with separate balls of yarn.

NEXT ROW: BO 6 (7, 8, 9) sts, work to neck; work to end of row.

BO 7 (8, 8, 9) sts at beg of next 2 rows.

left front

With larger needles and 2 strands each of A and B held tog, CO 51 (54, 57, 60) sts.

Knit 1 WS row.

NEXT (SET-UP) ROW: (RS) K1 (edge st), p10 (13, 16, 19) sts, pm, work Row 1 of Cable A over 6 sts, pm, p18 sts, pm, work Cable A over 6 sts, pm, p9, k1 (edge st).

NEXT ROW: K1 (edge st), k9, slm, work Row 2 of Cable A over 6 sts, slm, k18, slm, work Cable A over 6 sts, slm, k10 (13, 16, 19) sts, k1 (edge st).

Work 25 more rows in established patt.

SHAPE WAIST

NEXT (DEC) ROW: (RS) K1 (edge st), *purl to 2 sts before cable, p2tog, slm, work next row of Cable A over 6 sts, slm, p2tog; rep from * once more, purl to last st, k1 (edge st)—4 sts dec'd.

Rep dec row every 8 rows 4 more times—31 (34, 37, 40) sts rem, ending with a Row 8 of Cable A patt. Piece should measure about 11½" (29 cm) from CO edge.

NEXT ROW: (RS) K1 (edge st), p2 (5, 8, 11), slm, beg at right edge of chart and work Row 1 of chart over 27 sts and remove next 2 markers, slm, k1 (edge st).

NEXT ROW: K1 (edge st), slm, beg at center of chart and work Row 2 of chart over 27 sts, slm, k2 (5, 8, 11), k1 (edge st).

Cont in established patt until piece measures 17¼ (17¼, 17, 17)" (44 [44, 43, 43] cm from CO edge, ending with a WS row.

NEXT (INC) ROW: (RS) K1 (edge st), m1p, purl to marker, slm, work next row of chart over 27 sts, slm, k1 (edge st)—1 st inc'd.

Rep inc row every 6 rows 4 more times—36 (39, 42, 45) sts. Work new sts in rev St st. At the same time, remove rem markers on Row 56.

Sizes M (L, XL) only

NEXT ROW: (RS) Work to 1 st before chart sts, sl 1 st onto cn and hold in back, k3, p1 from cn, work 24 sts in established patt, work to end of row.

Rep last row every 8 rows 1 (3, 5) more time(s) to move 3 knit sts at right closer to edge, and cont rem inc.

All sizes

Cont even until piece measures 23¼ (23¼, 22¾, 22¾)" (59 [59, 58, 58] cm) from CO edge, ending with a WS row.

SHAPE ARMHOLE

BO at beg of RS rows 3 (3, 4, 4) sts once, 2 sts once. Dec 1 st at beg of RS rows 2 (3, 3, 4) times—29 (31, 33, 35) sts rem.

Cont even until armhole measures 4¾ (5¼, 5¾, 6)" (12 [13.5, 14.5, 15] cm), ending with a RS row.

SHAPE NECK

NEXT ROW: (WS) Work 8 (8, 9, 9) sts and place on holder for neck, work in established patt to end of row—21 (23, 24, 26) sts rem.

BO at beg of WS rows 3 sts once, 2 sts once, then 1 st 3 times—13 (15, 16, 18) sts rem.

Cont even until armhole measures 7 (7½, 8, 8¼)" (18 [19, 20.5, 21] cm), ending with a WS row.

SHAPE SHOULDER

BO at beg of next 2 RS rows 6 (7, 8, 9) sts once, then 7 (8, 8, 9) sts once.

right front

With larger needles and 2 strands each of A and B held tog, CO 51 (54, 57, 60) sts.

Knit 1 WS row.

NEXT (SET-UP) ROW: (RS) K1 (edge st), p9, pm, work Row 1 of Cable B over 6 sts, pm, p18, pm, work Cable B over 6 sts, pm, p10 (13, 16, 19), k1 (edge st).

NEXT ROW: K1 (edge st), k10 (13, 16, 19), slm, work Row 2 of Cable B over 6 sts, slm, k18, slm, work Cable B over 6 sts, slm, k9, k1 (edge st).

Work 25 more rows in established patt.

SHAPE WAIST

NEXT (DEC) ROW: (RS) K1 (edge st), *purl to 2 sts before cable, p2tog, slm, work next row of Cable B over 6 sts, slm, p2tog; rep from * once more, purl to last st, k1 (edge st)—4 sts dec'd.

Rep dec row every 8 rows 4 more times—31 (34, 37, 40) sts rem, ending with a Row 8 of Cable A patt. Piece should measure about 11½" (29 cm) from CO edge.

NEXT ROW: (RS) K1 (edge st), slm, beg at center of chart and work Row 1 of chart over 27 sts and remove next 2 markers, slm, p2 (5, 8, 11), k1 (edge st).

NEXT ROW: K1 (edge st), k2 (5, 8, 11), slm, beg at left edge of chart and work Row 2 of chart over 27 sts, slm, k1 (edge st).

Cont in established patt until piece measures 17¼ (17¼, 17, 17)" (44 [44, 43, 43] cm from CO edge, ending with a WS row.

NEXT (INC) ROW: (RS) K1 (edge st), purl to marker, slm, work next row of chart over 27 sts, slm, m1p, k1 (edge st)—1 st inc'd.

Rep inc row every 6 rows 4 more times—36 (39, 42, 45) sts. Work new sts in rev St st. At the same time, remove rem markers on Row 56.

Sizes M (L, XL) only

NEXT ROW: (RS) Work to last 3 chart sts, sl 3 sts onto cn and hold in front, p1 from cn, k3, work to end of row.

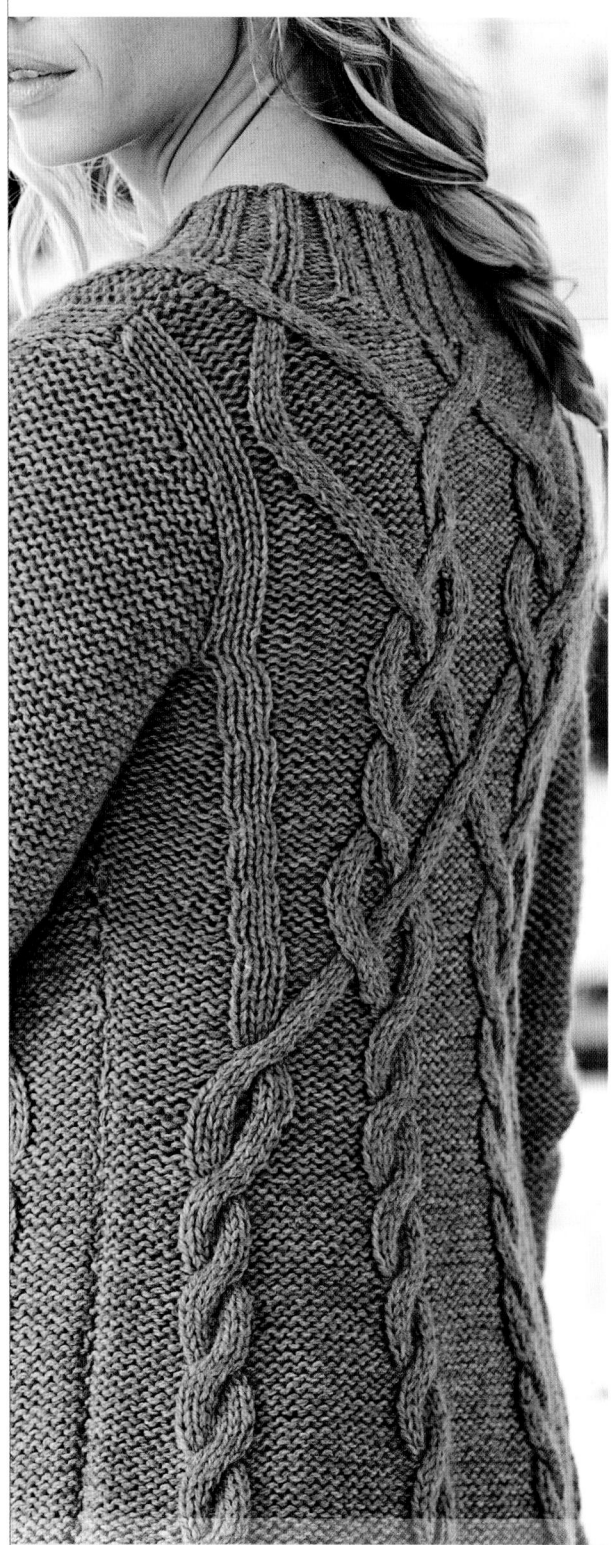

Rep last row every 8 rows 1 (3, 5) more time(s) to move 3 knit sts at left closer to edge, and cont rem inc.

All sizes

Cont even until piece measures 23¼ (23¼, 22¾, 22¾)" (59 [59, 58, 58] cm) from CO edge, ending with a RS row.

SHAPE ARMHOLE

BO at beg of WS rows 3 (3, 4, 4) sts once, 2 sts once. Dec 1 st at beg of WS rows 2 (3, 3, 4) times—29 (31, 33, 35) sts rem.

Cont even until armhole measures 4¾ (5¼, 5½, 6)" (12 [13.5, 14, 15] cm), ending with a WS row.

SHAPE NECK

NEXT ROW: (RS) Work 8 (8, 9, 9) sts and place on holder for neck, work in established patt to end of row—21 (23, 24, 26) sts rem.

BO at beg of RS rows 3 sts once, 2 sts once, then 1 st 3 times—13 (15, 16, 18) sts rem.

Cont even until armhole measures 7 (7½, 8, 8¼)" (18 [19, 20.5, 21] cm), ending with a RS row.

SHAPE SHOULDER

BO at beg of next 2 WS rows 6 (7, 8, 9) sts once, then 7 (8, 8, 9) sts once.

sleeves (make 2)

With smaller needles, CO 42 (42, 46, 46) sts.

ROW 1: (WS) P2, (2k, p2) to end of row.

ROW 2: (K2, p2) to last 2 sts, k2.

Cont in established rib patt until rib measures 2½" (6.5 cm), ending with a WS row.

Change to larger needles.

NEXT (DEC) ROW: (RS) P6 (5, 5, 7), *p2tog, p2 (4, 3, 4); rep from * 6 (4, 6, 4) more times, p2tog, purl to end of row—34 (36, 38, 40) sts rem.

Cont even in rev St st (purl RS rows, knit WS rows) until piece measures 6" (15 cm) from CO edge, ending with a WS row.

NEXT (INC) ROW: (RS) P1, m1p, purl to last st, m1p, p1—2 sts inc'd.

Rep inc row every 12 (12, 10, 8) rows 4 (4, 5, 6) more times—44 (46, 50, 54) sts.

Cont even until piece measures 18 (17¾, 17¼, 17)" (45.5 [45, 44, 43] cm) from CO edge, ending with a WS row.

SHAPE CAP
BO 3 sts at beg of next 2 rows, 2 sts at beg of next 2 (2, 2, 4) rows. Dec 1 st each end every RS row 5 (6, 7, 7) times. BO 2 sts at beg of next 2 rows, then 3 sts at beg of next 4 rows. BO rem 8 (8, 10, 10) sts.

finishing and edgings
Weave in ends. Block pieces to finished measurements.

Sew shoulder seams.

NECKBAND
With smaller needles and RS facing, knit 8 (8, 9, 9) held sts, pick up and k19 sts along right neck edge, knit 30 (30, 32, 32) held-back neck sts, pick up and k19 sts along left neck edge, then knit rem held 8 (8, 9, 9) sts—84 (84, 88, 88) sts.

ROW 1: (WS) K1 (edge st), p2, (k2, p2) to last st, k1 (edge st).

ROW 2: K1 (edge st), (k2, p2) to last 3 sts, k2, k1 (edge st).

Cont in established rib patt until neckband measures 2½" (6.5 cm). BO all sts loosely in rib.

BUTTONBAND
With smaller needles and RS facing, pick up and k126 (130, 130, 134) sts evenly along left front edge (about 3 sts for every 4 rows).

ROW 1: (WS) P2, (k2, p2) to the end.

ROW 2: K2 (p2, k2) to the end.

Cont in established rib patt until buttonband measures 1¼" (3.2 cm). BO all sts loosely in rib. Pm to mark placement of 8 buttonholes along right front edge, with first about ¾" (2 cm) down from neck and last about ¾" (2 cm) up from lower edge, and rem 6 evenly spaced in between.

BUTTONHOLE BAND
With smaller needles and RS facing, pick up and k126 (130, 130, 134) sts evenly along right front edge (about 3 sts for every 4 rows).

ROW 1: (WS) P2, (k2, p2) to the end.

ROW 2: K2 (p2, k2) to the end.

Work 1 more row in established rib patt.

NEXT (BUTTONHOLE) ROW: (RS) *Work in rib patt to marker, BO 2 sts for buttonhole; rep from * 7 more times, work in rib to end of row.

NEXT ROW: Work in established rib patt and CO 2 sts over each gap.

Cont in established rib patt until band measures 1¼" (3.2 cm). BO all sts loosely in rib.

Sew sleeve and side seams. Sew in sleeves. Sew buttons to buttonband opposite buttonholes.

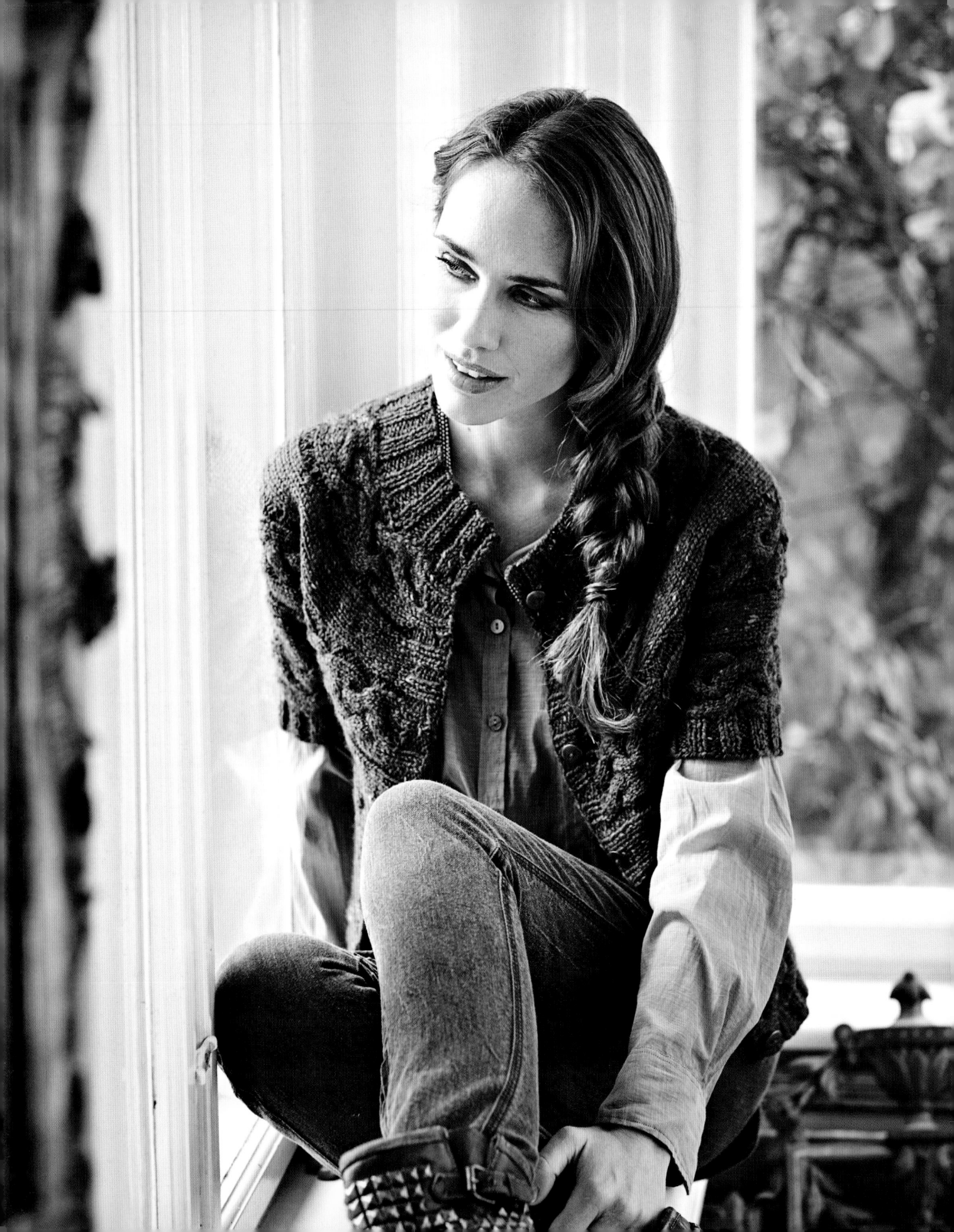

malika

bolero with side-to-side cables

This bolero is a snap to make smaller or larger because it's worked side to side, so you knit to the desired width!

FINISHED SIZE		S	M	L	XL
Bust with 1" (2.5 cm) overlap	in	33½	36¾	40	43¼
	cm	85	93.5	101.5	110
Length including neckband	in	18¾	18¾	18¾	18¾
	cm	47.5	47.5	47.5	47.5

YARN
Aran weight (#4 Medium).

Shown here: BC Garn Hamelton Tweed 1 (90% wool, 10% viscose; 109 yd [100 m]/50 g): #13, 7 (7, 8, 9) balls.

NEEDLES
Size U.S. 9 (5.5 mm): 32" (80 cm) circular (cir). Size U.S. 8 (5 mm): 24" (60 cm) cir.

Adjust needle size if necessary to obtain the correct gauge.

NOTIONS
Markers; cable needle (cn); stitch holders; tapestry needle; 7 buttons ¾" (19 mm) diameter.

GAUGE
21 sts and 25 rows = 4" (10 cm) in pattern on larger needles.

NOTES
This sweater is worked from side to side, beginning at the left front edge and ending at the right front edge.

The garment is shaped with short-rows as follows: work to the point where piece is to be turned, turn the piece without wrapping the next stitch, slip the first stitch, and tighten the yarn before working back. This method will help avoid holes.

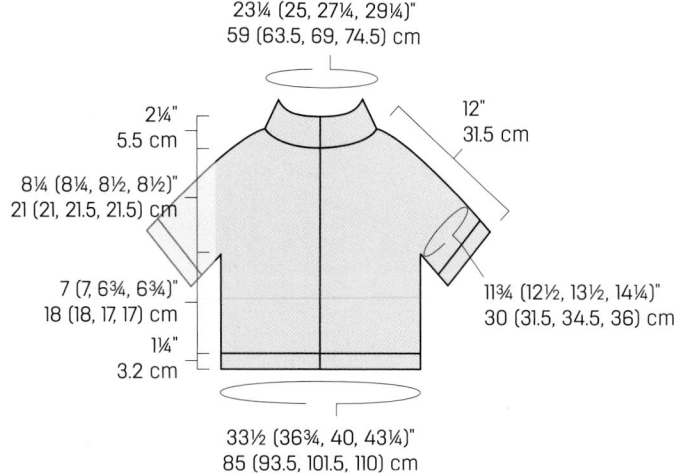

23¼ (25, 27¼, 29¼)"
59 (63.5, 69, 74.5) cm

2¼"
5.5 cm

12"
31.5 cm

8¼ (8¼, 8½, 8½)"
21 (21, 21.5, 21.5) cm

7 (7, 6¾, 6¾)"
18 (18, 17, 17) cm

1¼"
3.2 cm

11¾ (12½, 13½, 14¼)"
30 (31.5, 34.5, 36) cm

33½ (36¾, 40, 43¼)"
85 (93.5, 101.5, 110) cm

left front

With smaller cir needle, CO 56 sts. Do not join.

ROW 1: (WS) K1 (edge st), p2, (k2, p2) to last st, k1 (edge st).

ROW 2: (RS) K1 (edge st), (k2, p2) to last 3 sts, k2, k1 (edge st).

Work 4 more rows in established rib patt.

NEXT (INC) ROW: (WS) K1 (edge st), M1R, p2, (M1R, k1) twice, (M1R, p1) twice, M1R, (k2, p2) twice, *k2, M1R, p2, (M1R, k1) twice, (M1R, p1) twice, M1R, (k2, p2) twice; rep from * once more, k2, M1R, p2, (M1R, k1) twice, (M1R, p1) twice, M1R, k1 (edge st)—80 sts.

Change to larger cir needle.

ROW 1: (RS) K1 (edge st), work Row 1 of chart, k1 (edge st).

ROW 2: K1 (edge st), work Row 2 of chart, k1 (edge st).

Work 4 more rows in established patt.

*SHORT-ROW 1: Work 67 sts in established patt, place marker (pm) A, turn.

SHORT-ROW 2: Work back to edge.

SHORT-ROW 3: Work 59 sts in established patt, pm B, turn.

SHORT-ROW 4: Work back to edge.

SHORT-ROW 5: Work 37 sts in established patt, pm C, turn.

SHORT-ROW 6: Work back to edge.

Work 4 rows over all sts, slipping markers as you come to them*.

Rep from * to *, working to markers instead of placing new markers on each subsequent repeat, until piece measures 8¼ (9, 9¾, 10¾)" (21 [23, 25, 27.5] cm) from CO edge along beg of RS rows, and at the same time, cont crossing cables every 6 rows as shown in chart (because of short-rows, cable crosses may not always be on the same row for all cables). End with a WS row.

With RS facing, place last 43 (43, 45, 45) sts on holder for left sleeve—37 (37, 35, 35) sts rem. Work 3 rows even, pm in underarm edge for side of body, work 3 more rows. Place sts on holder.

left sleeve

NEXT ROW: (RS) With larger cir needle, CO 15 (15, 13, 13) sts for sleeve, then work 43 (43, 45, 45) held sts in established patt—58 sts.

Working new sts into patt, keeping first st and last st as edge sts, cont as follows: Work 2 rows even.

*SHORT-ROW 1: Work in established patt to marker B, turn.

SHORT-ROW 2: Work back to edge.

SHORT-ROW 3: Work in established patt to marker A, turn.

SHORT-ROW 4: Work back to edge.

Work 2 rows over all sts*.

Rep from * to * until sleeve measures 11¾ (12½, 13½, 14¼)" (30 [31.5, 34.5, 36] cm) from CO sleeve sts, ending with a WS row.

BO 15 (15, 13, 13) sleeve sts—43 (43, 45, 45) sts rem. Cut yarn.

back

Return held 37 (37, 35, 35) sts to left needle tip before yoke sts—80 sts. Attach yarn to beg with RS row and work from * to * same as for left front until piece measures 16½ (18, 19¾, 21¼)" (42 [45.5, 50, 54] cm) from side marker, ending with a WS row.

With RS facing, place last 43 (43, 45, 45) sts on holder for right sleeve—37 (37, 35, 35) sts rem. Work 3 rows even, pm in underarm edge for side of body, work 3 more rows. Place sts on holder.

right sleeve

NEXT ROW: (RS) With larger cir needle, CO 15 (15, 13, 13) sts for sleeve, then work 43 (43, 45, 45) held sts in established patt—58 sts.

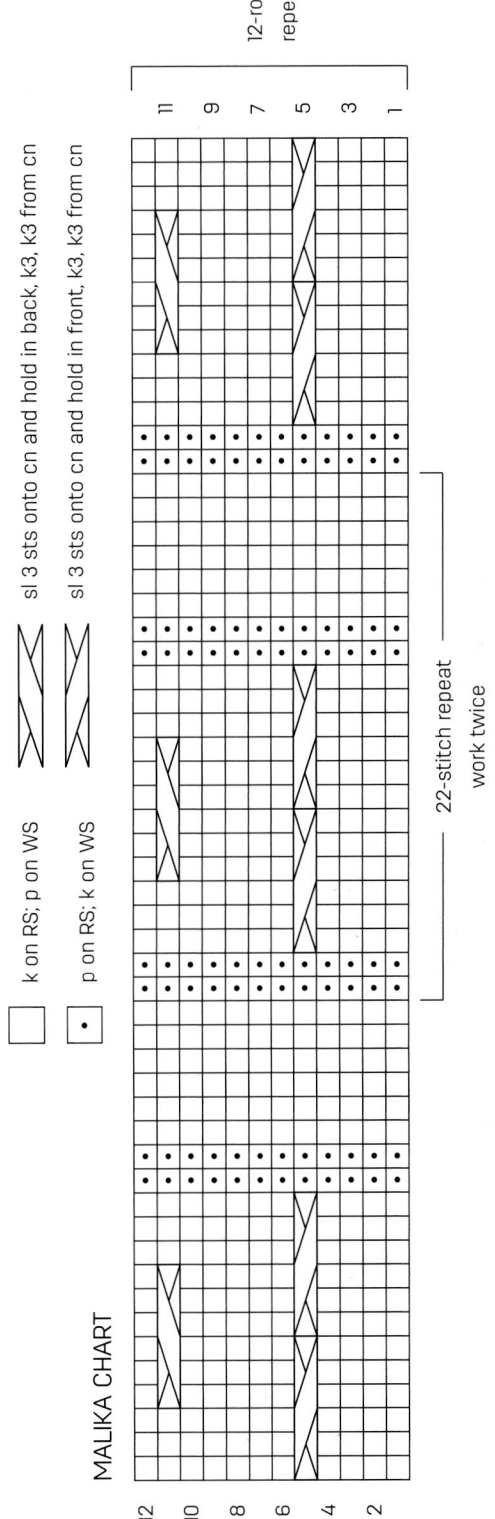

MALIKA CHART

Work right sleeve same as left sleeve. BO 15 (15, 13, 13) sleeve sts—43 (43, 45, 45) sts rem. Cut yarn.

right front

Return held 37 (37, 35, 35) sts to tip of left needle before yoke sts—80 sts. Attach yarn to beg with RS row and work from * to * same as for left front until piece measures 7¾ (8¾, 9½, 10¼)" (19.5 [22, 24, 26] cm) from side marker, ending with a WS row.

Change to smaller cir needle.

NEXT (DEC) ROW: (RS) K1 (edge st), (k2tog) twice, (p2tog) twice, (k2tog) twice, p2, *(k2, p2) twice, (k2tog) twice, (p2tog) twice, (k2tog) twice, p2; rep from * once more, (k2, p2) twice, (k2tog) twice, (p2tog) twice, (k2tog) twice, k1 (edge st)— 56 sts rem.

NEXT ROW: (WS) K1 (edge st), p2, (k2, p2) to last st, k1 (edge st).

NEXT (BUTTONHOLE) ROW: (RS) Work 8 sts in established rib, *BO 2 sts for buttonhole, work in established rib until there are 8 sts on tip of right needle after buttonhole gap; rep from * 3 more times, BO 2 sts for buttonhole, then work to end of row.

NEXT ROW: *Work in established rib to buttonhole gap, CO 2 sts over gap; rep from * 4 more times, then work to end of row.

Work 3 more rows in established rib. BO all sts loosely in rib.

neckband

With smaller cir needle and RS facing, pick up and k90 (94, 102, 106) sts evenly along neck edge and ends of front rib.

ROW 1: (WS) P2, (k2, p2) to end of row.

ROW 2: (RS) (K2, p2) to last 2 sts, k2.

Cont in established rib until neckband measures about ¾" (2 cm), ending with a WS row.

NEXT (BUTTONHOLE) ROW: (RS) K2, BO 2 sts for buttonhole, work in rib to end of row.

NEXT ROW: Work in established rib to buttonhole gap, CO 2 sts over gap, p2.

Cont in rib until neckband measures 2¼" (5.5 cm). BO all sts loosely in rib.

sleeve edgings (make 2)

With smaller cir needle and RS facing, pick up and k54 (58, 62, 66) sts evenly along lower edge of sleeve.

NEXT ROW: (WS) P2, (k2, p2) to end of row.

NEXT ROW: (RS) (K2, p2) to last 2 sts, k2.

Work 5 more rows in established rib. BO all sts loosely in rib.

finishing and edgings

Sew sleeve seams, leaving ¾" (2 cm) open at top of sleeve. Sew rem ¾" (2 cm) of sleeves to armholes.

BOTTOM EDGING

With smaller needle and RS facing, pick up and k162 (174, 186, 198) sts along the lower edge of body.

NEXT ROW: (WS) P2, (k2, p2) to end of row.

Work 2 more rows in established rib.

NEXT (BUTTONHOLE) ROW: (WS) Work in rib to last 4 sts, BO 2 sts for buttonhole, p1.

NEXT ROW: Work to buttonhole gap, CO 2 sts over gap, then work to end of row.

BO all sts loosely in rib.

Sew buttons to left front opposite buttonholes.

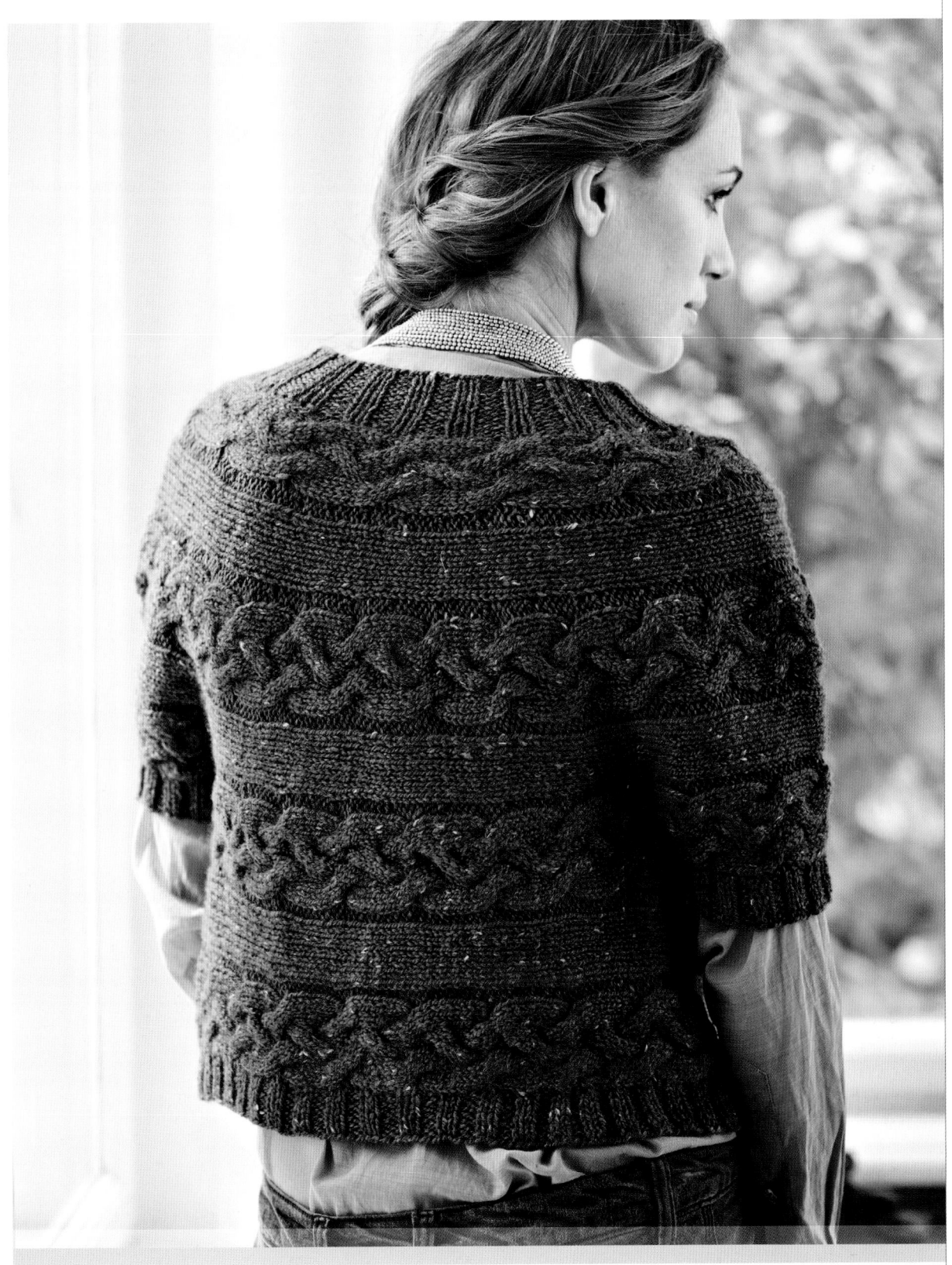

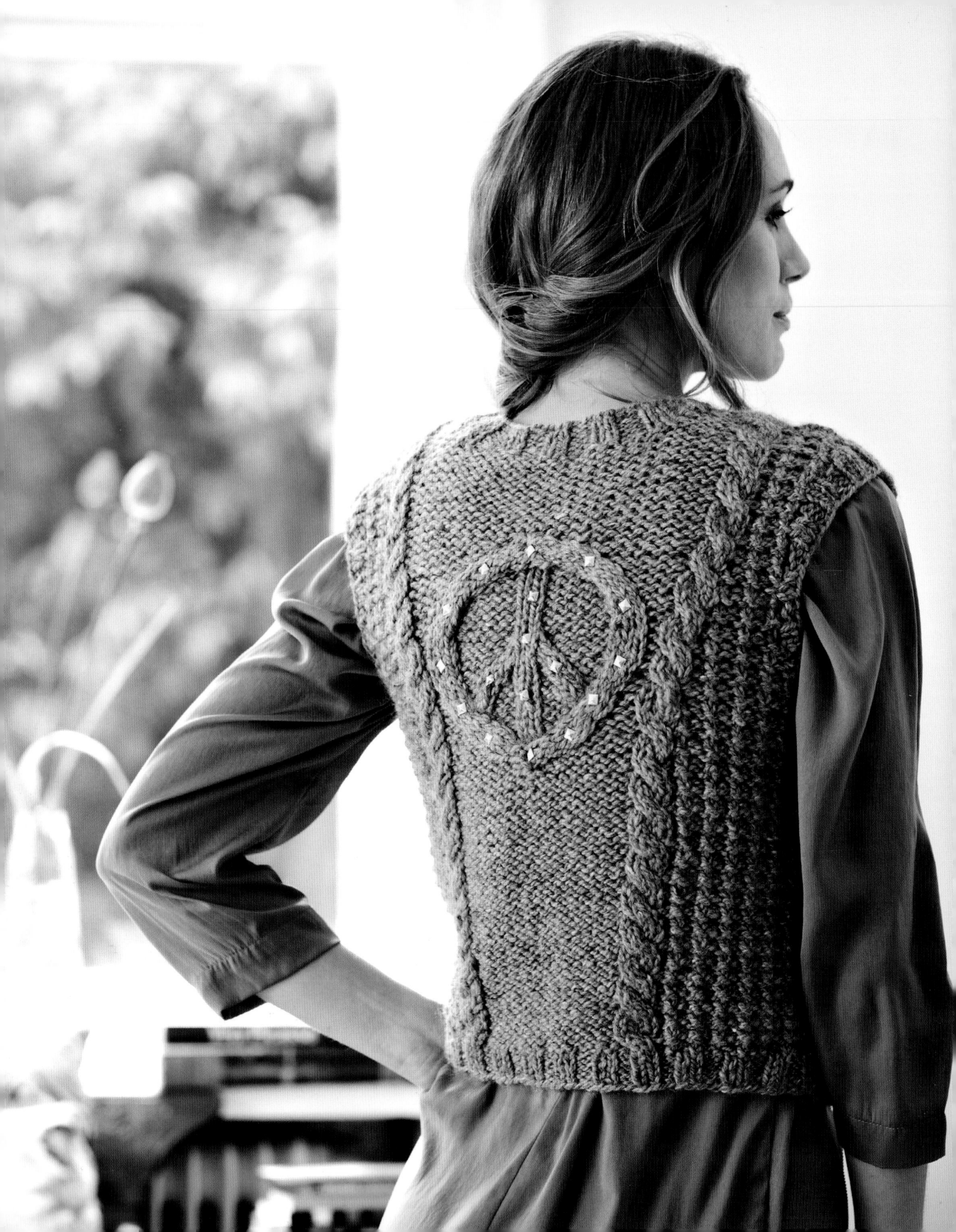

peace

vest with back symbol

A peace sign—interpreted here in cables—stands out on the back of this little vest. You'll embellish the symbol with pyramid studs.

FINISHED SIZE		S	M	L	XL
Bust	in	33½	35¾	38¾	41¾
	cm	85	91	98.5	106
Total length	in	18½	19	19¼	19¾
	cm	47	48.5	49	50

YARN
Bulky weight (#6 Super Bulky).

Shown here: BC Garn Hamelton Tweed 2 (90% wool, 10% viscose; 65 yd [60 m]/50 g): #HB15, 6 (7, 7, 8) balls.

NEEDLES
Sizes U.S. 10¾ and 11 (7 and 8 mm): straight. Size U.S. 10 (6 mm): 32" (80 cm) circular (cir).

Adjust needle size if necessary to obtain the correct gauge.

NOTIONS
Stitch holder; markers; cable needle (cn); tapestry needle; 5 buttons, about ½" (13 mm) diameter; 17 square rivets, about ¼" × ¼" (5 × 5 mm); small pliers.

GAUGE
11½ sts and 18 rows = 4" (10 cm) in St st on larger needles.

13 sts and 18 rows sts = 4" (10 cm) in pattern on larger needles.

stitch guide

LEFT CABLE (panel of 4 sts)
ROW 1: (RS) K4.
ROW 2: P4.
ROW 3: Sl 2 sts onto cn and hold in front, k2, k2 from cn.
ROW 4: P4.
Rep Rows 1–4 for patt.

RIGHT CABLE (panel of 4 sts)
ROW 1: (RS) K4.
ROW 2: P4.
ROW 3: Sl 2 sts onto cn and hold in back, k2, k2 from cn.
ROW 4: P4.
Rep Rows 1–4 for patt.

TEXTURE PATTERN (odd number of sts)
ROW 1: (RS) P1, *k1tbl, p1; rep from *.
ROW 2: Knit.
Rep Rows 1 and 2 for patt.

back

With size U.S. 10¾ (7 mm) needles, CO 54 (58, 62, 66) sts.

Sizes S and L

ROW 1: (WS) P2, *k2, p2; rep from * across.

ROW 2: K2, *p2, k2; rep from * across.

Sizes M and XL

ROW 1: (WS) K2, *p2, k2; rep from * across.

ROW 2: P2, *k2, p2; rep from * across.

All Sizes

Work 2 more rows in established rib. Work 1 more row of rib and dec 3 sts evenly across—51 (55, 59, 63) sts. Change to size U.S. 11 (8 mm) needles.

SET-UP ROW: (RS) Work Row 1 of Texture patt over 15 (17, 17, 19) sts, Row 1 of Left Cable over next 4 sts, next 13 (13, 17, 17) sts in rev St st (p on RS, k on WS), row 1 of Right Cable over next 4 sts, then Row 1 of Texture patt over rem 15 (17, 17, 19) sts.

Cont in established patt until piece measures about 4 (4, 4¼, 4¾)" (10 [10, 11, 12] cm) from CO edge, ending with a Row 4 of cable patt.

NEXT (INC) ROW: (RS) Work 19 (21, 21, 23) sts in established patt, M1, p13 (13, 17, 17), M1, work to end—2 sts inc'd.

Working new sts in rev St st, work 11 rows even.

NEXT (INC) ROW: (RS) Work 19 (21, 21, 23) sts in established patt, M1, p15 (15, 19, 19), M1, work to end—55 (59, 63, 67) sts, with 17 (17, 21, 21) sts in rev St st between cables.

Work 11 rows even.

NEXT ROW: (RS) Work to 1 st before cable, sl 1 st to cn and hold in back, k4 cable sts, p1 from cn, purl to next 4 cable sts, sl 4 sts to cn and hold in front, p1, k4 from cn, work in patt to end of row.

Rep last row every 8 rows 3 more times, working 1 fewer st before crossing cable. At the same time, when piece measures 8¼ (8¾, 9, 9½)" (21 [22, 23, 24] cm) from CO edge, end with a RS row. Mark center 19 sts.

NEXT ROW: (WS) Work to marker, slm, work Peace chart over next 19 sts, slm, work to end of row.

Cont in established patt until piece measures 10¾" (27.5 cm) from CO edge, ending with a WS row.

SHAPE ARMHOLE

BO 3 (3, 4, 4) sts at beg of next 2 rows, then 2 sts at beg of next 2 rows. Dec 1 st each end every RS row 1 (1, 2, 2) time(s)—43 (47, 47, 51) sts rem when all armhole shaping and chart are complete. Remove markers on last row of chart.

PEACE CHART

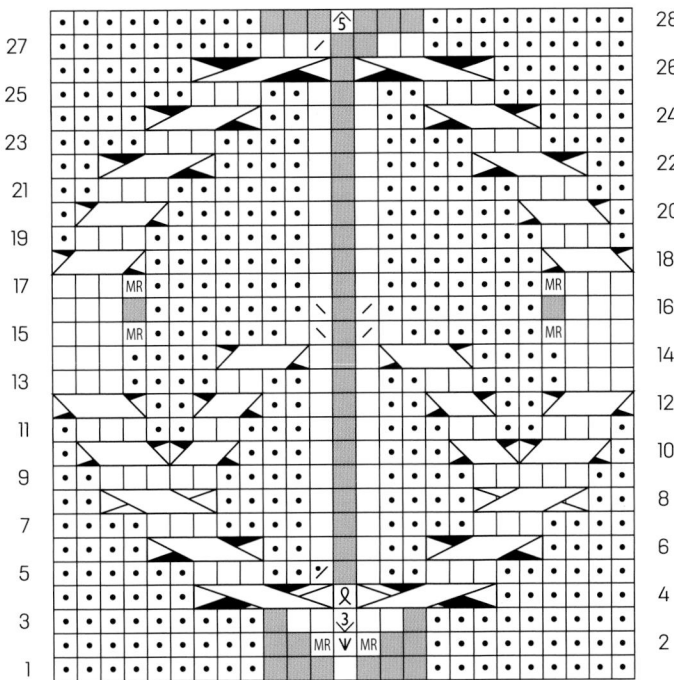

k on RS; p on WS

• p on RS; k on WS

ℓ k1tbl

∕ k2tog on RS; p2tog on WS

∖ ssk on RS; p2tog tbl on WS

⁄ p2tog on RS; k2tog on WS

MR M1R

③ (yo, k1, yo) in same st

v (k1tbl, k1) in next st, insert left needle tip under vertical strand between the 2 sts just knit, and k1tbl

⑤ sl 3 sts wyb, *pass 2nd st over first st, sl first st back to left needle tip, pass 2nd st over first st *, sl first st back to right needle tip; rep from * to * once more, purl rem st

sl 1 st onto cn and hold in back, k2, p1 from cn

sl 2 sts onto cn and hold in front, p1, k2 from cn

sl 1 st onto cn and hold in back, k3, p1 from cn

sl 3 sts onto cn and hold in front, p1, k3 from cn

sl 2 sts onto cn and hold in back, k3, k2 from cn

sl 3 sts onto cn and hold in front, k2, k3 from cn

sl 2 sts onto cn and hold in back, k3, p2 from cn

sl 3 sts onto cn and hold in front, p2, k3 from cn

sl 3 sts onto cn and hold in back, k3, p3 from cn

sl 3 sts onto cn and hold in front, p3, k3 from cn

sl 3 sts onto cn and hold in back, k3, then (p2, k1) from cn

sl 3 sts onto cn and hold in front, k1, p2, then k3 from cn

no stitch

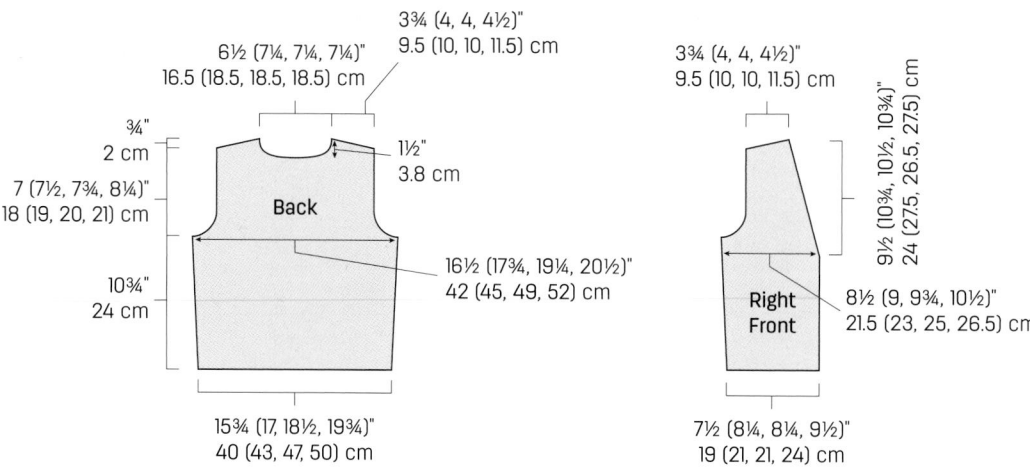

Cont even, working sts at center of back in rev St st, until armhole measures 6¼ (6¾, 7, 7½)" (16 [17, 18, 19] cm) ending with a WS row.

SHAPE NECK AND SHOULDERS

NEXT ROW: (RS) Work 14 (15, 15, 17) sts in established patt, place center 15 (17, 17, 17) sts on holder for neck, join a 2nd ball of yarn, and work to end—14 (15, 15, 17) sts rem for each side. Cont each side separately.

Work 1 WS row even.

NEXT ROW: Work to 2 sts before neck edge, k2tog; ssk, work to end—1 st dec'd each side.

NEXT ROW: BO 6 (6, 6, 7) sts, work to end.

NEXT ROW: BO 6 (6, 6, 7) sts, work to 2 sts before neck edge, k2tog; ssk, work to end.

NEXT ROW: BO rem 6 (7, 7, 8) sts; work to end.

NEXT ROW: BO rem 6 (7, 7, 8) sts.

left front

With size U.S. 10¾ (7 mm) needles, CO 27 (29, 31, 33) sts.

ROW 1: (WS) K1, *p2, k2; rep from * to last 2 (0, 2, 0) sts, p2 (0, 2, 0).

ROW 2: K2 (0, 2, 0), *p2, k2; rep from * to last st, k1.

Rep Rows 1 and 2 once more, then rep Row 1 once more and dec 2 sts evenly spaced—25 (27, 29, 31) sts.

Change to size U.S. 11 (8 mm) needles.

SET-UP ROW: (RS) Work Row 1 of Texture patt over first 15 (17, 17, 19) sts, work Row 1 of Left Cable over next 4 sts, work rev St st over rem 6 (6, 8, 8) sts.

Cont in established patt until piece measures about 4 (4, 4¼, 4¾)" (10 [10, 11, 12] cm) from CO edge, ending with a Row 4 of cable patt.

NEXT (INC) ROW: (RS) Work 19 (21, 21, 23) sts in established patt, M1, work in rev St st to end—1 st inc'd.

Working new st in rev St st, work 11 rows even.

Rep inc row—27 (29, 31, 33) sts.

Work 11 rows even.

NEXT ROW: (RS) Work to 1 st before cable, sl 1 st to cn and hold in back, k4 cable sts, p1 from cn, work to end of row.

Rep last row every 8 rows 3 more times. At the same time, when piece measures 9 (8¼, 8¾, 9)" (23 [21, 22, 23] cm) from CO edge, end with a RS row.

SHAPE NECK

NEXT (DEC) ROW: (WS) K1, k2tog, work to end of row—1 st dec'd.

Rep dec row every 4 rows 8 (9, 9, 9) more times. At the same time, when piece measures 10¾" (27.5 cm) from CO edge, end with a WS row.

SHAPE ARMHOLE

BO at armhole edge 3 (3, 4, 4) sts once, 2 sts once, then 1 st 1 (1, 2, 2) time(s)—12 (13, 13, 15) sts rem when all shaping is complete. Cont even until armhole measures 7 (7½, 7¾, 8¼)" (18 [19, 19.5, 21] cm) from CO edge, end with a WS row.

SHAPE SHOULDER

BO at beg of RS rows 6 (6, 6, 7) sts once, then 6 (7, 7, 8) sts once.

right front

With size U.S. 10¾ (7 mm) needles, CO 27 (29, 31, 33) sts.

ROW 1: (WS) P2 (0, 2, 0), *k2, p2; rep from * to last st, k1.

ROW 2: K1, *k2, p2; rep from * to last 2 (0, 2, 0) sts, k2 (0, 2, 0).

Rep Rows 1 and 2 once more, then rep Row 1 once more and dec 2 sts evenly spaced—25 (27, 29, 31) sts.

Change to size U.S. 11 (8 mm) needles.

SET-UP ROW: (RS) Work rev St st over first 6 (6, 8, 8) sts, Row 1 of Right Cable over next 4 sts, work Texture patt over rem 15 (17, 17, 19) sts.

Cont in established patt until piece measures 4 (4, 4¼, 4¾)" (10 [10, 11, 12] cm) from CO edge, ending with a Row 4 of cable patt.

NEXT (INC) ROW: (RS) Work to cable, M1, work in established patt to end of row—1 st inc'd.

Working new st in rev St st, work 11 rows even.

Rep inc row—27 (29, 31, 33) sts.

Work 11 rows even.

NEXT ROW: (RS) Work in established patt to cable, sl 4 cable sts to cn and hold in front, p1, k4 from cn, work to end of row.

Rep last row every 8 rows 3 more times. At the same time, when piece measures 9 (8¼, 8¾, 9)" (23 [21, 22, 23] cm) from CO edge, end with a WS row.

SHAPE NECK

NEXT ROW: (WS) Work to last 3 sts, ssk, k1—1 st dec'd.

Rep dec row every 4 rows 8 (9, 9, 9) more times. At the same time, when piece measures 10¾" (27.5 cm) from CO edge, end with a RS row.

SHAPE ARMHOLE

BO at armhole edge 3 (3, 4, 4) sts once, 2 sts once, then 1 st 1 (1, 2, 2) time(s)—12 (13, 13, 15) sts rem when all shaping is complete. Cont even until armhole measures 7 (7½, 7¾, 8¼)" (18 [19, 19.5, 21] cm), end with a RS row.

SHAPE SHOULDER

BO at beg of WS rows 6 (6, 6, 7) sts once, then 6 (7, 7, 8) sts once.

front bands

Sew shoulder seams.

With RS facing and size U.S. 10 (6 mm) cir needle, pick up and k35 (32, 34, 36) sts along right front

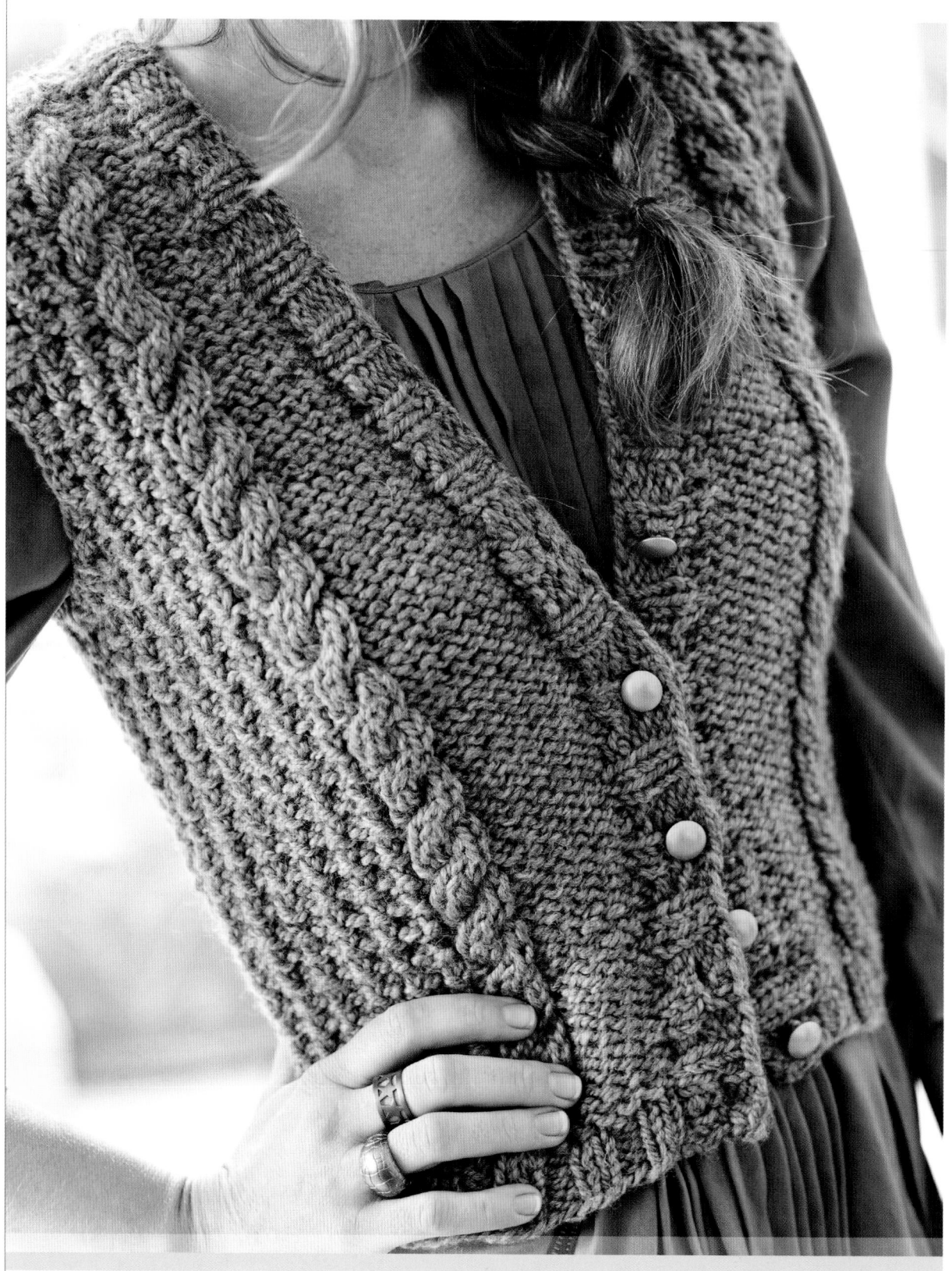

perfectly feminine knits

edge, 34 (38, 38, 38) sts along right neck to held sts, knit 15 (17, 17, 17) held back neck sts and inc 1 st at center of back, pick up and k34 (38, 38, 38) sts along left neck, then 35 (32, 34, 36) sts along left front edge—154 (158, 162, 166) sts.

NEXT ROW: (WS) P2, *k2, p2; rep from *.

NEXT ROW: *K2, p2; rep from * to last 2 sts, k2.

NEXT (BUTTONHOLE) ROW: Work in established rib to last 36 (32, 33, 36) sts, BO 2 sts, *work in rib until there are 6 (5, 5, 6) sts on right needle tip after buttonhole gap, BO 2 sts; rep from * 3 more times, work in rib to end.

NEXT ROW: Work in established rib and CO 2 sts over each gap.

Work 1 row even.

BO loosely in rib.

sleeve bands

With RS facing and using a size U.S. 10 (6 mm) cir needle, beg at center of underarm and pick up k29 (31, 33, 35) sts evenly to shoulder seam, then 29 (31, 33, 35) sts evenly to bottom of armhole—58 (62, 66, 70) sts.

SHORT-ROW 1: (WS) *P2, k2; rep from * 7 (8, 8, 9) more times, p2, turn.

SHORT-ROW 2: Yo, work 12 sts in established rib, turn.

SHORT-ROW 3: Yo, work 20 sts in rib, working yo together with next st to avoid leaving a hole, turn.

SHORT-ROW 4: Yo, work 28 sts in rib, working yo together with next st, turn.

NEXT ROW: Yo, work in rib to end of row, working yo together with next st.

BO all sts in rib, working last yo together with next st.

finishing

Weave in ends. Block pieces to finished measurements.

Sew side seams. Sew buttons to front band opposite buttonholes. Attach studs securely to the peace symbol, with 12 evenly spaced around the circle and the remaining 5 in the center lines (refer to the photo on page 120 for placement).

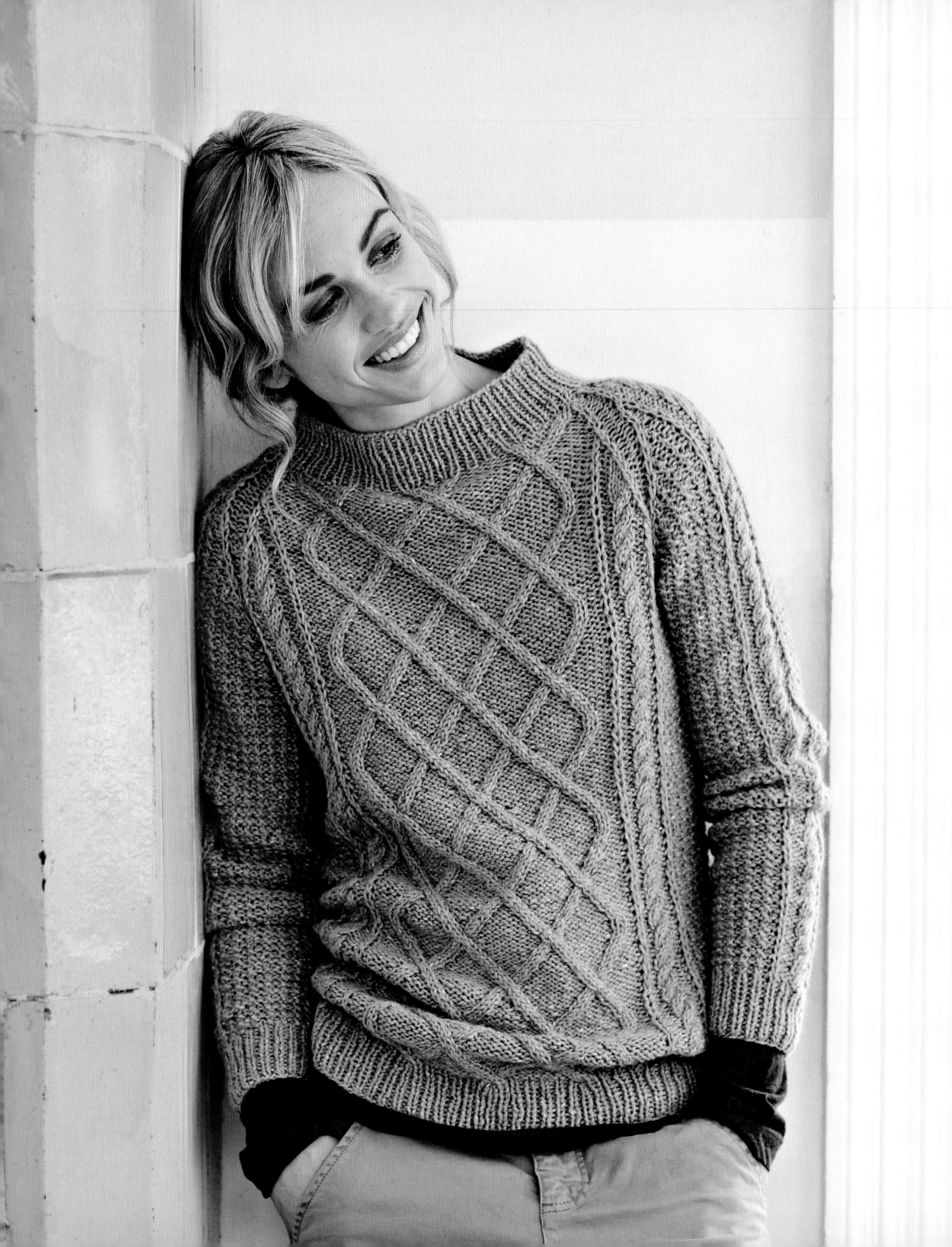

rosa

aran-pattern sweater

Lovely long cable patterns embellish a classic raglan worked in a wool tweed yarn. The design can be worked in two ways: a slightly longer and looser sweater shown in gray or the shorter, more fitted version in yellow.

FINISHED SIZE		S	M	L	XL
Short Version (Yellow) **Bust**	in	35¾	38½	41½	45
	cm	91	98	105.5	114.5
Total length	in	22¾	23	23¼	24½
	cm	58	58.5	59	62
Long Version (Gray) **Chest**	in	38¼	41¾	44¼	47½
	cm	97	106	112.5	120.5
Total length	in	25¼	25½	25¾	27
	cm	64	65	65.5	68.5

YARN

Worsted weight (#4 Medium).

Shown here: Gepard Loden (50% lambswool, 25% viscose, 25% alpaca; 120 yd [110 m]/50 g): yellow #603, 8 (9, 10, 11) balls for short version, and gray #820, 9 (10, 11, 12) balls for long version.

NEEDLES

Size U.S. 7 (4.5 mm): straight and 24" (60 cm) circular (cir).

Size U.S. 8 (5 mm): straight, and 24" and 32" (60 and 80 cm) cir.

Adjust needle size if necessary to obtain the correct gauge.

NOTIONS

Stitch holders; markers; two cable needles (cn); tapestry needle.

GAUGE

19 sts and 23 rows = 4" (10 cm) in St st or side patt on larger needles.

22 sts and 23 rows = about 4" (10 cm) in cable patt on larger needles.

stitch guide

BRIOCHE PATTERN *(panel of 4 sts)*
RND 1: Knit one in the row below (k1-b), p2, k1-b.
RND 2: K1, p2, k1.
Rep Rnds 1 and 2 for patt.

BRIOCHE DEC
Work to 3 sts before marker, insert tip of right needle kwise into 2nd st on left needle tip in the row below, then into first st on needle and k2tog (the brioche st and the st before it), p1, slm, p1, insert right needle tip pwise into next (brioche) st in the row below and sl st, p1, psso.

SHORT VERSION

back

With smaller needles, CO 93 (101, 111, 119) sts.

NEXT ROW: (WS) K1 (edge st), k1, *p1, k1; rep from * to last st, k1 (edge st).

NEXT ROW: (RS) K1 (edge st), *p1, k1; rep from * to last 2 sts, p1, k1 (edge st).

Cont in established rib patt until piece measures 4" (10 cm) from CO edge, ending with a WS row.

Change to larger needles.

NEXT (SET-UP) ROW: (RS) K1 (edge st), beg Row 1 at right edge of Chart A, work first st, next 2 sts 6 (8, 7, 9) times, work next 21 sts, next 14 sts 1 (1, 2, 2) time(s), work next 30 sts, next 2 sts 6 (8, 7, 9) times, work last st of chart, k1 (edge st).

Keeping edge sts in garter st (k every row), cont in established patt until piece measures 4¾" (12 cm) from CO edge, ending with a WS row.

SHAPE WAIST

NEXT (DEC) ROW: (RS) K1 (edge st), k2tog, work in established patt to last 3 sts, k2tog, k1 (edge st)— 2 sts dec'd.

Rep dec row every 8 rows 2 more times—87 (95, 105, 113) sts rem.

Cont even until piece measures 9" (23 cm) from CO edge, ending with a WS row.

NEXT (INC) ROW: (RS) K1 (edge st), M1, work in established patt to last st, M1, k1 (edge st)— 2 sts inc'd.

Rep inc row every 8 (8, 10, 10) rows 3 (3, 2, 2) more times—95 (103, 111, 119) sts.

Cont even until piece measures 15½" (39.5 cm) from CO edge, ending with a WS row.

BO 7 (9, 9, 11) sts at beg of next 2 rows—81 (85, 93, 97) sts rem. Place rem sts on holder.

front

Work front same as for back.

sleeves (make 2)

With smaller needles, CO 43 (43, 47, 47) sts.

NEXT ROW: (WS) K1 (edge st), *k1, p1; rep from * to last 2 sts, k2.

NEXT ROW: (RS) K1 (edge st), *p1, k1; rep from * to last 2 sts, p1, k1 (edge st).

Cont in established rib patt until piece measures 2½" (6.5 cm), ending with a WS row and inc 3 sts evenly across last row—46 (46, 50, 50) sts.

Change to larger needles.

NEXT (SET-UP) ROW: (RS) K1 (edge st), beg at right edge of Chart B, work first st, next 2 sts 8 (8, 9, 9) times, work next 10 sts, next 2 sts 8 (8, 9, 9) times, work last st of chart, k1.

CHART A

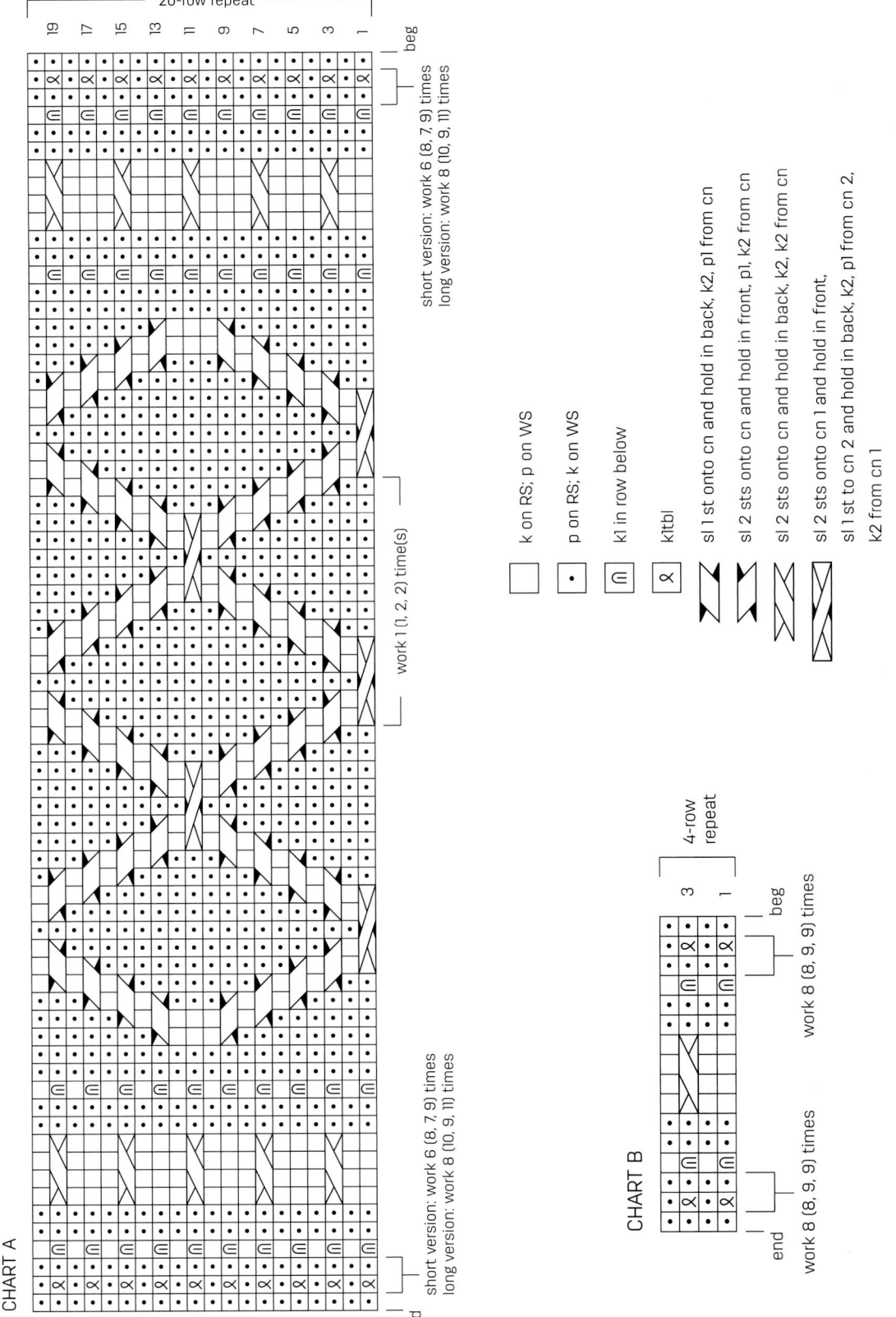

19 17 15 13 11 9 7 5 3 1

beg

short version: work 6 (8, 7, 9) times
long version: work 8 (10, 9, 11) times

work 1 (1, 2, 2) time(s)

short version: work 6 (8, 7, 9) times
long version: work 8 (10, 9, 11) times

end

☐ k on RS; p on WS

• p on RS; k on WS

⋒ k1 in row below

⋉ k1tbl

sl 1 st onto cn and hold in back, k2, p1 from cn

sl 2 sts onto cn and hold in front, p1, k2 from cn

sl 2 sts onto cn and hold in back, k2, k2 from cn

sl 2 sts onto cn 1 and hold in front,
sl 1 st to cn 2 and hold in back, k2, p1 from cn 2,
k2 from cn 1

CHART B

4-row
repeat

3

1

beg

work 8 (8, 9, 9) times

work 8 (8, 9) times

end

work 8 (8, 9) times

rosa 131

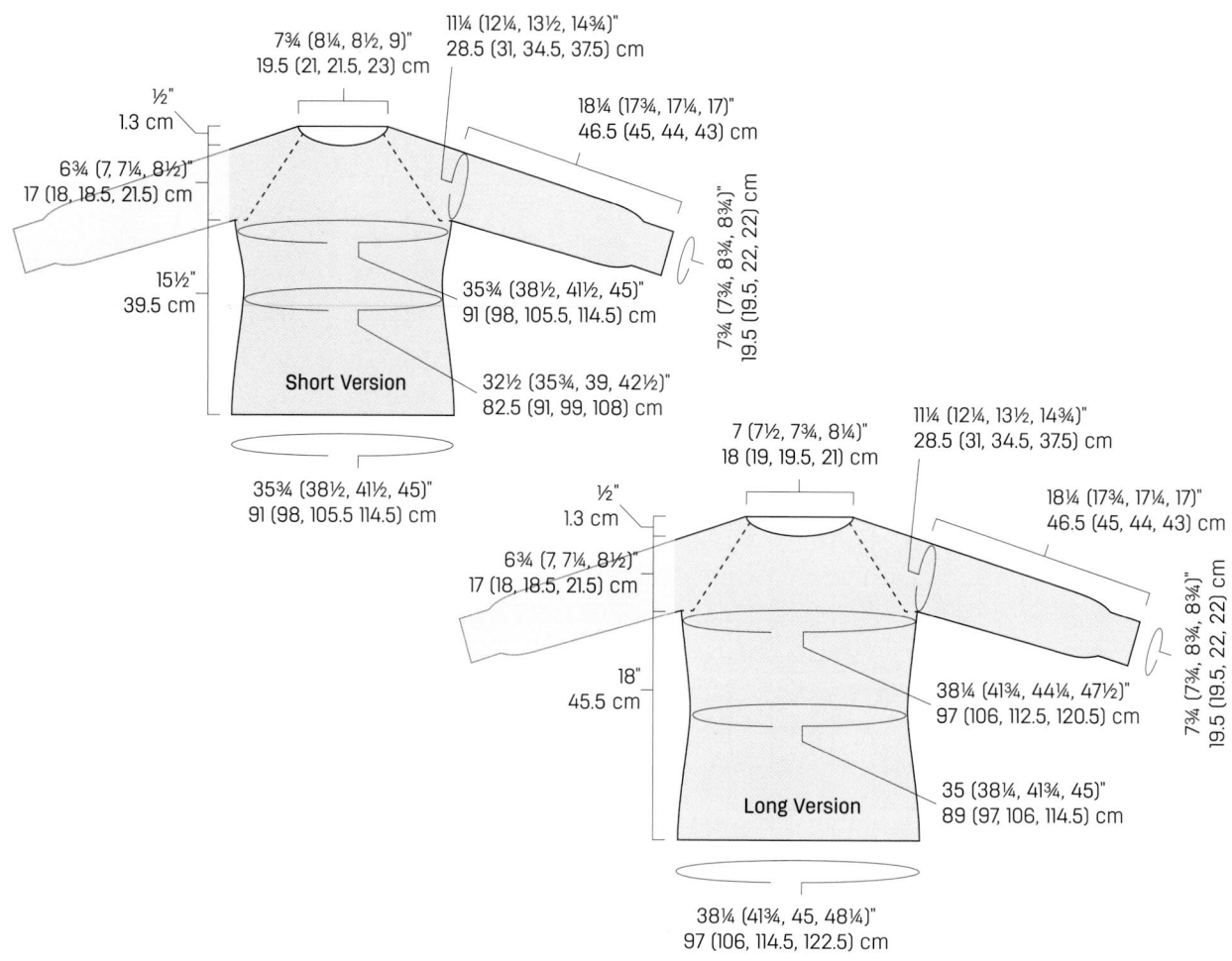

7¾ (8¼, 8½, 9)"
19.5 (21, 21.5, 23) cm

11¼ (12¼, 13½, 14¾)"
28.5 (31, 34.5, 37.5) cm

18¼ (17¾, 17¼, 17)"
46.5 (45, 44, 43) cm

½"
1.3 cm

6¾ (7, 7¼, 8½)"
17 (18, 18.5, 21.5) cm

7¾ (7¾, 8¾, 8¾)"
19.5 (19.5, 22, 22) cm

15½"
39.5 cm

35¾ (38½, 41½, 45)"
91 (98, 105.5, 114.5) cm

Short Version

32½ (35¾, 39, 42½)"
82.5 (91, 99, 108) cm

35¾ (38½, 41½, 45)"
91 (98, 105.5 114.5) cm

7 (7½, 7¾, 8¼)"
18 (19, 19.5, 21) cm

11¼ (12¼, 13½, 14¾)"
28.5 (31, 34.5, 37.5) cm

½"
1.3 cm

18¼ (17¾, 17¼, 17)"
46.5 (45, 44, 43) cm

6¾ (7, 7¼, 8½)"
17 (18, 18.5, 21.5) cm

7¾ (7¾, 8¾, 8¾)"
19.5 (19.5, 22, 22) cm

18"
45.5 cm

38¼ (41¾, 44¼, 47½)"
97 (106, 112.5, 120.5) cm

Long Version

35 (38¼, 41¾, 45)"
89 (97, 106, 114.5) cm

38¼ (41¾, 45, 48¼)"
97 (106, 114.5, 122.5) cm

Cont in established patt until piece measures 4¾ (4¾, 3½, 3¼)" (12 [12, 9, 8.5] cm) from CO edge, ending with a WS row.

NEXT (INC) ROW: (RS) K1 (edge st), M1, work in established patt to last st, M1, k1 (edge st)—2 sts inc'd.

Rep inc row every 10 (8, 8, 6) rows 6 (8, 9, 12) more times—60 (64, 70, 76) sts. Work new sts into patt.

Cont even until piece measures 18¼ (17¾, 17¼, 17)" (46.5 [45, 44, 43] cm), ending with a WS row and same cable patt row as back.

BO 7 (9, 9, 11) sts at beg of next 2 rows—46 (46, 52, 54) sts rem. Place rem sts on holder.

yoke

With RS facing, place sts for all pieces on larger size cir needle in this order: back, sleeve, front, sleeve—254 (262, 290, 302) sts; 81 (85, 93, 97) sts each for front and back, and 46 (46, 52, 54) sts for each sleeve. Place marker (pm) for beg of rnd and join for working in rnds.

NEXT (SET-UP) RND: *P1, k1, work 77 (81, 89, 93) sts in established patt, k1, p1, pm, p1, k1, work 42 (42, 48, 50) sts in established patt, k1, p1, pm; rep from * once more.

NEXT (DEC) RND: P1, insert right needle tip pwise into next (brioche) st in the row below and sl st, p1, psso, *work to 3 sts before next marker, Brioche Dec (see Stitch Guide), p1, sm; rep from * 2 more times, work to last 3 sts, insert tip of right needle kwise into second st on left needle tip in the row below, then into first st on needle and k2tog (the brioche st and the st before it), p1— 8 sts dec'd.

Rep dec rnd every other rnd 18 (19, 22, 23) more times—102 (102, 106, 110) sts rem; 43 (45, 47, 49) sts each for front and back, and 8 (6, 6, 6) sts for each sleeve. End with a dec rnd. Change to shorter cir needle when too few sts rem to work comfortably on longer needle.

SHAPE NECK

NEXT RND: Work back, left sleeve sts, and first 11 (12, 12, 13) sts of front in established patt, work next 21 (21, 23, 23) sts and place on holder for front neck, then work to end of rnd—81 (81, 83, 87) sts rem; 43 (45, 47, 49) sts for back, 11 (12, 12, 13) sts for each side of front, and 8 (6, 6, 6) sts for each sleeve.

Cut yarn and sl last 19 (18, 18, 19) sts from right needle tip to left needle tip (needle tips are at front neck edges). Rejoin yarn to beg with a RS row.

Cont raglan dec every RS row 4 times and at the same time, BO 3 sts at beg of next 8 rows—37 (41, 43, 47) sts rem; no sts rem for each front, 1 (2, 2, 3) st(s) rem for each sleeve, and 35 (37, 39, 41) sts rem for back. *Note: When too few sts rem at the front edges to work both BO and work raglan dec, BO only.*

finishing and neckband

NECKBAND

Change to smaller cir needle.

With RS facing, pick up and k16 sts along left neck edge, k21 (21, 23, 23) sts from front holder and dec 4 sts evenly over cables, pick up and k16 sts along right neck edge, then knit rem 37 (41, 43, 47) sts

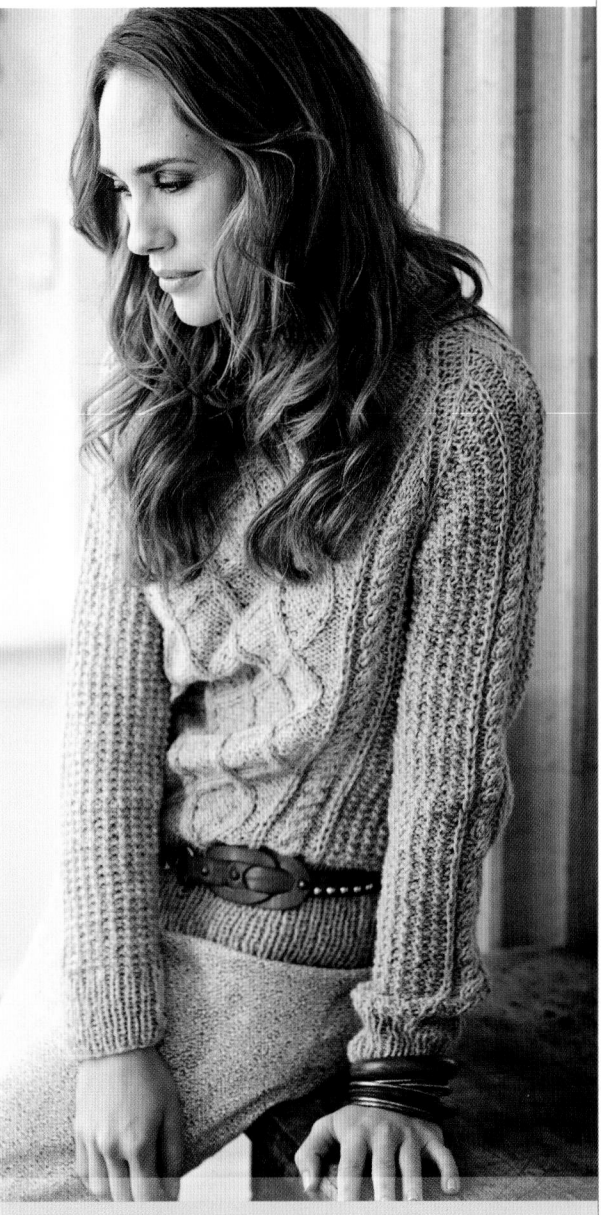

and dec 0 (4, 4, 4) sts evenly spaced over cables—86 (86, 90, 94) sts. Pm for beg of rnd and join for working in rnds.

Work in k1, p1 rib until neckband measures 2½" (6.5 cm). BO all sts loosely in rib.

Weave in ends. Sew sleeve and side seams. Sew underarm seams.

LONG VERSION

back

With smaller needles, CO 101 (109, 119, 127) sts.

NEXT ROW: (WS) K1 (edge st), k1, *p1, k1; rep from * to last st, k1 (edge st).

NEXT ROW: (RS) K1 (edge st), *p1, k1; rep from * to last 2 sts, p1, k1 (edge st).

Cont in established rib patt until piece measures 2½" (6.5 cm) from CO edge, ending with a WS row.

Change to larger needles.

NEXT ROW: (RS) K1 (edge st), beg Row 1 at right edge of Chart A, work first st, next 2 sts 8 (10, 9, 11) times, work next 21 sts, next 14 sts 1 (1, 2, 2) time(s), work next 30 sts, next 2 sts 8 (10, 9, 11) times, work last st of chart, k1 (edge st).

Keeping edge sts in garter st (k every row), cont in established patt until piece measures 4" (10 cm) from CO edge, ending with a WS row.

SHAPE WAIST

NEXT (DEC) ROW: (RS) K1 (edge st), k2tog, work in established patt to last 3 sts, k2tog, k1 (edge st)— 2 sts dec'd.

Rep dec row every 8 rows 3 more times—93 (101, 111, 119) sts rem.

Cont even until piece measures 11¾" (30 cm) from CO edge, ending with a WS row.

NEXT (INC) ROW: (RS) K1 (edge st), M1, work in established patt to last st, M1, k1 (edge st)— 2 sts inc'd.

Rep inc row every 8 rows 3 more times—101 (109, 119, 127) sts.

Cont even until piece measures 18" (45.5 cm) from CO edge, ending with a WS row.

BO 8 (10, 11, 13) sts at beg of next 2 rows—85 (89, 97, 101) sts rem. Place rem sts on holder.

front

Work front same as for back.

sleeves (make 2)

With smaller needles, CO 43 (43, 47, 47) sts.

NEXT ROW: (WS) K1 (edge st), *k1, p1; rep from * to last 2 sts, k2.

NEXT ROW: (RS) K1 (edge st), *p1, k1; rep from * to last 2 sts, p1, k1 (edge st).

Cont in established rib patt until piece measures 2½" (6.5 cm), ending with a WS row and inc 3 sts evenly across last row—46 (46, 50, 50) sts.

Change to larger needles.

NEXT (SET-UP) ROW: (RS) K1 (edge st), beg at right edge of Chart B, work first st, next 2 sts 8 (8, 9, 9) times, work next 10 sts, next 2 sts 8 (8, 9, 9) times, work last st of chart, k1.

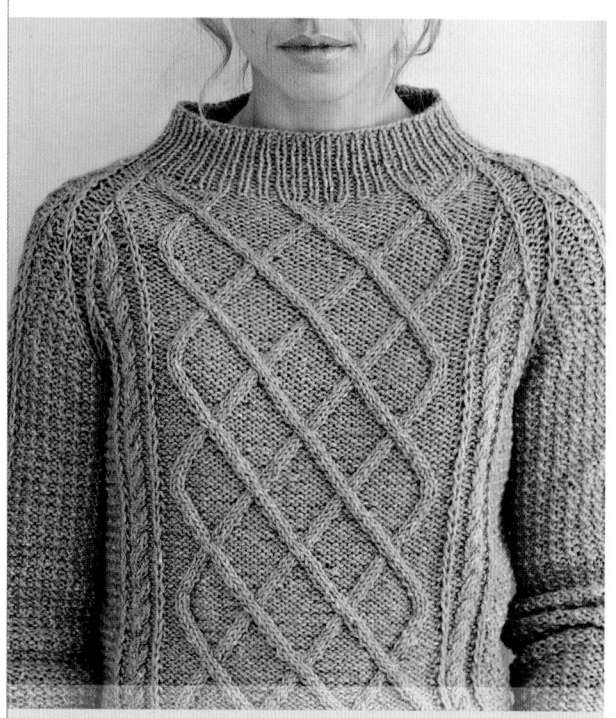

Cont in established patt until piece measures $4\frac{3}{4}$ ($4\frac{3}{4}$, $3\frac{1}{2}$, $3\frac{1}{4}$)" (12 [12, 9, 8.5] cm) from CO edge, ending with a WS row.

NEXT (INC) ROW: (RS) K1 (edge st), M1, work in established patt to last st, M1, k1 (edge st)—2 sts inc'd.

Rep inc row every 10 (8, 8, 6) rows 6 (8, 9, 12) more times—60 (64, 70, 76) sts. Work new sts into patt.

Cont even until piece measures $18\frac{1}{4}$ ($17\frac{3}{4}$, $17\frac{1}{4}$, 17)" (46.5 [45, 44, 43] cm), ending with a WS rows and same cable patt row as back.

BO 8 (10, 10, 12) sts at beg of next 2 rows—44 (44, 50, 52) sts rem. Place rem sts on holder.

yoke

With RS facing, place sts for all pieces on larger size cir needle in this order: back, sleeve, front, sleeve—258 (266, 294, 306) sts; 85 (89, 97, 101) sts each for front and back, and 44 (44, 50, 52) sts for each sleeve. Place marker (pm) for beg of rnd and join for working in rnds.

NEXT (SET-UP) RND: *P1, k1, work 81 (85, 93, 97) sts in established patt, k1, p1, pm, p1, k1, work 40 (40, 46, 48) sts in established patt, k1, p1, pm; rep from * once more.

NEXT (DEC) RND: P1, insert right needle tip pwise into next (brioche) st in the row below and sl st, p1, psso, *work to 3 sts before next marker, Brioche Dec (see Stitch Guide), p1, slm; rep from * 2 more times, work to last 3 sts, insert tip of right needle kwise into second st on left needle tip in the row below, then into first st on needle and k2tog (the brioche st and the st before it), p1—8 sts dec'd.

Rep dec rnd every other rnd 18 (19, 22, 23) more times—106 (106, 110, 114) sts rem; 47 (49, 51, 53) sts each for front and back, and 6 (4, 4, 4) sts for each sleeve. End with a dec rnd. Change to shorter cir needle when too few sts rem to work comfortably on longer needle.

SHAPE NECK

NEXT RND: Work back, left sleeve sts, and first 12 (13, 13, 14) sts of front in established patt, work next 23 (23, 25, 25) sts and place on holder for front neck, then work to end of rnd—83 (83, 85, 89) sts rem; 47 (49, 51, 53) sts for back, 12 (13, 13, 14) sts for each side of front, and 6 (4, 4, 4) sts for each sleeve.

Cut yarn and sl last 18 (17, 17, 18) sts from right needle tip to left needle tip (needle tips are at front neck edges). Rejoin yarn to beg with a RS row.

Cont raglan dec every RS row 4 times and at the same time, BO 3 sts at beg of next 8 rows—43 (47, 49, 51) sts rem; no sts rem for each side of front, 2 (3, 3, 3) st(s) rem for each sleeve, and 39 (41, 43, 45) sts rem for back. *Note: When too few sts rem at the front edges to work both BO and work raglan dec, BO only.*

finishing and neckband

NECKBAND

Change to smaller cir needle.

With RS facing, pick up and k14 sts along left neck edge, k23 (23, 25, 25) sts from front holder and dec 2 (4, 4, 4) sts evenly over cables, pick up and k14 sts along right neck edge, then knit rem 43 (47, 49, 51) sts and dec 2 (4, 4, 2) sts evenly spaced over cables—90 (90, 94, 98) sts. Pm for beg of rnd and join for working in rnds.

Work in k1, p1 rib until neckband measures $2\frac{1}{2}$" (6.5 cm). BO all sts loosely in rib.

Weave in ends. Sew sleeve and side seams. Sew underarm seams.

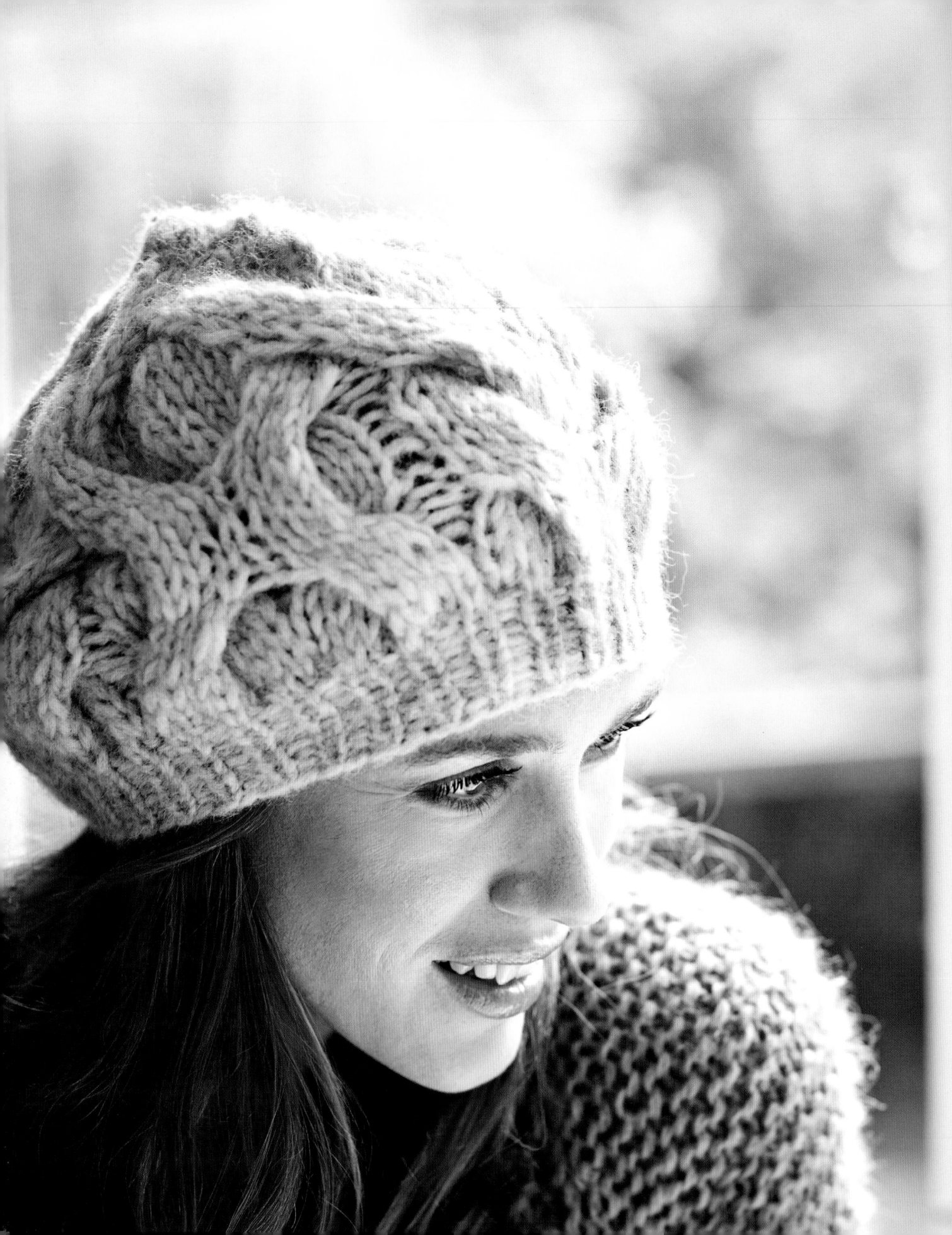

naja

cap with cables

Cables cross in all directions over the entire surface of this pert hat. It's rather easy to work at the beginning, but by the time you get to the top, you'll be feeling the challenge!

FINISHED SIZE
18" (45.5 cm) brim circumference and 9" (23 cm) tall.

YARN
Chunky weight (#5 Bulky).

Shown here: Gepard Puno (68% baby alpaca, 22% nylon, 10% merino wool; 120 yd [110 m]/50 g): gray #1311, 1 ball.

NEEDLES
Sizes U.S. 8 and 15 (5 and 10 mm): 16" (40 cm) circular (cir). Size U.S. 15 (10 mm): set of 5 dpn.

Adjust needle size if necessary to obtain the correct gauge.

NOTIONS
Marker; cable needle (cn); tapestry needle.

GAUGE
21 sts and 18 rnds = 4" (10 cm) in cable patt on larger needles.

cap

With smaller cir needle, CO 68 st. Place marker (pm) and join for working in rnds, being careful not to twist sts.

RND 1: *K1, p1; rep from *.

Rep Rnd 1 six more times.

NEXT (INC) RND: *K1, (p1, k1) in next st; rep from * around—102 sts.

Change to larger cir needle.

Work Rnds 1-15 of chart.

SHAPE TOP

Notes: The beginning of round shifts on Rnds 17, 18, 24, and 28 over the shaping of the top. Work each round as described, then begin the next round as indicated. Change to double-pointed needles when there are too few stitches to work comfortably on the circular needle.

RND 16 (DEC): *K16, k2tog, k14, ssk; rep from * 2 more times—96 sts rem.

RND 17: K4, *k8, sl 4 sts onto cn and hold in front, k4, k4 from cn; rep from * 4 more times, k8, sl 4 sts onto cn and hold in front, remove marker, k4, k4 from cn, pm. Beg of rnd has shifted 4 sts to the left.

RND 18: K95, sl 1, remove beg-of-rnd marker, sl last st from right needle tip back to left needle tip, pm. Beg of rnd has shifted 1 st to the right.

RND 19 (DEC): *Ssk, k6, k2tog, k6; rep from * 5 more times—84 sts rem.

RND 20: Knit.

RND 21 (DEC): *Ssk, k4, k2tog, k6; rep from * 5 more times—72 sts rem.

RND 22: Knit.

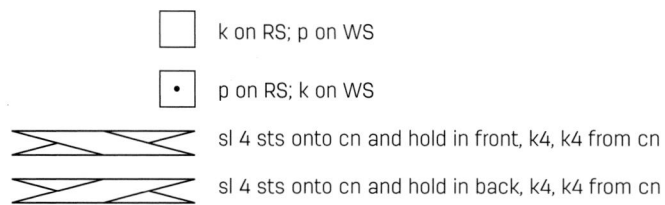

k on RS; p on WS

p on RS; k on WS

sl 4 sts onto cn and hold in front, k4, k4 from cn

sl 4 sts onto cn and hold in back, k4, k4 from cn

NAJA CHART

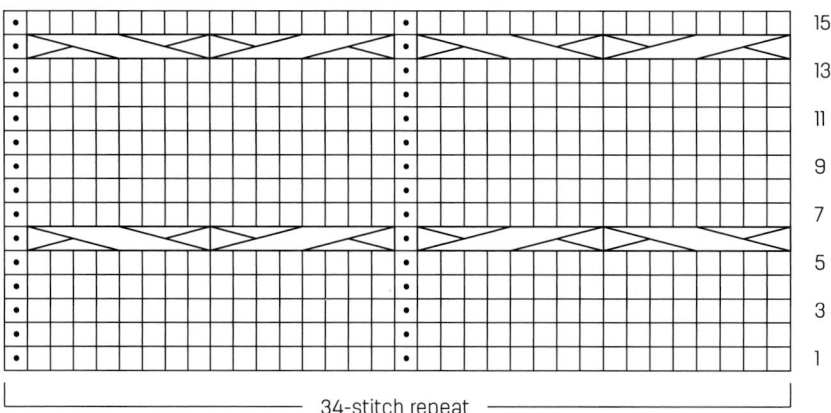

34-stitch repeat

RND 23 (DEC): *Ssk, k2, k2tog, k6; rep from *
5 more times—60 sts rem.

RND 24 (DEC): *Ssk, k2tog, k6; rep from * 4 more
times, ssk, k2tog, k3, sl 3, remove beg-of-rnd
marker, sl last 3 sts from right needle tip back to
left needle tip, pm—48 sts rem. Beg of rnd has
shifted 3 sts to the right.

RND 25: *Sl 4 sts onto cn and hold in back, k4, k4
from cn, k8; rep from * 2 more times.

RND 26: *K8, sl 4 sts onto cn and hold in back, k4,
k4 from cn; rep from * 2 more times.

RND 27: Knit.

RND 28 (DEC): K1, *k2, ssk, k2, k2tog; rep from *
4 more times, k2, ssk, k2, sl 1, remove marker, sl
last st from right needle tip back to left needle tip,
k2tog, pm—36 sts rem. Beg of rnd has shifted 1 st
to the left.

RND 29 (DEC): *K2, ssk, k2tog; rep from * 5 more
times—24 sts rem.

RND 30 (DEC): *K2, k2tog; rep from * 5 more
times—18 sts rem.

RND 31 (DEC): *K1, k2tog; rep from * 5 more
times—12 sts rem.

RND 32 (DEC): *K2tog; rep from * 5 more times—
6 sts rem.

Cut yarn, leaving an 8" (20.5 cm) tail. Thread tail
through rem sts, pull tight to close hole, fasten off
on WS.

finishing
Weave in ends.

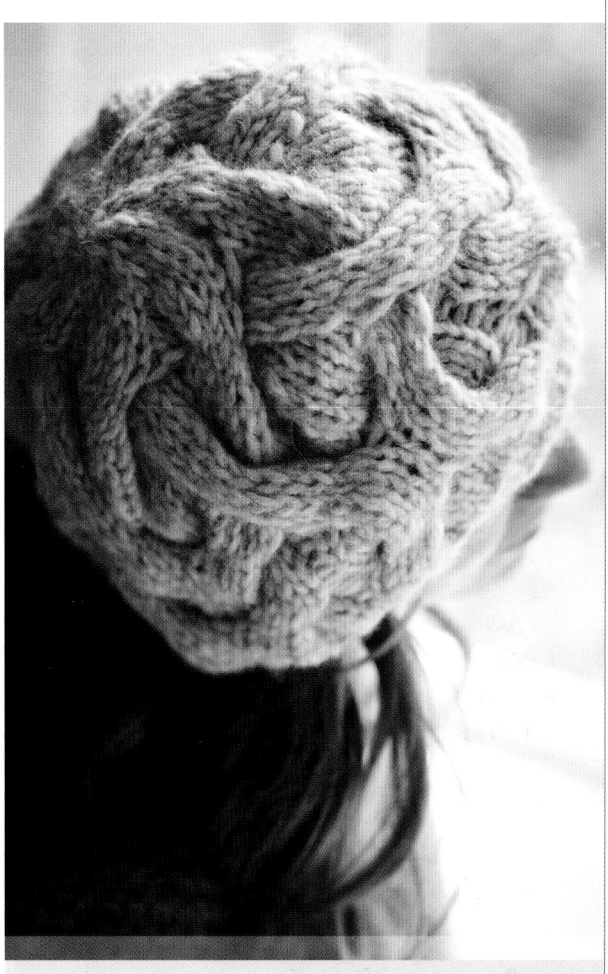

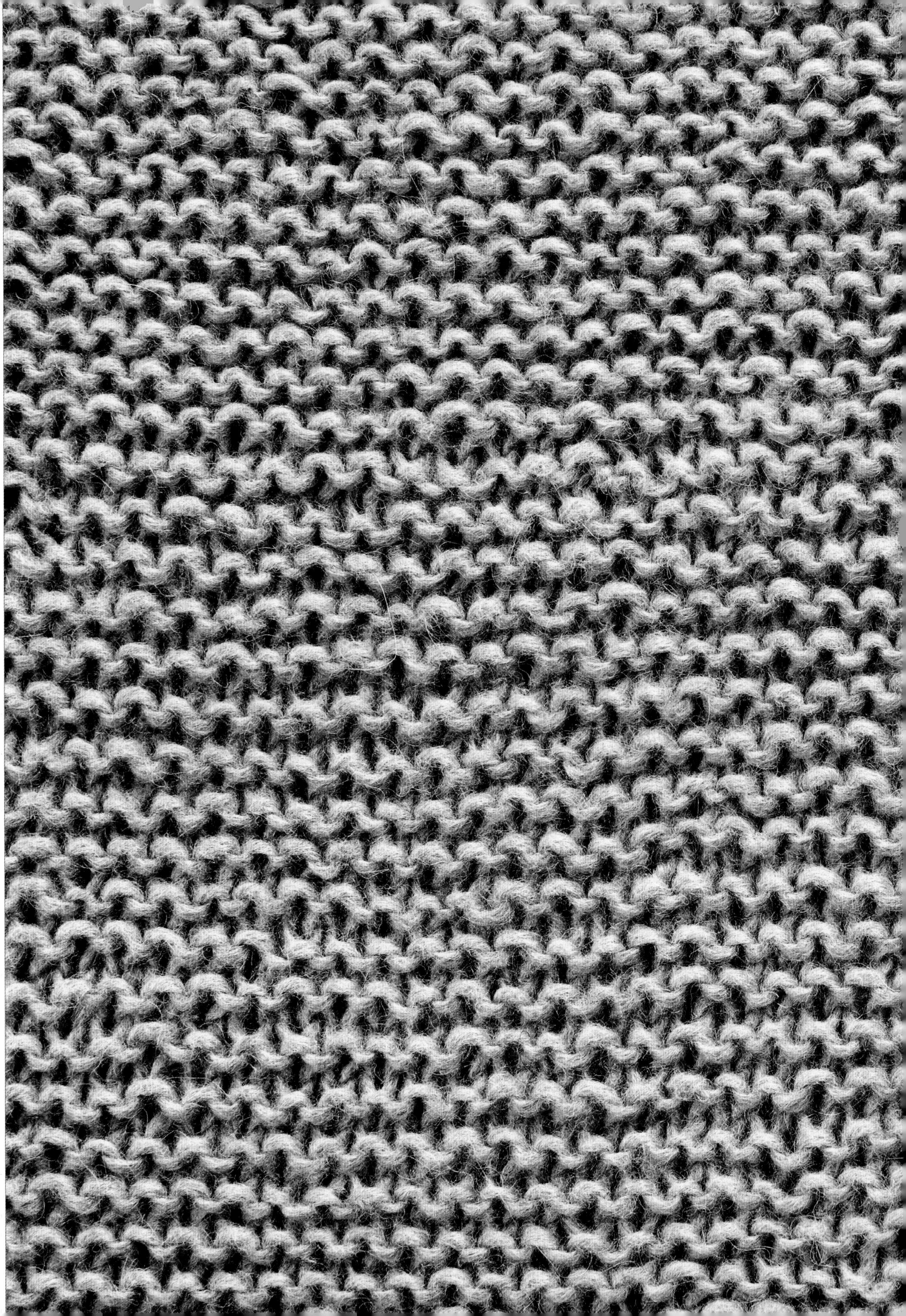

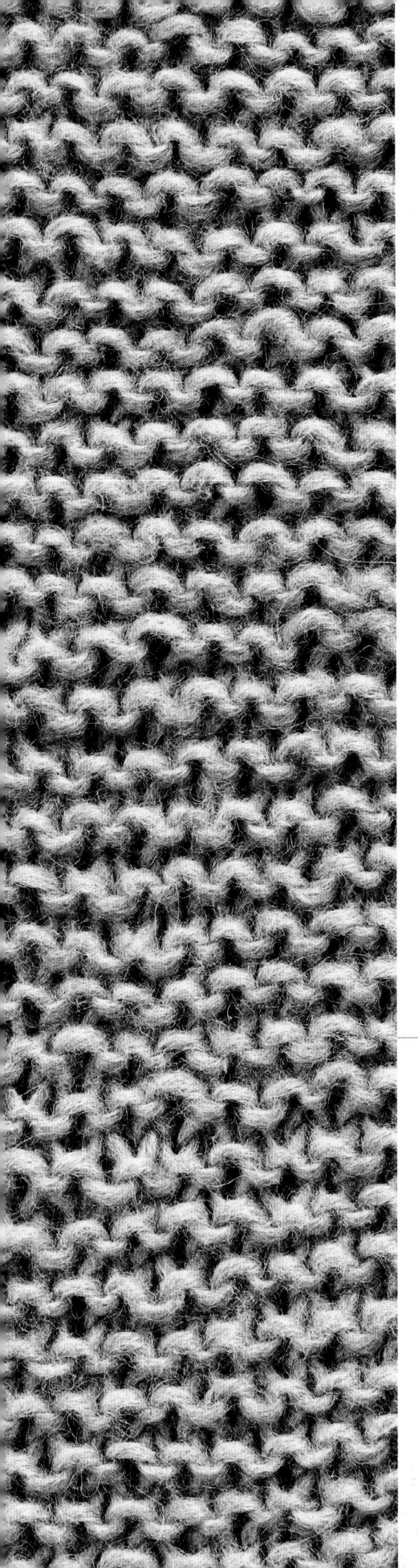

Garter Stitch

If you're new to knitting, garter stitch is a dream to do because you knit all the stitches on every row and avoid the slightly more difficult purl stitches. However, garter stitch doesn't have to be just a simple pattern. It can be combined with other techniques and provide, for example, a nice contrast to a feminine lace pattern.

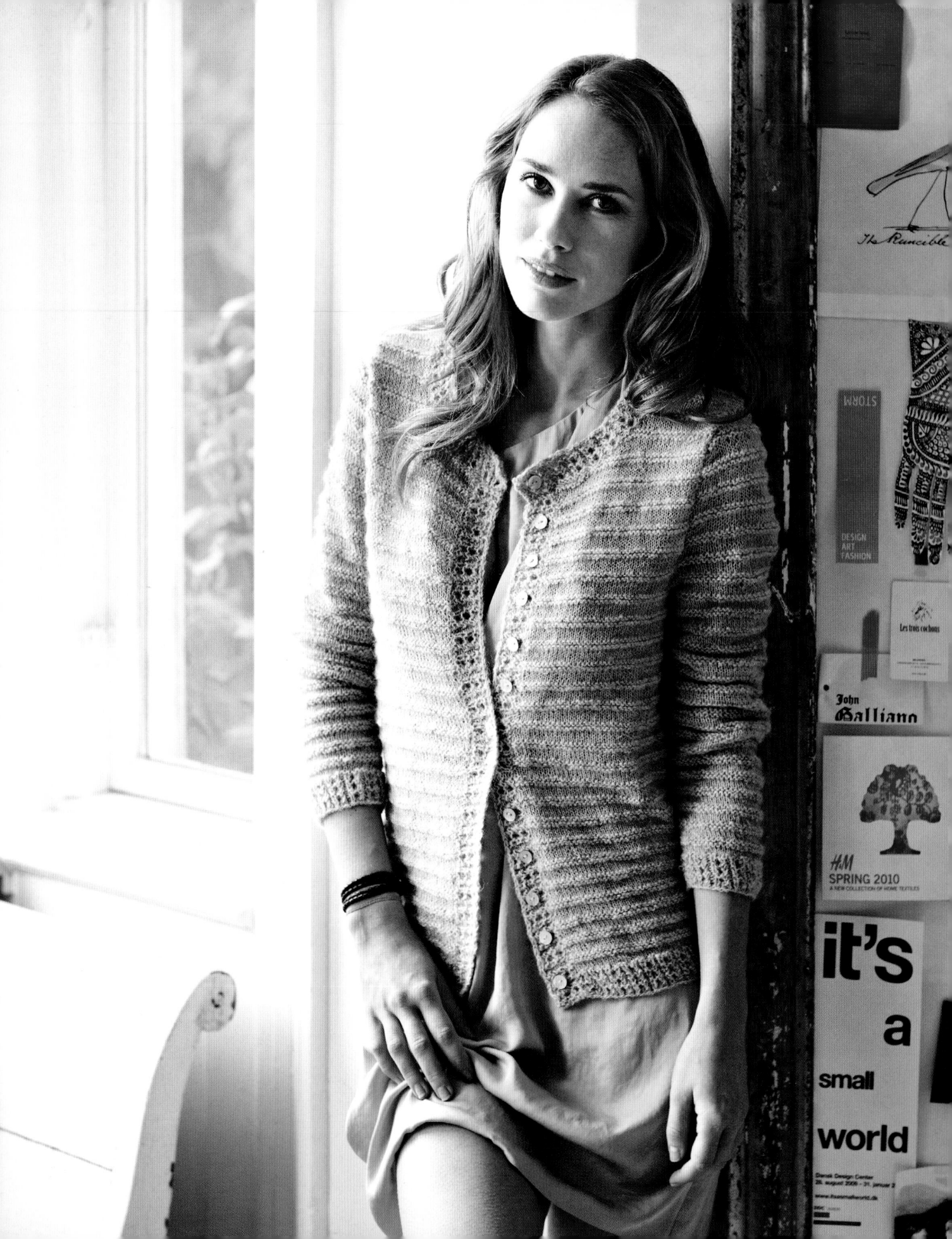

sigga

transparent stripes

This cardigan is worked with two different yarns in the same shade, to yield a delicate, single-color stripe-textured pattern. The sweater fits closely and has bracelet-length sleeves, as well as narrow edgings in a lace pattern.

FINISHED SIZE		S	M	L	XL
Bust	in	32¾	35½	38½	41¼
	cm	83	90	98	105
Total length	in	22¾	23¼	23½	24
	cm	58	59	59.5	61

YARN
Laceweight (#0 Lace).

Shown here: Isager Alpaca 1 (100% alpaca; 437 yd [400 m]/50 g): light gray #2s (A), 3 (4, 4, 4) skeins.

Isager Spinni (100% wool; 330 yd [302 m]/50 g): light gray #2s (B): 3 (3, 3, 4) skeins.

NEEDLES
Size U.S. 2.5 (3 mm): straight.

Adjust needle size if necessary to obtain the correct gauge.

NOTIONS
Markers; holders; tapestry needle; 13 buttons about ½" (13 mm) diameter.

GAUGE
23 sts and 33 rows = 4" (10 cm) in stripe pattern.

NOTE
The pattern used in this sweater will stretch after hanging, so hold the garment vertically when measuring the pieces.

stitch guide

LACE RIB PATTERN (*multiple of 4 sts + 1, worked with 1 strand each A and B held tog*)
ROW 1: (WS) K1, *p3, k1; rep from *.
ROWS 2 AND 4: (RS) P1, *k3, p1; rep from *.
ROW 3: K1, *p1, yo, p2tog, k1; rep from *.
ROW 5: Knit.
Rep Rows 2–5 for patt.

STRIPE PATTERN
ROWS 1 AND 3: (RS) With 1 strand of A, knit.
ROWS 2 AND 4: With 1 strand of A, purl.
ROWS 5–8: With 1 strand each of A and B held tog, knit.
Rep Rows 1–8 for patt.

back

With 1 strand each of A and B held tog, CO 95 (103, 111, 119) sts, and work in lace rib:

ROW 1: (WS) K1 (edge st), work Row 1 of Lace Rib patt to last st, k1 (edge st).

ROW 2: K1 (edge st), work Row 2 of Lace Rib patt to last st, k1 (edge st).

Work Rows 3–5 of Lace Patt, then rep Rows 2–5 two more times.

Cont in stripe pattern until piece measures 2¼" (5.5 cm) from CO edge, ending with a WS row.

NEXT (DEC) ROW: (RS) K1, ssk (or ssp to maintain patt), work in established patt to last 3 sts, k2tog (or p2tog to maintain patt), k1—2 sts dec'd.

Rep dec row every 1½" (3.8 cm) 3 more times—87 (95, 103, 111) sts rem. Cont even until piece measures 10¼" (26 cm) from CO edge, ending with a WS row.

NEXT (INC) ROW: (RS) K1, M1 (or m1p to maintain patt), work in established patt to last st, M1 (or m1p to maintain patt), k1—2 sts inc'd.

Rep inc row every 1¼" (3.2 cm) 3 more times—95 (103, 111, 119) sts. Cont even until piece measures 15" (38 cm) from CO edge, ending with a WS row.

SHAPE ARMHOLES

BO 4 sts at beg of next 2 rows, 3 sts at beg of next 0 (0, 2, 2) rows, 2 sts at beg of next 4 (4, 2, 4) rows. Dec 1 st each end every RS row 2 (3, 3, 2) times—75 (81, 87, 93) sts rem.

Cont even until armhole measures 7 (7½, 7¾, 8¼)" (18 [19, 19.5, 21] cm), ending with a WS row. Mark center 39 (41, 43, 45) sts.

SHAPE NECK AND SHOULDERS

NEXT ROW: (RS) BO 6 (6, 7, 8) sts, work in established patt to marked sts, place center 39 (41, 43, 45) sts on holder for neck, join a second set of yarns and work to end of row.

NEXT ROW: BO 6 (6, 7, 8) sts, work to neck; work to end of row—12 (14, 15, 16) sts rem for each shoulder. Work both sides at same time with separate balls of yarn.

BO 6 (7, 7, 8) sts at beg of next 2 rows, then 6 (7, 8, 8) sts at beg of next 2 rows.

left front

With 1 strand each of A and B held tog, CO 46 (50, 54, 58) sts.

ROW 1: (WS) K1 (edge st), *p3, k1; rep from * to last st, k1 (edge st).

ROWS 2 AND 4: K1 (edge st), *p1, k3; rep from * to last st, k1 (edge st).

ROW 3: K1 (edge st), *p1, yo, p2tog, k1; rep from * to last st, k1 (edge st).

ROW 5: Knit.

Rep Rows 2–5 two more times.

Cont in stripe pattern until piece measures 2¼" (5.5 cm) from CO edge, ending with a WS row.

NEXT (DEC) ROW: (RS) K1, ssk (or ssp to maintain patt), work in established patt to last st, k1—1 st dec'd.

Rep dec row every 1½" (3.8 cm) 3 more times—42 (46, 50, 54) sts rem. Cont even until piece measures 10¼" (26 cm) from CO edge, ending with a WS row.

NEXT (INC) ROW: (RS) K1, M1 (or m1p to maintain patt), work in established patt to last st, k1—1 st inc'd.

Rep inc row every 1¼" (3.2 cm) 3 more times—46 (50, 54, 58) sts. Cont even until piece measures 15" (38 cm) from CO edge, ending with a WS row, matching stripe to left side of back.

SHAPE ARMHOLES

BO at beg of RS rows 4 sts once, 3 sts 0 (0, 1, 1) time, 2 sts 2 (2, 1, 2) time(s), then 1 st 2 (3, 3, 2) times—36 (39, 42, 45) sts rem.

Cont even until armhole measures 4¼ (4¾, 5, 5½)" (11 [12, 12.5, 14] cm), ending with a WS row.

SHAPE NECK

NEXT ROW: (RS) Work 28 (30, 32, 34) sts in established patt, place rem 8 (9, 10, 11) sts on holder for neck.

BO at beg of WS rows 3 sts once, 2 sts twice, then 1 st 3 times—18 (20, 22, 24) sts rem.

Cont even until armhole measures 7 (7½, 7¾, 8¼)" (18 [19, 19.5, 21] cm), ending with a WS row.

SHAPE SHOULDER

BO at beg of RS rows 6 sts 3 (1, 0, 0) time(s), 7 sts 0 (2, 2, 0) times, then 8 sts 0 (0, 1, 3) time(s).

right front

With 1 strand each of A and B held tog, CO 46 (50, 54, 58) sts.

ROW 1: (WS) K1 (edge st), *k1, p3; rep from * to last st, k1 (edge st).

ROWS 2 AND 4: K1 (edge st), *k3, p1; rep from * to last st, k1 (edge st).

ROW 3: K1 (edge st), *k1, p1, yo, p2tog; rep from * to last st, k1 (edge st).

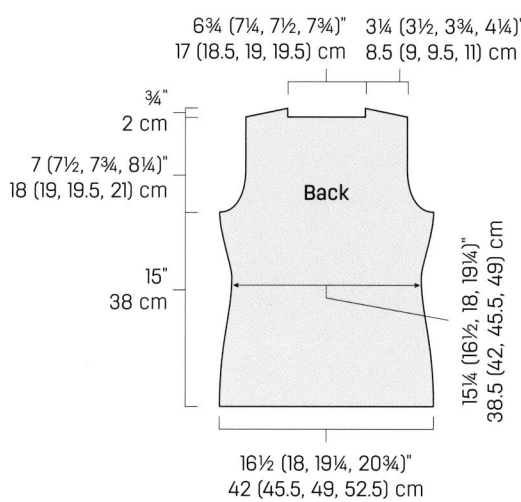

6¾ (7¼, 7½, 7¾)"
17 (18.5, 19, 19.5) cm   3¼ (3½, 3¾, 4¼)"
8.5 (9, 9.5, 11) cm

¾"
2 cm

7 (7½, 7¾, 8¼)"
18 (19, 19.5, 21) cm

Back

15"
38 cm

15¼ (16½, 18, 19¼)"
38.5 (42, 45.5, 49) cm

16½ (18, 19¼, 20¾)"
42 (45.5, 49, 52.5) cm

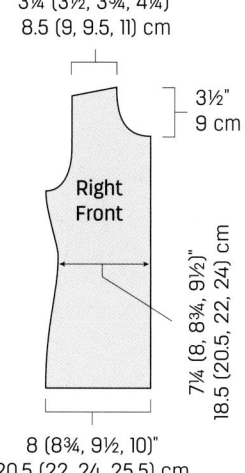

3¼ (3½, 3¾, 4¼)"
8.5 (9, 9.5, 11) cm

3½"
9 cm

Right Front

7¼ (8, 8¾, 9½)"
18.5 (20.5, 22, 24) cm

8 (8¾, 9½, 10)"
20.5 (22, 24, 25.5) cm

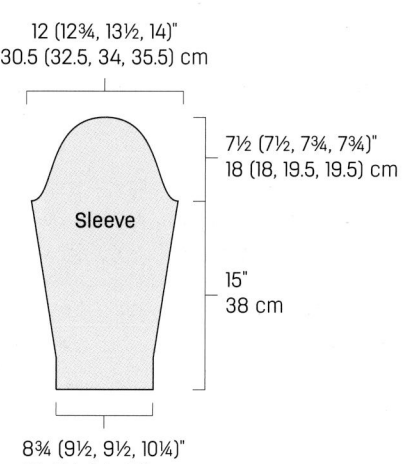

12 (12¾, 13½, 14)"
30.5 (32.5, 34, 35.5) cm

7½ (7½, 7¾, 7¾)"
18 (18, 19.5, 19.5) cm

Sleeve

15"
38 cm

8¾ (9½, 9½, 10¼)"
22 (24, 24, 26) cm

ROW 5: Knit.

Rep Rows 2–5 two more times.

Cont in stripe pattern until piece measures 2¼" (5.5 cm) from CO edge, ending with a WS row.

NEXT (DEC) ROW: (RS) K1, work in established patt to last 3 sts, k2tog (or p2tog to maintain patt), k1—1 st dec'd.

Rep dec row every 1½" (3.8 cm) 3 more times— 42 (46, 50, 54) sts rem. Cont even until piece measures 10¼" (26 cm) from CO edge, ending with a WS row.

NEXT (INC) ROW: (RS) K1, work in established patt to last st, M1 (or m1p to maintain patt), k1— 1 st inc'd.

Rep inc row every 1¼" (3.2 cm) 3 more times— 46 (50, 54, 58) sts. Cont even until piece measures 15" (38 cm) from CO edge, ending with a RS row, matching stripe to right side of back.

SHAPE ARMHOLES
BO at beg of WS rows 4 sts once, 3 sts 0 (0, 1, 1) time, 2 sts 2 (2, 1, 2) time(s), then 1 st 2 (3, 3, 2) times—36 (39, 42, 45) sts rem.

Cont even until armhole measures 4¼ (4¾, 5, 5½)" (11 [12, 12.5, 14] cm), ending with a RS row.

SHAPE NECK
NEXT ROW: (WS) Work 28 (30, 32, 34) sts in established patt, place rem 8 (9, 10, 11) sts on holder for neck.

BO at beg of RS rows 3 sts once, 2 sts twice, then 1 st 3 times—18 (20, 22, 24) sts rem.

Cont even until armhole measures 7 (7½, 7¾, 8¼)" (18 [19, 19.5, 21] cm), ending with a RS row.

SHAPE SHOULDER
BO at beg of WS rows 6 sts 3 (1, 0, 0) time(s), 7 sts 0 (2, 2, 0) times, then 8 sts 0 (0, 1, 3) time(s).

sleeves (make 2)
With 1 strand each of A and B held tog, CO 51 (55, 55, 59) sts.

ROW 1: (WS) K1 (edge st), work Row 1 of Lace Rib patt to last st, k1 (edge st).

ROW 2: K1 (edge st), work Row 2 of Lace Rib patt to last st, k1 (edge st).

Work Rows 3–5 of Lace Rib patt, then rep Rows 2–5 two more times.

Cont in stripe pattern until piece measures 2¼" (5.5 cm), ending with a WS row.

NEXT (INC) ROW: (RS) K1, M1 (or m1p to maintain patt), work in established patt to last st, M1 (or m1p to maintain patt), k1—2 sts inc'd.

Rep inc row every 1¼ (1¼, 1, 1)" (3.2 [3.2, 2.5, 2.5] cm) 8 (8, 10, 10) more times—69 (73, 77, 81) sts.

Cont even until piece measures 15" (38 cm) from CO edge, ending with a WS row and matching patt stripe to back.

SHAPE CAP
BO 4 sts at beg of next 2 rows, then 2 sts at beg of next 6 rows—49 (53, 57, 61) sts rem.

NEXT (DEC) ROW: (RS) K1, ssk (or ssp to maintain patt), work in established patt to last 3 sts, k2tog (or p2tog to maintain patt), k1—2 sts dec'd.

Rep dec row every 6 rows 8 more times. BO 2 sts at beg of next 2 (2, 4, 2) rows, then 3 sts at beg of next 2 (2, 2, 4) rows—21 (25, 25, 27) sts rem.

BO rem sts.

finishing

Weave in ends. Block pieces to finished measurements.

Sew shoulder seams. Sew sleeve and side seams. Sew in sleeves, matching stripes on sleeves with body as closely as possible.

BUTTONBAND

With RS facing and 1 strand each of A and B held tog, pick up and k101 (101, 105, 105) sts (about 4 sts for every 8 rows) evenly along left front edge.

ROW 1: (WS) Knit.

ROWS 2 AND 4: K1 (edge st), k3, *p1, k3; rep from * to last st, k1 (edge st).

ROW 3: K1 (edge st), p1, yo, p2tog, *k1, p1, yo, p2tog; rep from * to last st, k1 (edge st).

Rep Rows 1-4 one more time, then rep Rows 1-3 one more time. BO in patt.

BUTTONHOLE BAND

Work same as for buttonband.

NECKBAND

With RS facing and 1 strand each of A and B held tog, pick up and k7 sts along end of band, knit 8 (9, 10, 11) held sts, pick up and k38 sts along right neck to held back sts, knit 39 (41, 43, 45) held sts, pick up and k38 sts along left neck to held sts, knit 8 (9, 10, 11) held sts, pick up and k7 sts along end of band—145 (149, 153, 157) sts.

ROW 1: (WS) Knit.

ROWS 2 AND 4: *P1, k3; rep from * to last st, p1.

ROW 3: K1, yo, p2tog, *k1, p1, yo, p2tog; rep from * to end of row.

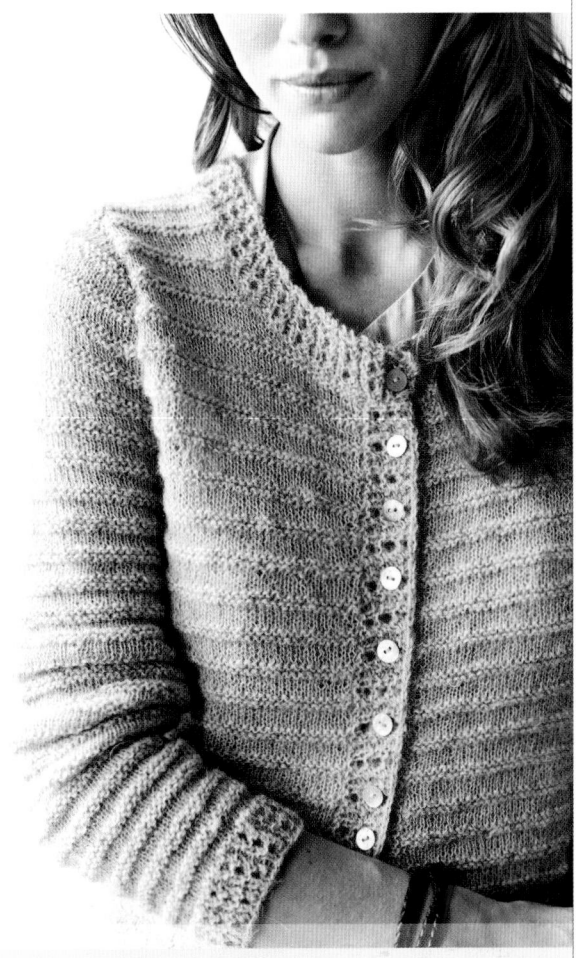

Rep Rows 1-4 one more time, then rep Rows 1-3 one more time. BO in patt. Sew 1 button to left end of neckband and rem buttons to every other rep of lace rib patt of buttonband, using yo for buttonholes.

Sew 12 buttons evenly along left front band and 1 button on end of neckband, using holes in lace rib as buttonholes.

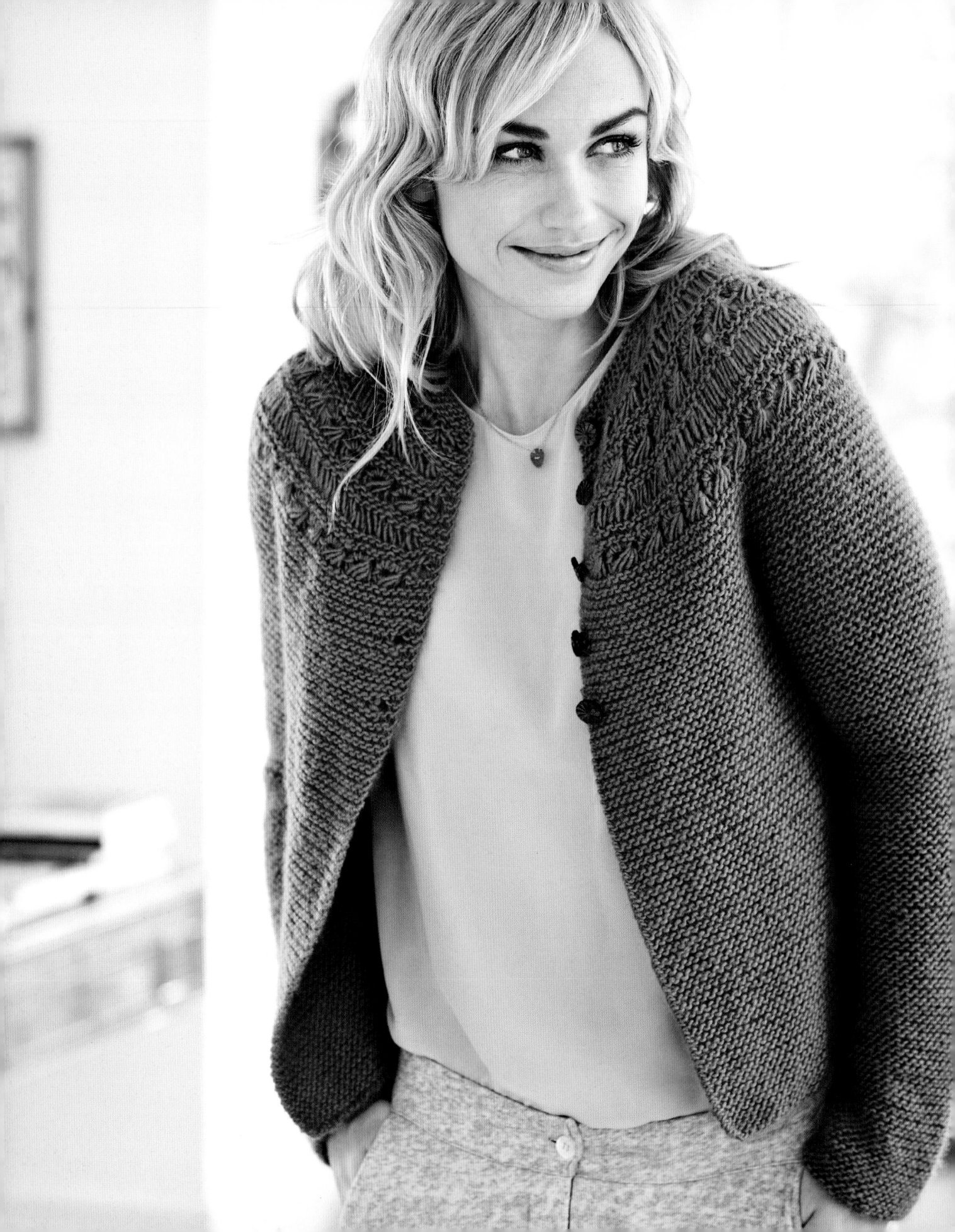

lulu

garter-stitch cardigan with elongated stitches

Here's a fun technique: wrap the yarn twice around the needle, then later drop the extra yarnovers! The pattern stripes of long, open stitches provide a feminine contrast to the ridges on this garter-stitch cardigan. On alternate pattern stripes, the long open stitches are crossed, producing a crochet-like motif with a fine texture.

FINISHED SIZE		S	M	L	XL
Bust with 1" (2.5 cm) overlap	in	34¼	37¾	40½	44
	cm	87	96	103	112
Total length at center of back	in	18¾	19¼	19¾	20¼
	cm	47.5	49	50	51.5

YARN
Aran weight (#4 Medium).

Shown here: Onion Camel+Merino (70% merino wool, 30% camel; 120 yd [110 m]/50 g): petroleum blue #905, 9 (10, 11, 12) balls.

NEEDLES
Size U.S. 8 (5 mm): straight. Sizes U.S. 7 and 8 (4.5 and 5 mm): 32" (80 cm) circular (cir).

Adjust needle size if necessary to obtain the correct gauge.

NOTIONS
Stitch holders; markers; tapestry needle; 5 buttons ¾" (19 mm) diameter.

GAUGE
18 sts and 32 rows = 4" (10 cm) in garter st on larger needles.

stitch guide

PATTERN WITH LONG STITCHES
(multiple of 4 sts)

ROW 1: (RS) *K1 wrapping yarn around needle twice; rep from * across.

ROW 2: *Sl 4 sts to right needle tip dropping extra yo, place these 4 sts back on left needle tip, insert right needle tip in these 4 sts as if to k4tog and work (k1, p1) twice in these same sts; rep from * across.

ROWS 3–6: Knit, working dec and buttonholes as described in patt.

ROW 7: Rep Row 1.

ROW 8: Knit, dropping extra yo.

ROWS 9 AND 10: Knit, working dec and buttonholes as described in patt.

BUTTONHOLE

(RS) K2, BO 2 sts, knit to end of row; on next row, knit to gap, CO 2 sts over gap from previous row.

back

With straight needles, CO 76 (84, 90, 98) sts.

Work in garter st (knit every row) until piece measures 10¾ (11, 11½, 11¾)" (27.5 [28, 29, 30] cm) from CO edge, ending with a WS row.

BO 7 (8, 9, 10) sts at beg of next 2 rows—62 (68, 72, 78) sts rem.

Place rem sts on holder.

left front

With straight needles, CO 41 (45, 48, 52) sts.

Work in garter st until piece measures 10¾ (11, 11½, 11¾)" (27 [28, 29, 30] cm) ending with a WS row.

NEXT ROW: (RS) BO 7 (8, 9, 10) sts, knit to end of row—34 (37, 39, 42) sts rem.

Knit 1 row even.

Place rem sts on holder.

right front

Work right front same as left front until piece measures 10¾ (11, 11½, 11¾)" (27.5 [28, 29, 30] cm) ending with a RS row.

NEXT ROW: (WS) BO 7 (8, 9, 10) sts, knit to end of row—34 (37, 39, 42) sts rem.

Place rem sts on holder.

sleeves (make 2)

With straight needles, CO 38 (40, 40, 42) sts.

Work in garter st until piece measures 2¼ (2, 3¼, 1½)" (5.5 [5, 8.5, 3.8] cm), ending with a WS row.

NEXT (INC) ROW: (RS) K1, m1, knit to last st, m1, k1—2 sts inc'd.

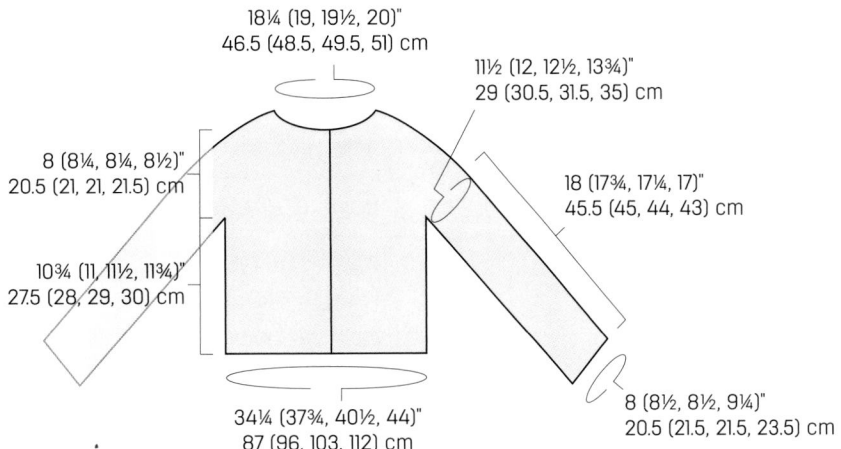

18¼ (19, 19½, 20)"
46.5 (48.5, 49.5, 51) cm

11½ (12, 12½, 13¾)"
29 (30.5, 31.5, 35) cm

8 (8¼, 8¼, 8½)"
20.5 (21, 21, 21.5) cm

18 (17¾, 17¼, 17)"
45.5 (45, 44, 43) cm

10¾ (11, 11½, 11¾)"
27.5 (28, 29, 30) cm

34¼ (37¾, 40½, 44)"
87 (96, 103, 112) cm

8 (8½, 8½, 9¼)"
20.5 (21.5, 21.5, 23.5) cm

Rep inc row every 18 (16, 12, 12) rows 6 (7, 8, 9) more times—52 (56, 58, 62) sts.

Cont even until piece measures 18 (17¾, 17¼, 17)" (45.5 [45, 44, 43] cm) from CO edge, ending with a WS row.

BO 7 (8, 9, 10) sts at beg of next 2 rows—38 (40, 40, 42) sts rem.

Place rem sts on holder.

yoke

With RS facing, place held sts for each piece on larger cir needle in this order: right front, sleeve, back, sleeve, left front—206 (222, 230, 246) sts.

Cont in garter st and make buttonholes on rows indicated for your size.

ROW 1: (RS) K33 (36, 38, 41) right front sts, k2tog and place marker (pm) on this st, k36 (38, 38, 40) sleeve sts, k2tog and pm on this st, k60 (66, 70, 76) back sts, k2tog and pm on this st, k36 (38, 38, 40) sleeve sts, k2tog and mark this st, knit rem 33 (36, 38, 41) left front sts—202 (218, 226, 242) sts rem; 33 (36, 38, 41) sts for each front, 60 (66, 70, 76) sts for back, 36 (38, 38, 40) sts for each sleeve, and 4 raglan sts. Move raglan markers up as you work.

ROW 2: Knit.

ROW 3: Make buttonhole for size S only, knit.

ROW 4: Knit.

ROW 5: Make buttonhole for sizes M and L only, *knit to 2 sts before marked st, k2tog, knit marked st, ssk; rep from * 3 more times, knit to end of row—8 sts dec'd.

ROW 6: Knit.

ROW 7: Make buttonhole for size XL only, rep Row 5—8 sts dec'd.

ROW 8: Knit.

ROW 9: *Knit to 2 sts before marked st, k2tog, knit marked st, ssk; rep from * 3 more times, knit to end of row—8 sts dec'd.

ROW 10: Knit.

Rep last 2 rows 0 (1, 1, 2) more time(s)—178 (186, 194, 202) sts; 30 (32, 34, 36) sts for each front, 54 (58, 62, 66) sts for back, 30 sts for each sleeve, and 4 raglan sts.

Knit 4 rows even.

NEXT (BUTTONHOLE) ROW: Knit, making button-hole for all sizes.

Knit 9 more rows even, removing raglan m on last row.

Cont in pattern as follows:

ROW 1: (RS) K5, work Row 1 of patt with Long sts to last 5 sts, k5.

ROW 2: K5, work Row 2 of patt with Long sts to last 5 sts, k5.

ROW 3: Knit, making buttonhole for all sizes.

ROW 4: Knit.

Row 5 (dec): K12 (16, 2, 6), *k2tog, k6; rep from * to last 6 (10, 0, 4) sts, knit to end of row—158 (166, 170, 178) sts rem.

ROW 6: Knit.

ROW 7: K5, work Row 7 of patt with Long sts to last 5 sts, k5.

ROW 8: K5, work Row 8 of patt with Long sts to last 5 sts, k5.

Row 9 (dec): K12 (16, 2, 6), *k2tog, k5; rep from * to last 6 (10, 0, 4) sts, knit to end of row—138 (146, 146, 154) sts rem.

ROW 10: Knit.

ROWS 11-14: Rep Rows 1-4.

Row 15 (dec): K12 (16, 16, 6), *k2tog, k4; rep from * to last 6 (10, 10, 4) sts, knit to end of row—118 (126, 126, 130) sts rem.

ROW 16: Knit.

ROWS 17 AND 18: Rep Rows 7 and 8.

Row 19 (dec): K12 (16, 16, 6), *k2tog, k3; rep from * to last 6 (10, 10, 4) sts, knit to end of row—98 (106, 106, 106) sts rem.

ROW 20: Knit.

ROWS 21 AND 22: Rep Rows 1 and 2.

ROW 23: Change to smaller cir needle. Knit and dec 11 (16, 14, 12) sts evenly spaced across to last 5 sts, k5—87 (90, 92, 94) sts rem.

ROW 24: Rep Row 4.

ROWS 25-28: Knit.

BO all sts kwise.

finishing

Weave in ends.

Sew sleeve and side seams using a half-stitch seam allowance. Sew underarm seams. Sew buttons to left front opposite buttonholes.

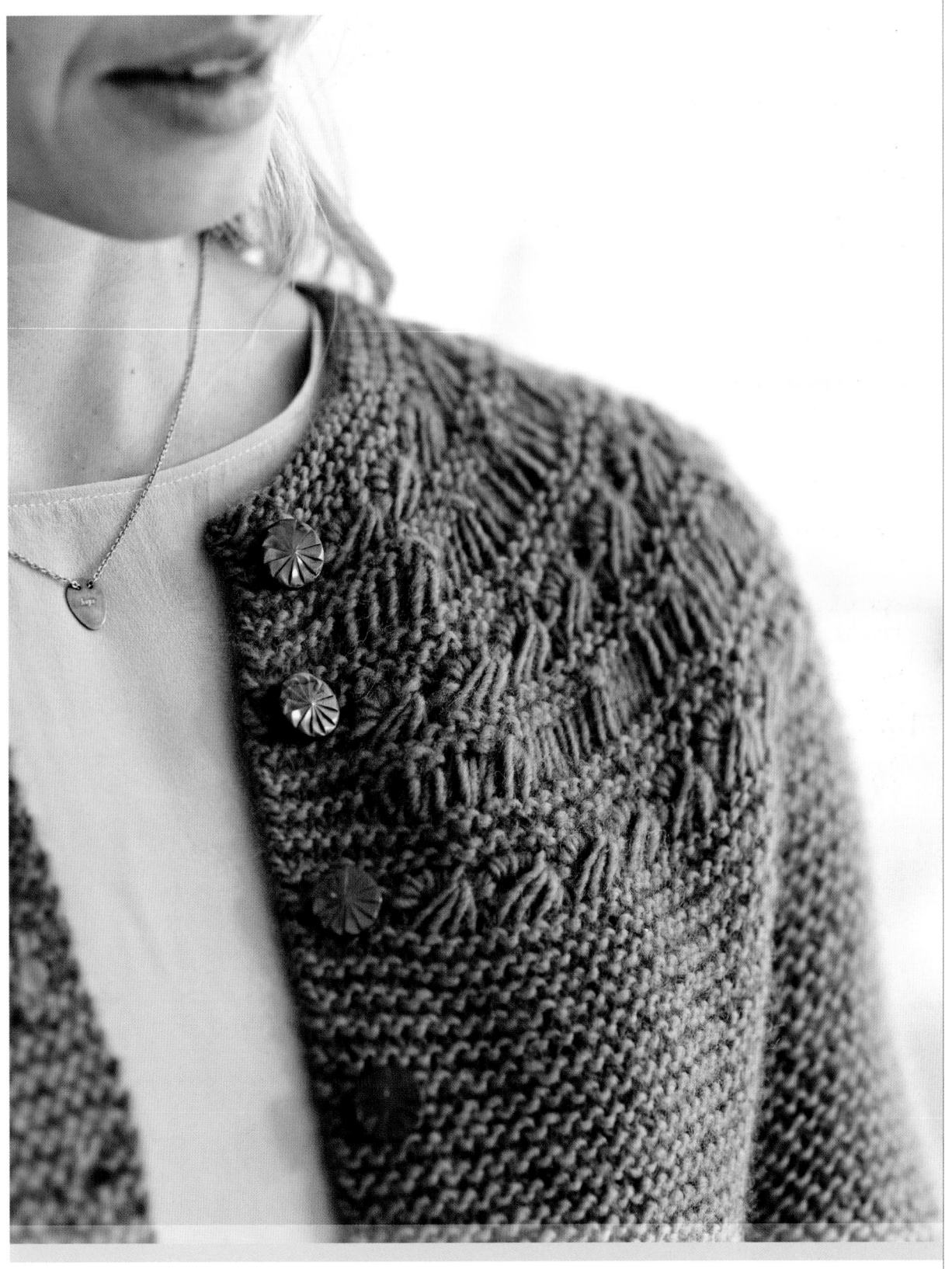

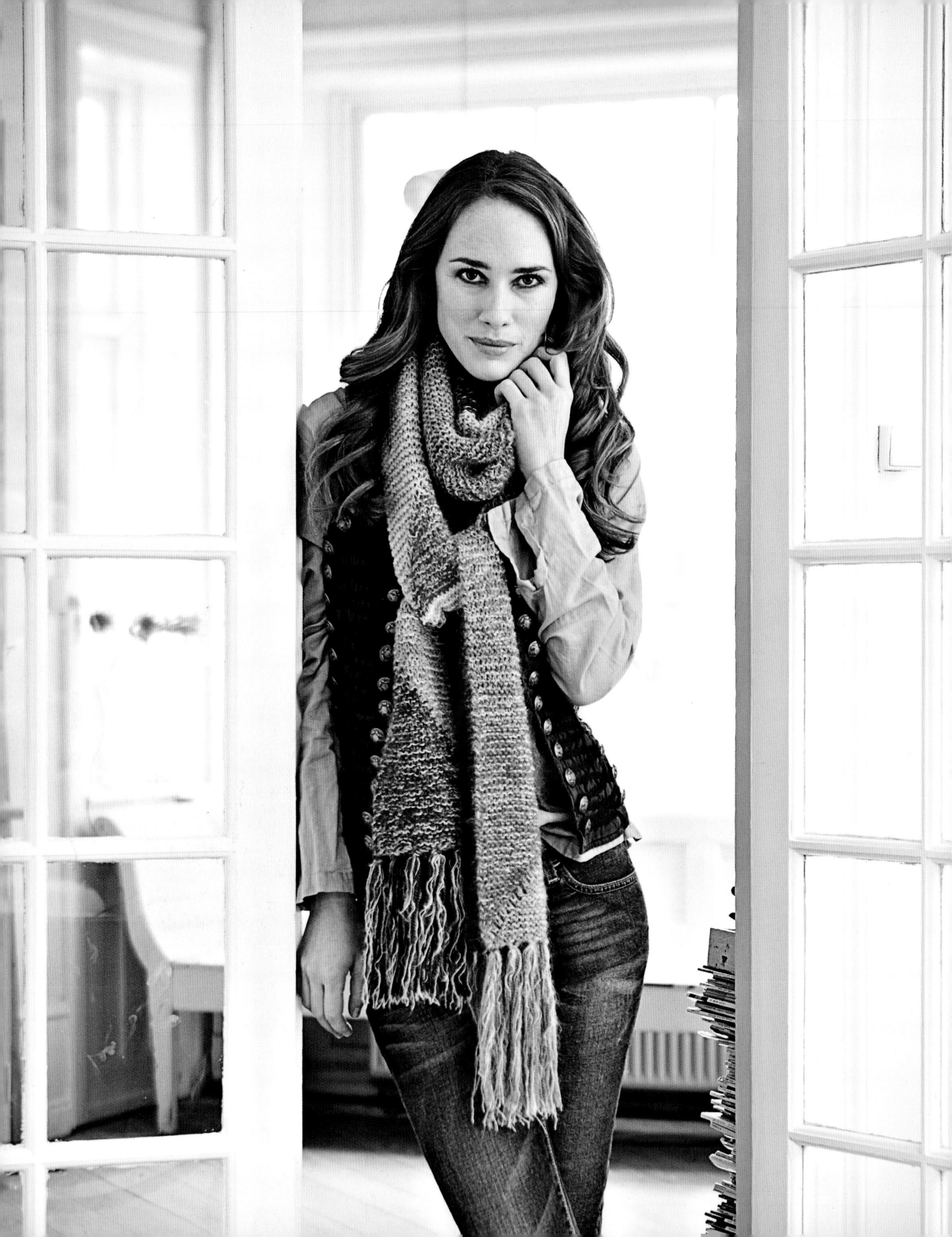

tira

triangles scarf

A fine mohair yarn, knitted in combination
with each of the colors forming the graphic
triangles, lends an overall tweedy look.

FINISHED SIZE
8¼" × 102¾" (21 × 261 cm) or
desired length, plus fringe.

YARN
Lace and DK weights
(#0 Lace–#3 Light).

Shown here: BC Garn Semilla (100%
organic wool; 175 yd [160 m]/50 g):
1 ball each of orange #115 (A);
green #133 (B); natural #01 (C);
navy blue #114 (D); purple #108 (E);
blue #111 (F); pink #104 (G); aqua
#120 (H).

Permin Angel (70% kid mohair,
30% silk; 229 yd [210 m]/25 g):
sand #03 (I), 3 balls.

NEEDLES
Size U.S. 10 (6 mm): straight.

*Adjust needle size if necessary to
obtain the correct gauge.*

NOTIONS
Tapestry needle.

GAUGE
16 sts and 26½ rows = 4" (10 cm)
in garter st with 1 strand each of
lace- and DK-weight yarn held
together. 1 triangle measures
about 10¼" (26 cm) long.

NOTES
The scarf is worked with 1 strand
each of Angel and Semilla
held together throughout, and
only the color changes for the
Semilla yarn will be mentioned
in the instructions (see diagram,
page 157).

When referring to the diagram,
read right-side "rows" from right
to left and wrong-side "rows" from
left to right. Read diagram "rows"
from bottom to top.

scarf

Holding 1 strand each of I and B tog, CO 33 sts.

ROW 1: (WS) Knit.

ROW 2: (RS) K32, drop B but do not cut, join A, with I and A held tog, k1. *Note: There is no need to twist colors when changing yarns because the work is held together by the mohair yarn.*

ROW 3: K1 with A, drop A and pick up B, knit to end of row.

ROW 4: K31 with B, drop B and pick up A, knit to end of row.

ROW 5: K2 with A, drop A and pick up B, knit to end of row.

ROWS 6-65: Cont as established, working 1 more st with A every 2 rows. Cut B at end of last row.

ROWS 66 AND 67: Knit with A. Cut A.

ROWS 68 AND 69: Join F and knit.

ROW 70: Join C, k1 with C, k32 with F.

ROW 71: K32 with F, k1 with C.

ROW 72: K2 with C, k31 with F.

ROW 73: K31 with F, k2 with C.

ROWS 74-133: Cont as established, working 1 st more with C every 2 rows. Cut F at end of last row.

ROWS 134 AND 135: Knit with C. Cut C.

ROWS 136 AND 137: Join G and knit.

ROWS 138-203: Join H and rep Rows 2-67, working 1 st more with H every 2 rows. Cut G and H.

ROWS 204 AND 205: Join C and knit.

ROWS 206-271: Join D and rep Rows 70-135, working 1 st more with D every 2 rows. Cut C and D.

ROWS 272 AND 273: Join A and knit.

ROWS 274-339: Join F and rep Rows 2-67, working 1 st more with F every 2 rows. Cut A and F.

ROWS 340 AND 341: Join B and knit.

ROWS 342-407: Join C and rep Rows 70-135, working 1 st more with C every 2 rows. Cut B and C.

ROWS 408 AND 409: Join E and knit.

ROWS 410-475: Join H and rep Rows 2-67, working 1 st more with H every 2 rows. Cut E and H.

ROWS 476 AND 477: Join D and knit.

ROWS 478-543: Join G and rep Rows 70-135, working 1 st more with G every 2 rows. Cut D and G.

ROWS 544 AND 545: Join C and knit.

ROWS 546-611: Join B and rep Rows 2-67, working 1 st more with B every 2 rows. Cut C and B.

ROWS 612 AND 613: Join E and knit.

ROWS 614-679: Join D and rep Rows 70-135, working 1 st more with D every 2 rows. Cut E. Piece should measure about 102¾" (261 cm).

BO kwise with D.

finishing

Weave in ends. Block to finished measurements.

FRINGE

Cut 45 strands each of B and I, each about 17¾" (45 cm) long. With 5 strands of each yarn held tog, attach 9 fringes to CO edge. Rep with D and I for BO edge.

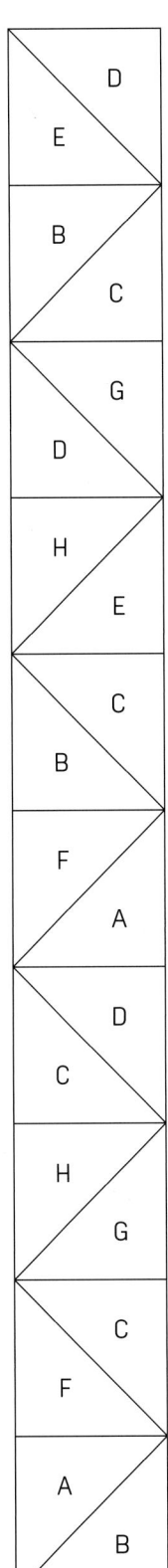

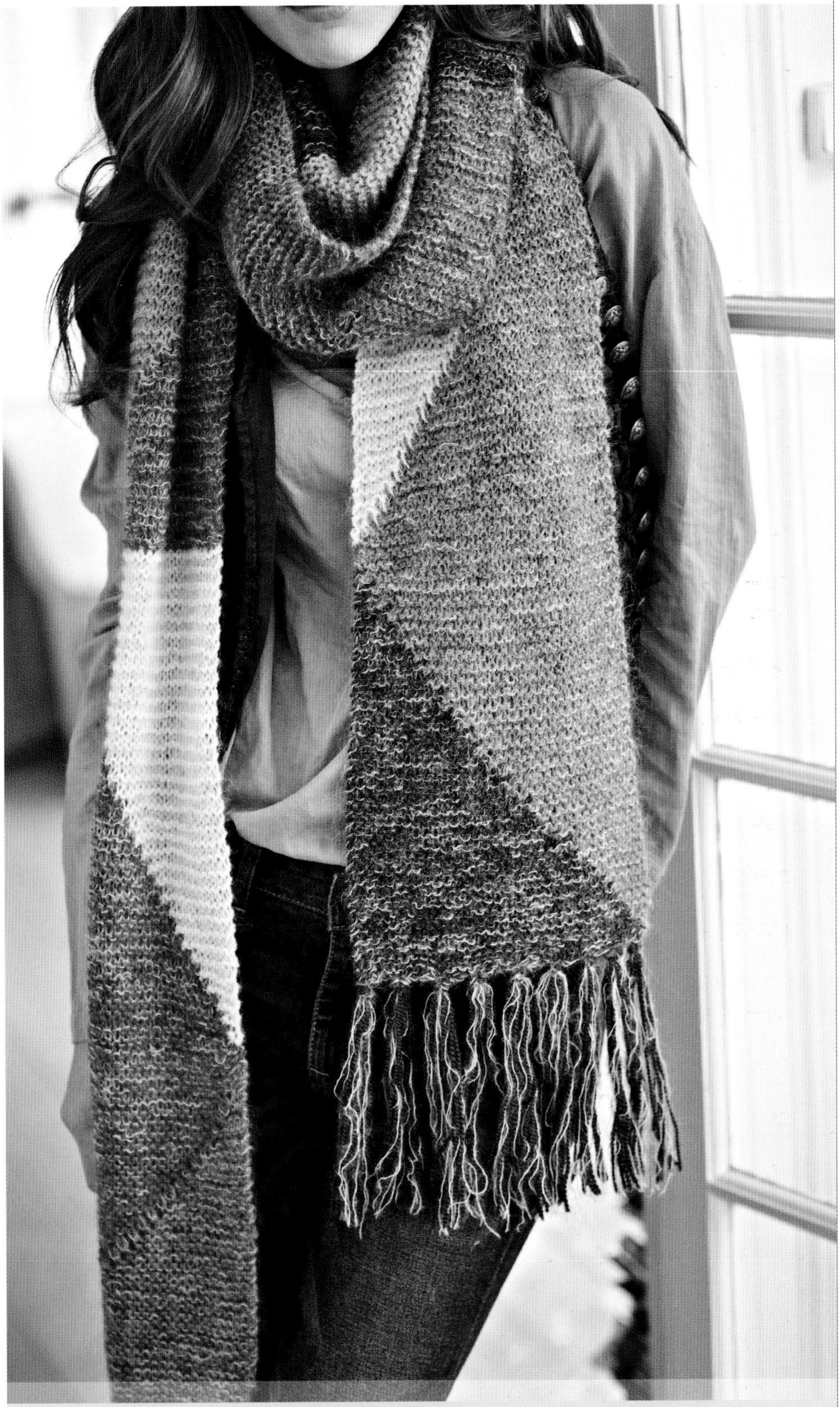

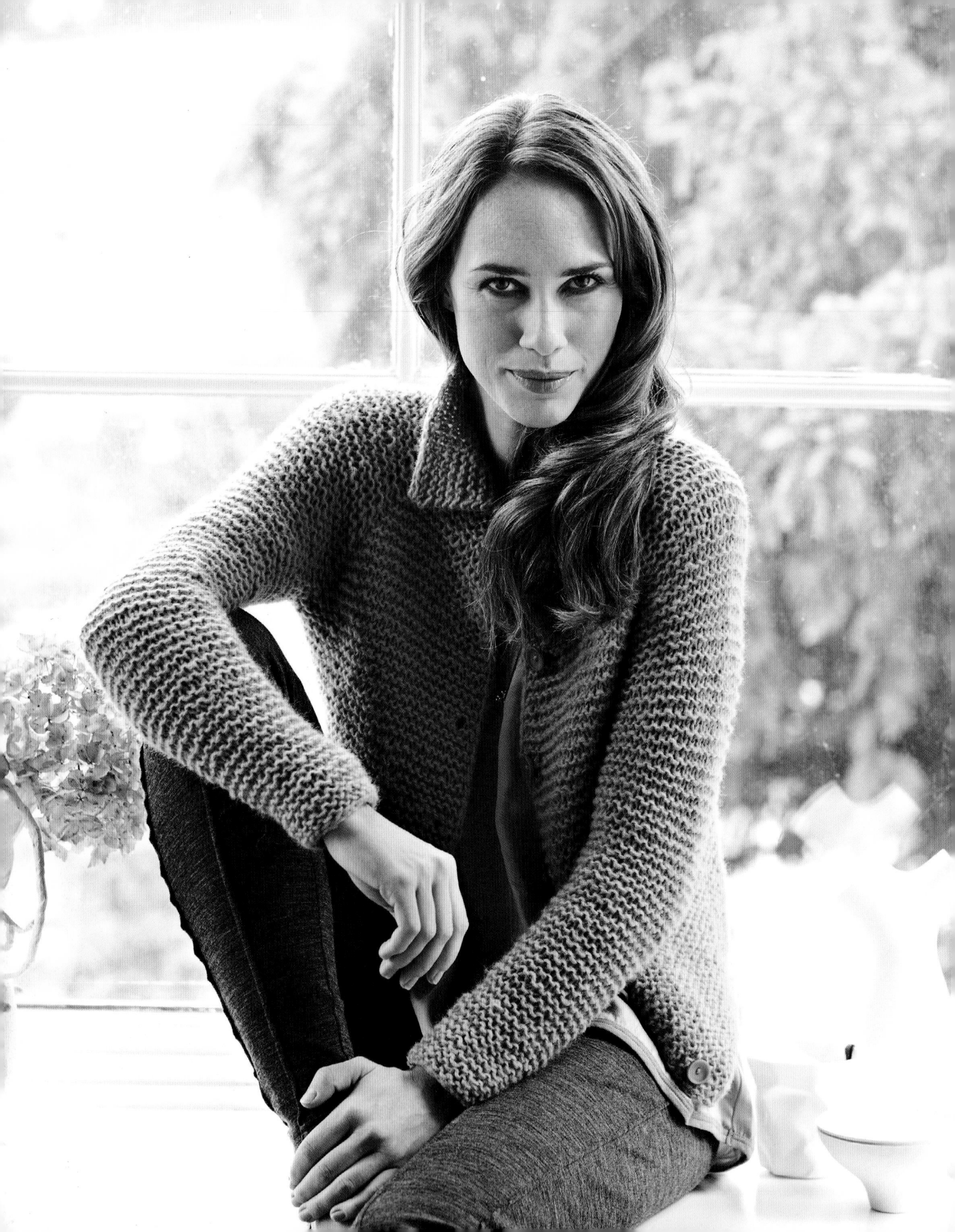

ria

garter-stitch sweater with or without a collar

It doesn't get any easier than this cardigan, which is knitted from the neck down, back and forth on a circular needle. The collar, if you want one, is worked last.

FINISHED SIZE		S	M	L	XL
Ochre Cardigan Bust including 1¼" (3.2 cm) overlap	in	34½	37½	40½	43
	cm	87.5	95	103	109
Total length	in	20	20½	21¼	21¾
	cm	51	52	54	55
Gray Cardigan Bust including 1¼" (3.2 cm) overlap	in	37½	40¾	44	46¾
	cm	95	103.5	112	118.5
Total length	in	19	19¾	20¼	20½
	cm	48.5	50	51.5	52

YARN
For Ochre Cardigan with Collar
Chunky weight (#5 Bulky).

Shown here: Gepard Puno (68% baby alpaca, 22% mixed synthetic fiber, 10% merino wool; 120 yd [110 m]/50 g): ochre #345, 5 (6, 6, 7) balls.

For Gray Cardigan without Collar
Chunky weight (#5 Bulky).

Shown here: Sandnes Garn Alfa (85% pure new wool, 15% mohair; 65 yd [60 m]/50 g): gray #1042 (A), 10 (12, 13, 14) balls; ochre #2427 (B), 1 ball.

NEEDLES
Size U.S. 11 (8 mm): straight and 32" (80 cm) circular (cir). Size U.S. 10¾ (7 mm): straight.

Adjust needle size if necessary to obtain the correct gauge.

con't.

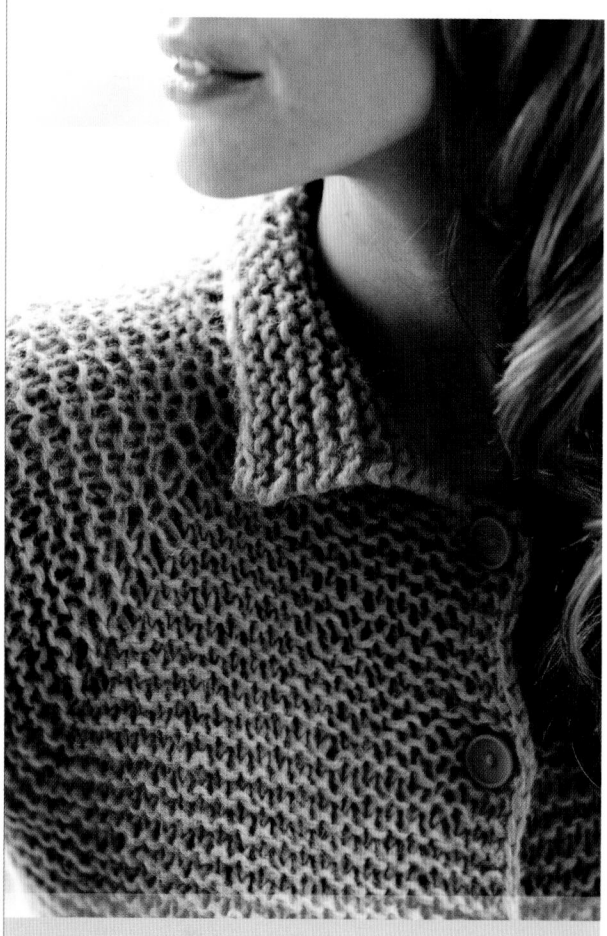

CARDIGAN WITH COLLAR

yoke

With larger cir needle, CO 58 (60, 64, 64). Knit 2 rows a little tightly.

NEXT (BUTTONHOLE) ROW: (RS) Knit to last 4 sts, k2tog, yo, k2.

Knit 1 WS row.

NEXT (INC) ROW: K12 (12, 13, 13) sts for left front, yo, k1 and place marker (pm) on st for raglan, yo, k6 (7, 7, 7) sts for sleeve, yo, k1 and pm on st for raglan, yo, k18 (18, 20, 20) sts for back, yo, k1 and pm on st for raglan, yo, k6 (7, 7, 7) sts for sleeve, yo, k1 and pm on st for raglan, yo, knit rem 12 (12, 13, 13) sts—8 sts inc'd.

NEXT ROW: Knit, working each yo through back loop.

Rep last 2 rows 11 (13, 13, 15) more times and at the same time, work buttonholes every 18 rows 5 more times—154 (172, 176, 192) sts; 24 (26, 27, 29) sts for each front, 42 (46, 48, 52) sts for back, 30 (35, 35, 39) sts for each sleeve, and 4 raglan sts.

NEXT (INC) ROW: (RS) Knit to marker, yo, k32 (37, 37, 41), yo, knit to next marker, yo, k32 (37, 37, 41), yo, knit to end of row—4 sts inc'd.

Rep inc row every RS row 2 (2, 3, 3) more times—166 (184, 192, 208) sts; 27 (29, 31, 33) sts for each front, 48 (52, 56, 60) sts for back, 30 (35, 35, 39) sts for each sleeve, and 4 raglan sts.

NEXT ROW: (WS) K27 (29, 31, 33), *BO marked st, knit to next marked st; rep from * twice more, BO marked st, knit to end—162 (180, 188, 204) sts; 27 (29, 31, 33) sts for each front, 48 (52, 56, 60) sts for back, and 30 (35, 35, 39) sts for each sleeve.

DIVIDE BODY AND SLEEVES

NEXT ROW: (RS) Knit left front sts, place 30 (35, 35, 39) sleeve sts on holder, CO 7 (8, 9, 9), knit

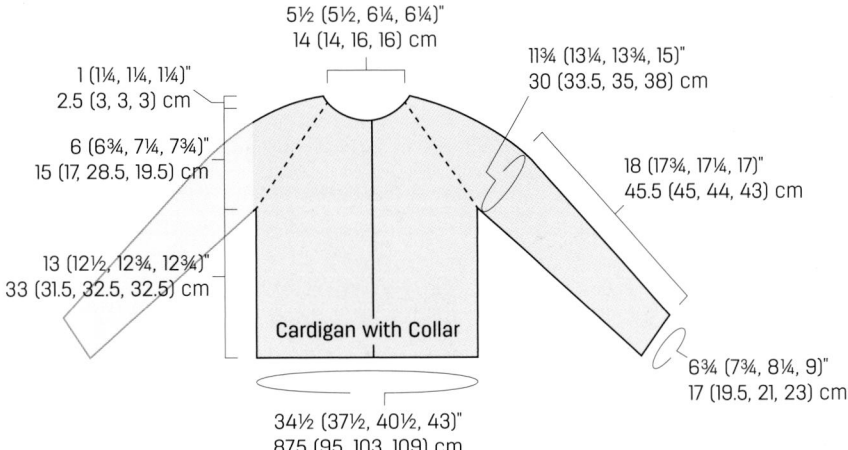

Cardigan with Collar

- 5½ (5½, 6¼, 6¼)"
  14 (14, 16, 16) cm
- 11¾ (13¼, 13¾, 15)"
  30 (33.5, 35, 38) cm
- 1 (1¼, 1¼, 1¼)"
  2.5 (3, 3, 3) cm
- 6 (6¾, 7¼, 7¾)"
  15 (17, 28.5, 19.5) cm
- 18 (17¾, 17¼, 17)"
  45.5 (45, 44, 43) cm
- 13 (12½, 12¾, 12¾)"
  33 (31.5, 32.5, 32.5) cm
- 6¾ (7¾, 8¼, 9)"
  17 (19.5, 21, 23) cm
- 34½ (37½, 40½, 43)"
  87.5 (95, 103, 109) cm

back sts, place 30 (35, 35, 39) sleeve sts on holder, CO 7 (8, 9, 9) sts, knit right front sts—116 (126, 136, 144) sts.

body

Cont even in garter st (knit every row) until piece measures 19 (19¼, 20, 20½)" (48.5 [49, 51, 52] cm) from CO edge, and cont rem buttonholes. BO all sts.

sleeves (make 2)

With larger cir needle and RS facing, return held 30 (35, 35, 39) sleeve sts to larger cir needle, CO 4 (4, 5, 5) sts, knit sleeve sts, CO 4 (4, 5, 5) sts—38 (43, 45, 49) sts.

Cont in garter st for 1½" (3.8 cm), ending with a WS row.

NEXT (DEC) ROW: (RS) K1, k2tog, knit to last 3 sts, k2tog, k1—2 sts dec'd.

Rep dec row every 12 (10, 10, 8) rows 7 (8, 8, 9) more times—22 (25, 27, 29) sts rem.

Cont even until sleeve measures 18 (17¾, 17¼, 17)" (45.5 [45, 44, 43] cm) from armhole. BO rem sts.

collar

With smaller needles and RS facing, working as close to CO edge as possible to avoid an obvious seam, skip first 2 sts, pick up and k1 st in each CO st to last 2 sts—54 (56, 60, 60) sts.

NEXT ROW: (WS) Knit and dec 4 (4, 6, 6) sts evenly spaced across row—50 (52, 54, 54) sts rem.

Cont even in garter st until collar measures 1¼" (3.2 cm). Change to larger straight needles. Cont even until collar measures about 3" (7.5 cm). BO all sts loosely.

finishing and edgings

Weave in ends. Sew sleeve seams using finer yarn in same color, sewing as close to edge as possible, making sure not to tighten the stitches as you work. Sew underarm seams.

FRONT EDGING

With smaller needles and RS facing, pick up and k1 st in each garter ridge along front edge, picking up sts as close to edge as possible, and, at the same time, BO knitwise as you're picking up sts. Work edging on rem front edge same as for first edging.

Sew buttons to front edge opposite buttonholes.

CARDIGAN WITHOUT COLLAR

yoke

With larger cir needle and A, CO 58 (60, 64, 64). Knit 2 rows a little tightly.

NEXT (BUTTONHOLE) ROW: (RS) Knit to last 4 sts, k2tog, yo, k2.

Knit 1 WS row.

NEXT (INC) ROW: K12 (12, 13, 13) sts for left front, yo, k1 and place marker (pm) on st for raglan, yo, k6 (7, 7, 7) sts for sleeve, yo, k1 and pm on st for raglan, yo, k18 (18, 20, 20) sts for back, yo, k1 and pm on st for raglan, yo, k6 (7, 7, 7) sts for sleeve, yo, k1 and pm on st for raglan, yo, knit rem 12 (12, 13, 13) sts—8 sts inc'd.

NEXT ROW: Knit.

Rep last 2 rows 11 (13, 13, 15) more times and at the same time, work buttonholes every 16 rows 5 more times—154 (172, 176, 192) sts; 24 (26, 27, 29) sts for each front, 42 (46, 48, 52) sts for back, 30 (35, 35, 39) sts for each sleeve, and 4 raglan sts.

NEXT (INC) ROW: (RS) Knit to marker, yo, k32 (37, 37, 41), yo, knit to next marker, yo, k32 (37, 37, 41), yo, knit to end of row—4 sts inc'd.

Rep inc row every RS row 2 (2, 3, 3) more—166 (184, 192, 208) sts; 27 (29, 31, 33) sts for each front, 48 (52, 56, 60) sts for back, 30 (35, 35, 39) sts for each sleeve, and 4 raglan sts.

NEXT ROW: (WS) K27 (29, 31, 33), *BO marked st, knit to next marked st; rep from * twice more, BO marked st, knit to end—162 (180, 188, 204) sts; 27 (29, 31, 33) sts for each front, 48 (52, 56, 60) sts for back, and 30 (35, 35, 39) sts for each sleeve.

DIVIDE BODY AND SLEEVES

NEXT ROW: (RS) Knit left front sts, place 30 (35, 35, 39) sleeve sts on holder, CO 7 (8, 9, 9), knit back sts, place 30 (35, 35, 39) sleeve sts on holder, CO 7 (8, 9, 9) sts, knit right front sts—116 (126, 136, 144) sts.

body

Cont even in garter st (knit every row) until piece measures 18 (18½, 19, 19¼)" (45.5 [47, 48.5, 49] cm) from CO edge, and cont rem buttonholes. BO all sts.

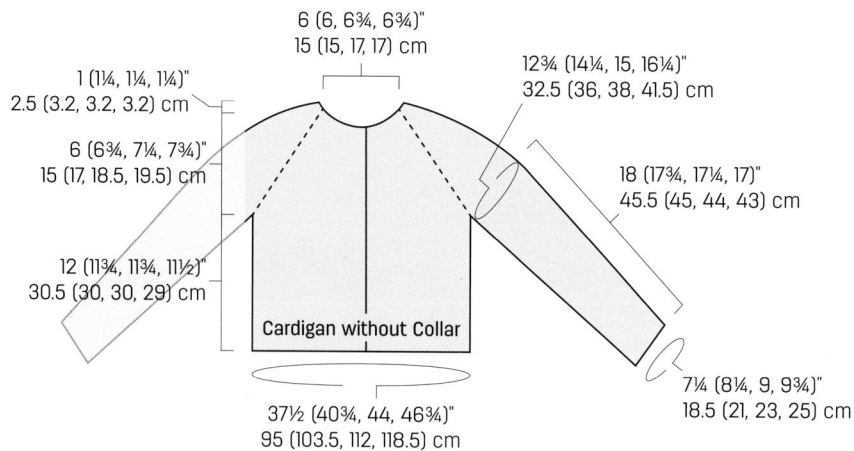

1 (1¼, 1¼, 1¼)"
2.5 (3.2, 3.2, 3.2) cm

6 (6, 6¾, 6¾)"
15 (15, 17, 17) cm

12¾ (14¼, 15, 16¼)"
32.5 (36, 38, 41.5) cm

6 (6¾, 7¼, 7¾)"
15 (17, 18.5, 19.5) cm

18 (17¾, 17¼, 17)"
45.5 (45, 44, 43) cm

12 (11¾, 11¾, 11½)"
30.5 (30, 30, 29) cm

Cardigan without Collar

37½ (40¾, 44, 46¾)"
95 (103.5, 112, 118.5) cm

7¼ (8¼, 9, 9¾)"
18.5 (21, 23, 25) cm

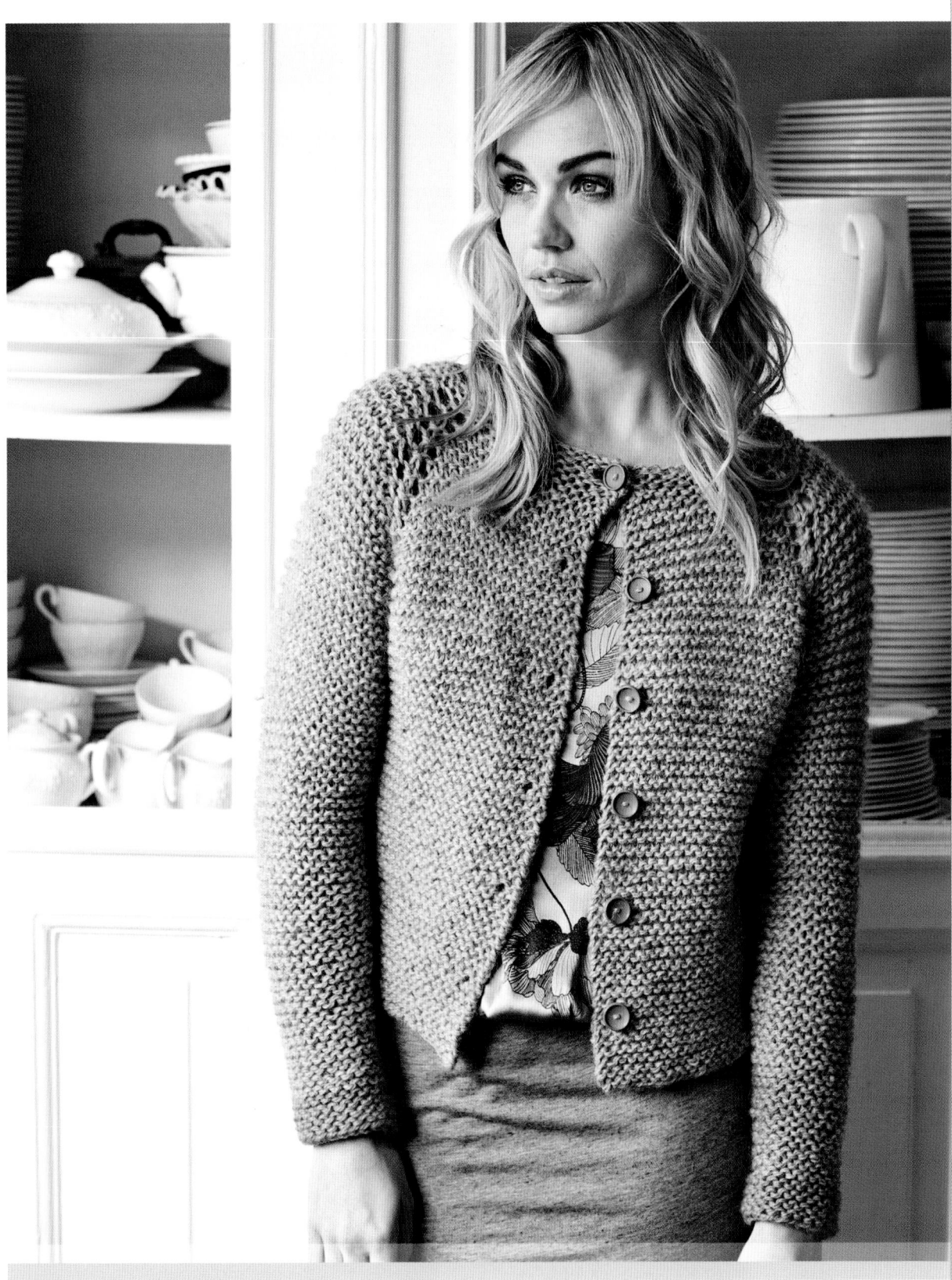

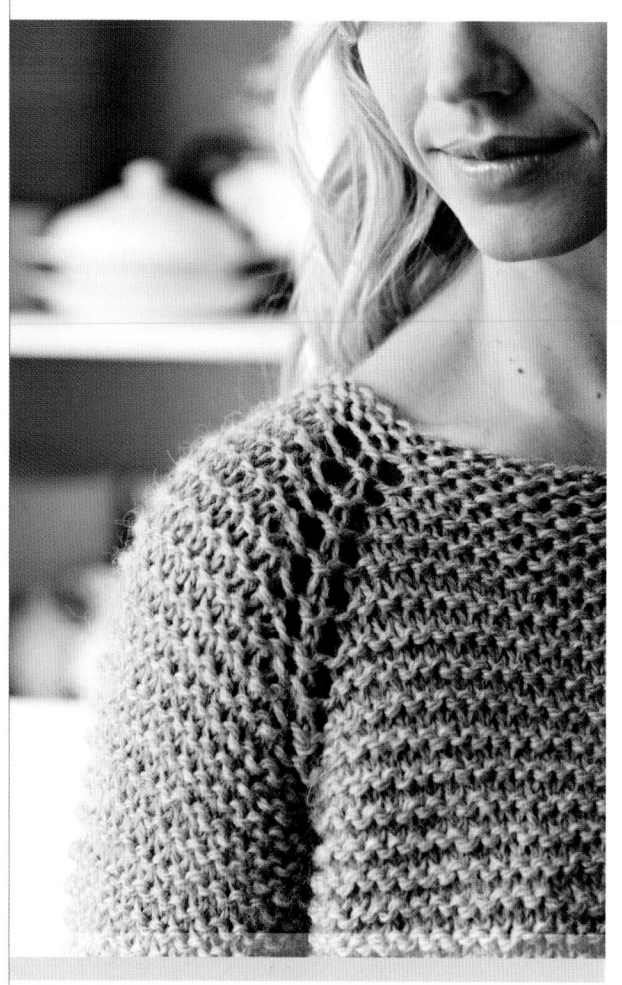

sleeves (make 2)

With larger cir needle and A, return held 30 (35, 35, 39) sleeve sts to larger cir needle with RS facing, CO 4 (4, 5, 5) sts, knit sleeve sts, CO 4 (4, 5, 5) sts—38 (43, 45, 49) sts.

Cont in garter st for 1½" (3.8 cm), ending with a WS row.

NEXT (DEC) ROW: (RS) K1, k2tog, knit to last 3 sts, k2tog, k1—2 sts dec'd.

Rep dec row every 12 (10, 10, 8) rows 7 (8, 8, 9) more times—22 (25, 27, 29) sts rem.

Cont even until sleeve measures about 16½ (16¼, 15¾, 15½)" (42 [41.5, 40, 39.5] cm) from armhole. Change to B. Cont even until sleeve measures 18 (17¾, 17¼, 17)" (45.5 [45, 44, 43] cm) from armhole. BO rem sts.

finishing and edgings

Weave in ends. Sew sleeve seams using finer yarn in same color, sewing as close to edge as possible, making sure not to tighten the stitches as you work. Sew underarm seams. Sew buttons to front edge opposite buttonholes.

Sources for Yarn

IN THE USA

ISAGER
TUTTO Opal-Isager
218 Galisteo St.
Santa Fe, NM 87501
(505) 982-8356
www.knitisager.com

PERMIN
Distributed by Wichelt Imports Inc.
N162 Hwy. 35
Stoddard, WI 54658
www.wichelt.com

ROWAN YARNS
Distributed by Westminster Fibers Inc.
165 Ledge St.
Nashua, NH 03060
(800) 445-9276
www.westminsterfibers.com

SANDNES GARN
Distributed by Swedish Yarn Inc.
PO Box 2069
126 Wade St.
Jamestown, NC 27282
(800) 331-5648
www.swedishyarn.com

OUTSIDE THE USA

BC GARN
Albuen 56 A
6000 Kolding
Denmark
www.bcgarn.dk

CANARD
www.mohairbycanard.com

FILCOLANA
Vandværksvej 10
8620 Kjellerup
Denmark
www.filcolana.dk

GEPARD OG GRIGNASCO
Gl. Jernbanevej 7
2800 Lyngby
Denmark
www.gepardgarn.dk

**HJELHOLT'S ULDSPINDERI APS
(HJELHOLT'S WOOL MILL)**
Svendborg Landevej 43
5874 Hesselager
Denmark
www.hjelholt.dk

ONION
Bøssebjerg 3
4500 Nykøbing Sj
Denmark
www.onion.dk

QIVIUT APS
Box 600
3911 Sisimiut
Greenland
www.qiviutonline.com

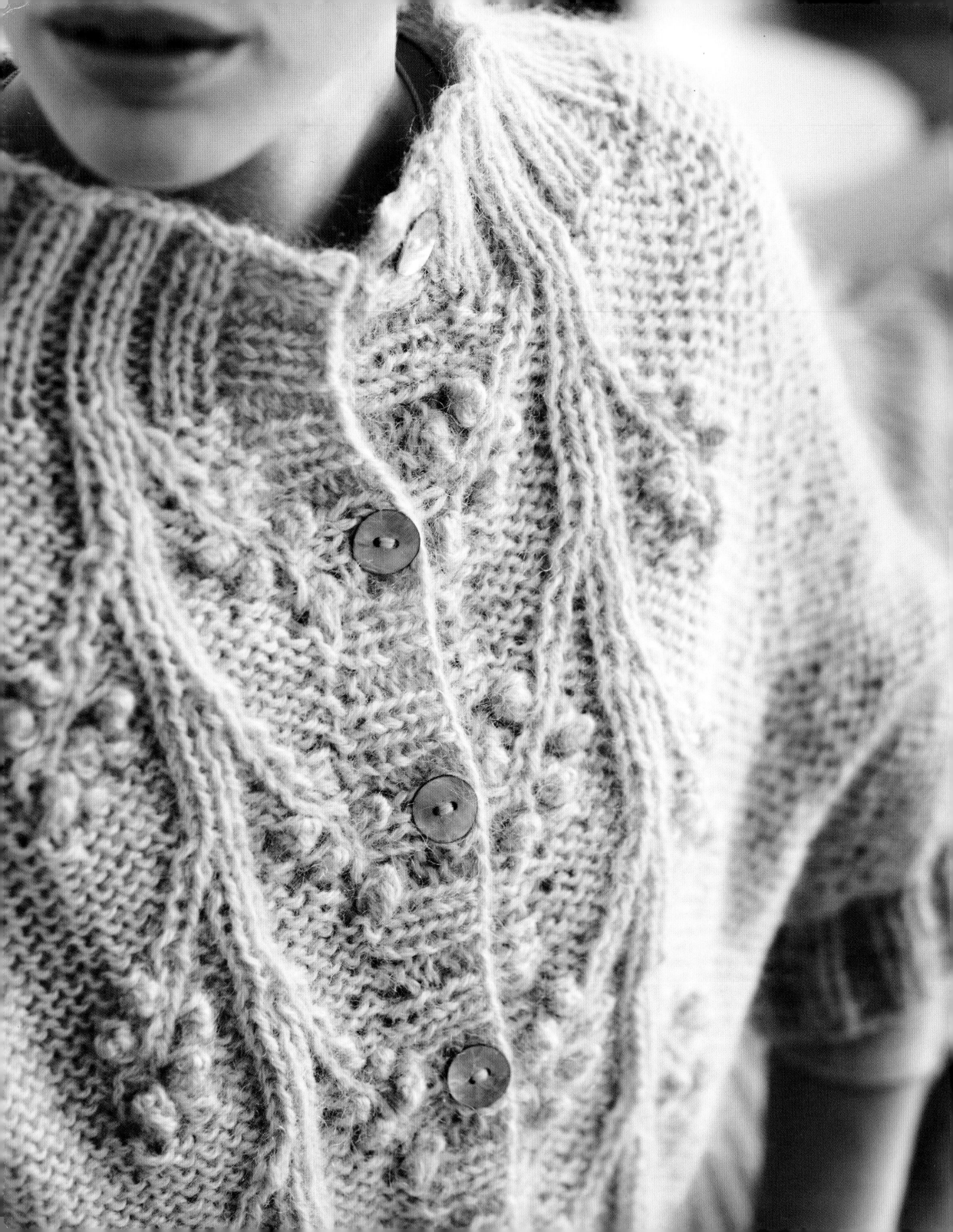

Index

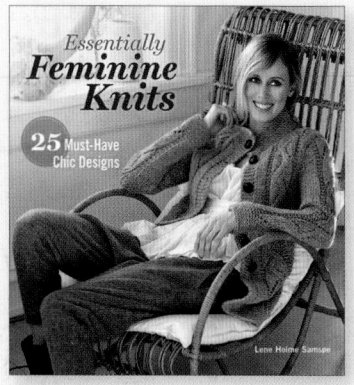
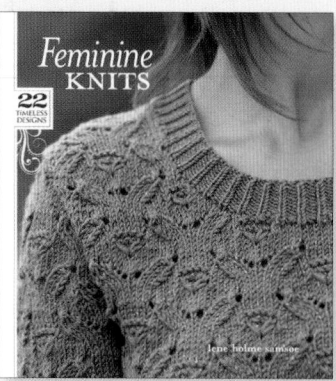
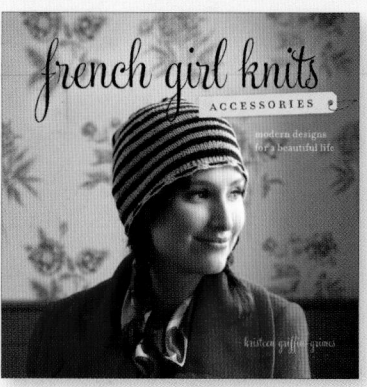
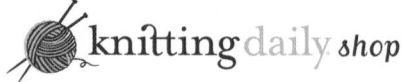
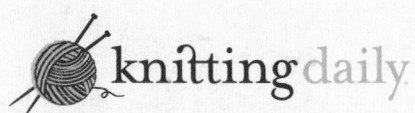